MASCULINITIES AND DISPLACEMENT
IN THE MIDDLE EAST

MASCULINITIES AND DISPLACEMENT IN THE MIDDLE EAST

Syrian Refugees in Egypt

Magdalena Suerbaum

I.B. TAURIS

LONDON • NEW YORK • OXFORD • NEW DELHI • SYDNEY

I.B. TAURIS
Bloomsbury Publishing Plc
50 Bedford Square, London, WC1B 3DP, UK
1385 Broadway, New York, NY 10018, USA
29 Earlsfort Terrace, Dublin 2, Ireland

BLOOMSBURY, I.B. TAURIS and the I.B. Tauris logo
are trademarks of Bloomsbury Publishing Plc

First published in Great Britain 2021
This paperback edition published in 2022

Cover design: Adriana Brioso

Cover image: taken by
Agata Skowronek and Mohammad Al Bdewi

A catalogue record for this book is available from the British Library.

A catalog record for this book is available from the Library of Congress.

ISBN: HB: 978-1-8386-0404-2
          PB: 978-0-7556-3525-2
          ePDF: 978-1-8386-0405-9
          eBook: 978-1-8386-0406-6

Series: Gender and Islam

Typeset by Integra Software Services Pvt. Ltd.

To find out more about our authors and books visit www.bloomsbury.com
and sign up for our newsletters.

CONTENTS

ACKNOWLEDGEMENTS

Writing this book has been an intense, challenging and exciting journey. I owe my deepest gratitude to various people, who helped me through this endeavour. First and foremost, I would like to thank the Syrian and Egyptian men and women I met in Egypt and who decided to share their experiences, memories, opinions and daily lives with me. I am thankful that I was received with respect and hospitality, and that many Syrian men and women opened up to me and made this work possible by sharing, explaining and allowing me to follow them through parts of their lives and memories.

I am truly thankful for the wonderful support and guidance provided by Ruba Salih who followed this project from the outset. I would like to express my deepest gratitude for her thorough and challenging feedback. I would also like to thank Nadje Al-Ali, Caroline Osella, Elena Fiddian-Qasmiyeh and in particular Samuli Schielke for their critical feedback and support.

A number of people read early drafts of chapters and gave feedback, or served as sounding boards for burgeoning arguments and ideas. I am deeply indebted to Veronica Ferreri, Robin Steedman, Sabiha Allouche, Gustavo Barbosa, Haje Keli, Laurie Lijnders and Jan-Jonathan Bock. In particular, I wish to extend a big thank you to Donata Kremsner and Kim J. Zinngrebe who did not only read and comment on the text in its different versions, but also helped me through this episode of my life with countless deep conversations.

Sophie Rudland has been a wonderful editor. I appreciate her enthusiasm, support and understanding. Her comments as well as the feedback of the reviewers she selected for the manuscript have very much enriched the book.

Some of the material of this book has appeared in earlier publications. An earlier version of Chapter 2 appeared in 2018 in *Men & Masculinities*. Some of the arguments presented in Chapters 2, 3 and 4 appeared in 2018 in *Signs: Journal of Women in Culture and Society* and in 2017 in *META: Middle East-Topics and Arguments*. Many thanks are due to the editors and anonymous reviewers of these publications. I would also like to thank the participants and organizers of the Workshops 'Arab Masculinities: Anthropological Reconceptions' that took place in Oxford in 2017 and 'Talking 'bout my Generation: Concepts of Youth and Generation in Research on the MENA Region and Beyond' in Marburg in 2016 for their comments and feedback.

For his love, positive energy, wisdom, belief in me and support in tough moments, I wish to thank my husband, Mohammad Al Bdewi. I feel deeply grateful and extremely lucky to have found his companionship. Our wonderful daughter Mira has been the joy of my life since she was born. Mohammad and Mira have brought so much happiness, ease and love to my life. I am also deeply thankful for the love, encouragement and care of my siblings Johanna, Judith and Matthias and my parents Ingrid and Paul-Hans Suerbaum. I am thankful for their belief in me and their enthusiasm for my work.

To Mohammad and Mira

INTRODUCTION: STUDYING MASCULINITIES, MIDDLE-CLASSNESS AND RELATIONS TO THE STATE DURING FORCED DISPLACEMENT

One evening in October 2014, when I had been doing fieldwork for almost three months in Cairo, after we had eaten and shared shisha, Fadi decided to show me his workplace. He was a Syrian man in his early twenties, and on arriving in Egypt in 2012 he had had to interrupt his studies in order to support his family. His dream was to become an engineer; however, when I met him he was working in the lingerie shop that belonged to a distant relative, on a busy street in an affluent neighbourhood of Cairo. After he showed me the tiny, neat shop that sold women's tights, nightgowns, underwear and socks, we strolled down the street, absorbed in a conversation about his work and his struggle to simultaneously prepare for his final exams in high school, which he had to retake because his Syrian high school diploma was not accepted in Egypt. We were passing an old woman who was sitting on the sidewalk begging. In a monotone voice, she kept asking for help and because of her accent and the way she was dressed I identified her as Egyptian. Fadi, without interrupting our discussion, slowed down and gave her some coins. He made no comment as to his action and continued walking down the street. Only a couple of weeks later, I was waiting for Abu Khalid in the crowded streets of another wealthy and busy Cairene district. I had met Abu Khalid at the beginning of my fieldwork. He was introduced to me as a community leader in 6th of October City, a satellite town around 30 kilometres outside Cairo, where many Syrians had settled since late 2011. He said he was trying to help Syrian families in need by raising awareness, funds and donations, and this was the reason for our short meeting. As we walked down the road to find a taxi or mini-bus so that we could both return to our homes, an Egyptian child approached us. The boy asked for money and Abu Khalid gave him a couple of Egyptian Pounds before continuing on his way.

Early in my fieldwork, their little, undramatic acts of giving left me utterly at odds with my own preconceptions, ideas and positioning of the 'helpless' refugee. They engaged my interest in the location of the receiving society vis-à-vis 'the refugee', the position of 'the refugee' in the social hierarchy, power relations between 'the refugee man' and Egyptian women, and the agency and self-perception of 'the refugee'. Moreover, these episodes sparked my wish to take a closer look at help and being helped and that 'the refugee' ought to be on the receiving side. At that moment, at the beginning of my fieldwork, these two situations would significantly guide future encounters with Syrian men and women. They made me ask my Syrian contacts specific questions, such as: 'Do you feel like a refugee?' and 'What does it mean to be a refugee for you?' A couple of months later, I had gathered enough material to connect these incidents with more explicit references as to who was, in the eyes of many Syrians, a 'real' refugee, namely the one who needed help, who begged and was dependent on others. Conversely, a respectable Syrian man was the one who was financially independent and able to provide help and donations to others. I started to read both Syrian men's acts of giving as performances with the aim to claim incompatibility with the refugee label in front of me. Remembering these incidents five years later, while revising this introduction for its publication in book form, I consider them to be evocative of many more themes that are relevant for this book: They bring to the forefront questions of class and wealth, of receiving and giving help, of masculinities as conscious performances and practices, of my positionality in the field and of the relations between Syrians and Egyptians.

This book is about the situation of Syrians who came to Egypt after the Syrian uprising[1] in 2011, and to whom the label 'refugee' is usually ascribed by national and international aid organizations, UNHCR, the Egyptian government, and by national and international media. In the first place, this book deals with Syrian men and the challenges they face during forced displacement in Egypt. By exploring their attempts to create distance from being constructed as refugees, this book delves into Syrian men's perceptions of ideal manhood. Furthermore, there is a focus on Syrian men as (un)successful participants in the Egyptian labour market, their perception of working women and unemployment. I analyse how Syrian men faced up to changes in marriage patterns and how they dealt with their sense of 'not being groom enough' when meeting potential Syrian brides and their families in Egypt. Furthermore, his book traces how Syrian men experienced the uprising in their home country, how they remembered growing up under an authoritarian regime and how they come to terms with leaving behind their home country. I investigate Syrian men's understanding of sectarianism and its impact on their daily lives. Finally, I explore Syrian men's interactions with the Egyptian and Syrian states, their sense and strategies of approaching state authorities, and how fear of the Syrian surveillance system travelled with Syrian men to Egypt and informed their lives there.

This book presents formations of refugeeness[2] by paying close attention to 'the refugee' as a classed, gendered person who is defined by his history as well as his current living conditions and future aspirations. Experiencing forced displacement does not follow fixed meanings and consequences. People respond differently to their displacement and live it in various, sometimes contradicting ways (Malkki 1995). (Forced) displacement is an existential experience (Jackson 2013; Lems 2016; Ramsay 2019) produced from living in 'situations of enforced change' (Ramsay 2019: 6). Furthermore, it should be defined as a 'temporal state of liminality' (Ramsay 2019: 5) that pulls people out of 'the teleology of their own lives' (Ramsay 2019: 7). Syrian displacement in Egypt at the time of my ethnographic fieldwork in 2014/2015 was deeply informed by the recentness of the conflict and the uncertainty of its development. Forced displacement relates, following Lubkemann (2008: 193), to 'the transformation of lifescapes in ways that render essential life projects harder to achieve'. According to Lubkemann's reasoning, the condition of displacement includes loss of access to social, material and symbolic resources that were once available. Among Syrian refugee men in Egypt, loss of access to resources that were once taken for granted and the recognition of this loss were gradual processes aggravating over time. As the chapter structure shows, the here and now in Egypt and the past in Syria were equally present in Syrian men's minds. In almost all the chapters, there is a back and forth between foci and topics concerning their everyday lives in Egypt and their past in Syria showing their inherent interconnectedness. According to Loizos (2007: 193), 'forced migration introduces a different kind of time, disjunctive in the sense of dividing experience into Before and After periods'. This was not the case among Syrian refugee men in Egypt: there were no coherence and linearity in what defined as 'before' and 'after', rather past and present were often muddled, sinuous and intertwined. In addition to Ramsay's argument that people are not in control of 'the teleology of their own lives' (2019: 7) anymore, Lems (2016: 320) offers a reason for this muddle: she argues that place does not cease to exist even in contexts of displacement and that it defines relations to the present and current location.

As far as my use of the term 'refugee' is concerned, I understand it as a category, definition and marker of identity that has legal, material and symbolic implications. I follow Malkki's (1995: 496) conceptualization that the superficial classification as refugee can merely be understood as a broad, descriptive, legal rubric hiding behind its façade a myriad of socioeconomic statuses, biographies and psychological conditions. Through the dynamic, contradictory and not always consensual process of labelling as a refugee, one 'becomes' rather than 'is' a refugee. Furthermore, I start from the premise that the meaning of refugeeness in a specific social context is determined by individual agency (Ong 2003). Aihwa Ong (2003) focuses on power relations involved in the shaping of refugees and citizens in the United States arguing that refugees are subjects to a series of determining codifications and administrative rulings that govern how 'they should be assessed and treated, and how they should think of themselves and their actions' (2003: 16). Basing her argument on Foucault, she stresses that refugees are both subjected to objectifying modes of knowledge and power and engaged in self-making by struggling against imposed knowledges and practices.

The main endeavour of this book is the analysis of notions of masculinities. It asks how men meet expectations and attempt to materialize the social norms that define them as men in a context of forced displacement. I present several strategies of forming masculinities that I observed, such as processes of othering,[3] the creation of hierarchies, masculinization against women and the combination of various registers of manhood according to urgencies and possibilities. Furthermore, I detect various challenges to ideals of manhood that were prevalent among Syrian men:

for instance, Syrian men had difficulties to prove in front of themselves and others that they could adhere to images of provider, protector and military masculinities. I argue in this book that in the context of forced displacement constructions of masculinities prove to be tensile, elastic, responsive and adaptive. Moreover, I use masculinity as a lens to understand pressing issues that were of relevance in Syrian men's lives. Thus, this book draws particular attention to Syrian men's notion of class belonging and status. I show that class needs to be dealt with thoroughly in accordance with displaced people's self-positioning and by focusing not only on their socioeconomic situation during forced displacement, but also on their pasts and their strivings for the future. Through a focus on masculinity, I also analyse Syrian men's changing perceptions of citizenship, contact to state institutions and relationship to the nation state. Ultimately, I suggest that formations, practices and representations of masculinities during forced displacement should be understood as inherently intersectional, relational and deeply ingrained in the respective context.

Throughout this book, I apply intersectionality as a lens to explore how Syrian men in Egypt made sense of forced displacement and how they strategized to create an acceptable version of masculinity for themselves. Intersectionality as a concept, strategy, methodology and research paradigm has travelled widely and has influenced various disciplines (Henry 2017). Its core concept was introduced by black feminist, legal scholar Kimberley Crenshaw (1991: 1245) who argues that a focus on intersectionality is needed 'to account for the multiple grounds of identity when considering how the social world is constructed'. She stresses that oppression can never be reduced to a single cause, such as being a woman or being working-class. Rather, an intersectional analysis shows that oppression has its roots in different, intermeshed social grounds and emphasizes how different social identities influence each other. An intersectional approach should however not include essentialization, naturalization and the mere creation of an additive 'list of social divisions' to which an individual is assumed to belong and to which explanatory power is ascribed. Instead, there is a need to pay close attention to differences among individuals and how the specific historical situations in which individuals find themselves cause differential access to resources and diverse forms of oppression (Yuval-Davis 2006: 199/200). Relevant critique has been voiced regarding the use of this concept: Hasso (2018) stresses that intersectionality does not take into account how colonial and imperial relations as well as modern state laws impact on gender. And Henry (2017) urges researchers to avoid using 'intersectionality merely as a way of capturing multiple differences and their effects on individuals'. Rather, intersectionality reveals systems of oppressions and should be taken to bring to the fore existing gender regimes and patriarchal power relations, that is 'the flipside of intersectionality coin, that of privileges, benefits and power gains' (2017). Looking at masculinities from an intersectional lens means to analyse how forms of social differentiation, such as class, race or age, influence, form and shape masculinities. Masculinities are understood to vary for different ethnic groups and to be potentially damaged or strengthened by its specific intersection with class, ethnicity, age, etc. (Christensen and Jensen

2014: 69). Furthermore, an intersectional lens is crucial to grasp the formation of masculine identities as strategies and performances which emerge within distinct local contexts and in certain social and sensual realms drawing on specific sources and capacities available from one's surroundings (Hopkins and Noble 2009: 813–16). Applying an intersectional perspective thus helps to highlight the significance of a man's position in his life, including his marital and parental status, for an analysis of the construction of masculinities. Engaging in an intersectional analysis of how Syrian refugees constructed themselves as men has turned the spotlight on the importance of social class, especially an association with middle-class life. Another relevant aspect that impacted on their lives was their uncertain, ambivalent and paradoxical relationship with the Egyptian and Syrian states.

Syrians in Egypt

Syrians had a historical presence in Egypt long before the uprising in 2011 and the consequent arrival of many thousands fleeing Syria. The first wave that came to Egypt in the eighteenth century consisted mainly of Greek Catholics. A second wave of immigration of Christian Maronites, Greek Orthodox Christians and Muslims started in the middle of the nineteenth century and ended with the First World War (Philipp 1985). By 1914, about 35,000 Syrians of different socioeconomic and educational backgrounds were living in Egypt, most of whom were Christians and a minority were Muslim (Booth 2011: 228). They automatically received Egyptian citizenship unless they explicitly opted for another one. However, after the Second World War several laws were imposed, and national and religious tendencies became more prominent so that the lives of minorities in Egypt worsened and many left (Abdulhaq 2016: 195). During the period of the UAR, again, many Syrian professionals and businessmen left Egypt because of Gamal Abdel Nasser's socialist political system (Barbir 1986 cited in Ayoub and Khallaf 2014: 20).

At the end of 2011 and in 2012, when Syrians began arriving in Egypt, having fled the rising violence and insecurity in their home country, then-President Muhammad Morsi and his Muslim Brotherhood allies supported the Syrian uprising and there was a welcoming attitude within Egyptian society, especially among Egypt's ageing Nasserist generation, young liberal activists, the Muslim Brotherhood and Anti-Alawite Islamists (Ali 2012). Morsi announced Egypt's full support for the Syrian uprising, emphasized an open-door policy for Syrians entering Egypt and granted Syrians full access to public services. Since Egypt has no policy of encampment, Syrians settled all over Egypt, predominantly in the governorates of Cairo, Alexandria, Damietta and Mansoura (Ayoub and Khallaf 2014: 7). In August 2013, immediately after Morsi was toppled, visa restrictions for Syrians were imposed. Furthermore, Syrian refugees became the subject of a government-organized media campaign that labelled them as 'terrorists', allies of the Muslim Brotherhood and supporters of Morsi. This generated an increase in xenophobia and discrimination against Syrian refugees in the Egyptian population, which was still affecting them in their daily lives, albeit to a lesser extent, when I began conducting my research in August 2014. Because of the demonization of the Muslim Brotherhood driven by President al-Sisi's regime, being considered a supporter or sympathizer could seriously damage one's reputation or could even be dangerous. This had a direct impact on the conditions of Syrian refugees in Egypt, since the majority of Islamic charities that had provided them with major support were shut down in the summer of 2013. I witnessed how the head of a Syrian private nursery in which I volunteered, a woman of Syrian-Egyptian descent wearing a face veil and a long black dress, became the object of rumours that she was a supporter of the Muslim Brotherhood, so she had to close the nursery and move to another place in the spring of 2015.

After the public campaigns that fuelled anti-Syrian sentiments in 2013, there appeared to be a new trend in the Egyptian media in 2015 that used the plight of the Syrians as a political tool to expand the support for the military and al-Sisi's regime. Riham Sa'id, an Egyptian broadcaster, for instance, posted a video of herself handing food and clothes to Syrian refugees in a Lebanese camp. After having complained about the Syrians and how they disrespectfully grabbed the donated items, she described their plight and their behaviour as the fate of a people whose country was destroyed. The clip ends with the broadcaster praising Egypt's armed forces (AlNahar TV 2015). Another time, Sa'id used the picture of Syrian-Kurdish toddler Aylan washed up on the shore to make the point that Egyptians should support the army. As described critically by a journalist of *Madamasr*, Sa'id said that the military was fighting on the Egyptian borders to prevent such a tragedy from happening and asked the rhetorical question of who could be still against the army (Magid 2015). When I discussed these video clips with Mahhmud, a tour guide in his thirties, whom I had got to know in Syria and met again in Cairo where we spent a lot of time together, he said to me: 'they use us as a lesson' meaning that in Egypt the Syrian civil war was taken as a tool to promote the people's support for the regime.

Another trend can be observed in official speeches and statements by al-Sisi and his government: in an article by *Daily News Egypt* the regime presented itself, despite the economic difficulties Egypt was facing, as selflessly supporting their 'brothers from Syria, Iraq, Yemen, Sudan, South Sudan, Ethiopia and Eritrea' (Youssef 2015). In a speech in September 2015, al-Sisi said that Egypt had accepted at least '500,000 people of our brothers from Syria'.[4] He continued: 'The UN counted only 130,000. No one heard our voice. And no one heard our voice when we welcomed them.' In this speech, al-Sisi further highlighted that the Egyptian state had to be prevented from becoming a 'refugee state'. Nevertheless, he stressed that refugees in Egypt would be treated as if they were Egyptians, since they had access to all social, educational and health services (MENA 2015). The public statements by the Egyptian regime gloss over the fact that al-Sisi's government introduced major restrictions in 2013, effectively denying Syrian refugees access to Egypt. Likewise, the emphasis on free access to education is a euphemism, since Syrians who want to enrol their children in Egyptian public schools or universities must first meet several requirements. Muhannad, a student of dentistry in his early twenties, founded an NGO that I will call *Fursa* in this book. *Fursa*'s aim was to help Syrians in Egypt to gain access to education. Muhannad explained the challenging process of enrolment to me: Syrian students were not able to enrol at an Egyptian university unless they could present their birth certificate, Syrian high school diploma and a letter from the Syrian embassy in Egypt. In the context of a community who fled from a civil war, such requirements effectively diminish the number of Syrian students who can successfully enrol in Egyptian universities and schools.

Yet another discourse has recently developed around the Syrian presence in Egypt: successful Syrian entrepreneurs were praised in the Egyptian media for their resilience and creativity in making a living in Egypt. For instance, the Egyptian TV show *Kalam Tani* (Dream TV Egypt 2017) dealt with the productivity and creativity of the Syrians in 6th of October City vis-à-vis the 'idleness' of the Egyptians.

Egypt's refugee regime

Egypt has been host to refugee movements from various countries in the twentieth and twenty-first centuries, among them Armenians, Palestinians, Iraqis, Sudanese, Eritreans, Somalis and Ethiopians (Davis et al. 2017). Egypt signed both the 1951 Refugee Convention and its 1967 Protocol as well as the Organisation of African Unity Convention Governing the Specific Aspects of Refugee Problems in Africa in 1969 (Kagan 2011: 10). In the absence of a national asylum system, registration, documentation, refugee status determination and provision for assistance are conducted by UNHCR based on a Memorandum of Understanding between the Egyptian government and UNHCR in 1954 (UNHCR 2011a: 142). The country stipulated several reservations to the 1951 Convention, specifically regarding articles related to personal status, universal primary education, public relief and assistance, as well as to employment and social security (Rowe 2009: 9). These reservations have enabled the government to consider refugees as foreigners, who can be excluded from several basic rights (Al-Sharmani and Grabska 2009: 459). For instance, refugees' rights to employment fall under domestic statuses applicable to foreigners in general and require sponsorship by an employer, legal residence and travel documents, proof of specialized skills that do not put them in competition with Egyptian workers, HIV tests, and the payment of processing fees (Rowe 2009: 9). This means that legal employment is only accessible to the extremely small, educated elite who can meet these rigid requirements, while the vast majority of refugees in Egypt survive economically only because the Egyptian authorities have tolerated unauthorized labour (Kagan 2011: 18/19). If refugees manage to find employment, they are often unable to report cases of exploitation to state officials due to fear of detention, abuse or deportation (Fiddian 2006: 301). Another challenge refugees face due to their categorization as foreigners is the high level of rent foreigners in Egypt are expected to pay. While nationals fall under a rent-protection law, foreigners have to pay between ten to fifteen times more (Briant and Kennedy 2004: 439). A further restriction to refugee life in Egypt is the exclusion of most refugee children from state-funded education with the exception of Sudanese and, since 2012, Syrian refugee children (see Norman 2016: 34). Several community schools, mainly operated by church-based organizations, try to fill this gap for refugee children of other nationalities. However, these 'refugee schools' are not accredited by the Egyptian Ministry of Education (Kagan 2011: 17). Since the public education system that Syrians are in principle allowed to access is overburdened, Syrians often turn to schools run by community-based organizations (Davis et al. 2017: 30).

Based on the memorandum signed in 1954, UNHCR conducts refugee status determination on behalf of the Egyptian government but must obtain approval from the government as to which nationalities are eligible for asylum (Norman 2015: 85). Consequently, an asylum seeker entering Egypt must register with UNHCR for protection and eligibility for assistance. The individual then receives the 'yellow card' – the proof of asylum-seeking intent that enables the person to stay in Egypt under the protection of UNHCR until a refugee status determination interview is scheduled. With the 'yellow card', one needs to register with the Egyptian Ministry of Foreign Affairs and receives a residence permit that must be renewed every six months at the respective city hall (Ayoub and Khallaf 2014: 9). Even though refugees can stay indefinitely and have access to residence permits from the government, local integration is difficult and naturalization impossible. Repatriation and resettlement are considered the only permanent solutions for refugees in Egypt (Kagan 2011: 26). Syrians in Egypt receive prima facie refugee status when they register with UNHCR. However, many Syrians avoid the residency permit given to refugees and obtain instead residency permits on the basis of their children's enrolment in Egyptian public schools (Davis et al. 2017: 30).

Doing fieldwork

I conducted ethnographic fieldwork from August 2014 to September 2015 in various neighbourhoods in Cairo and in the satellite town 6th of October City, approximately 30 kilometres away from Cairo.[5] In Cairo, I knew and met Syrians in various neighbourhoods, such as in the expensive gated communities of Rehab and Medinaty, in upper- and middle-class areas, such as al-Maʿadi, Dokki and Medinat Nasr, and in lower middle-class neighbourhoods, such as Faysal and Haram. In 6th of October City, Syrians lived in the affluent neighbourhoods close to the Husari Mosque. I also visited families in the extremely poor areas of Masakin ʿUthman or Bayt al-ʿAʾila. 6th of October City (which has been often referred to in national and international media as 'little Damascus') has attracted many Syrians to move there over the past years because of the availability of Syrian goods and restaurants, the presence of various aid organizations, affordable rent and the possibility to avoid engagement with Egyptian neighbours. Syrian contacts of mine decided where they wanted to meet me. Most of them invited me to their homes; others preferred to meet me in a café or restaurant in their neighbourhood. I did not visit men-only spaces, such as the *ahwa* which is a coffee shop in which mostly men gather to smoke, drink tea and watch football.

My Syrian interlocutors hailed from various villages and cities in Syria and were of different ages. As far as my interlocutors' religious and ethnic background is concerned: apart from one man who identified as Christian, I only met Syrians who presented themselves to me as Sunni Muslims. Most Syrian Muslims I met were knowledgeable with regard to Islamic rules and traditions; pursued a lifestyle in accordance with Sunni religious ethics; and followed religious obligations like praying, fasting during Ramadan and paying almsgiving. In terms of religious affiliation, I thus analyse the narratives and arguments of a group that presented itself as homogeneous to me. Regarding their legal status in Syria, I met one family whose roots were Palestinian. This family held a special legal status in both Syria and Egypt. Apart from this family, all the other Syrians I met were Syrian citizens: their belonging to the Syrian nation was unchallenged.[6]

The field site: Cairo

Conducting research among refugees who lived self-settled in a mega city created a specific situation and posed significant hurdles.[7] My image of Cairo is that of a cosmopolitan, crowded, dirty and loud city that never sleeps; its streets blocked with buses, trucks, taxis and donkey carts; the smell of exhaust and garbage in the air; and the sound of honking that barely stops even at night. Looking at Cairo from the perspective of a village in Northern Egypt, Schielke (2015: 10) describes it as 'the place to be' within the country, where the financial, political and cultural elites converge. It is the place that promises wealth, career, power, culture and glamour, even though the path of social advancement in the capital is in fact difficult. Indeed, despite its glamorous, cosmopolitan reputation in the countryside, many parts of Cairo cannot fulfil this promise: some of the urban poor and the middle-class poor live in cemeteries, on rooftops and on public lands on the outskirts of Cairo, creating informal communities. Greater Cairo hosts more than 111 informal settlements where more than 6 million people have created homes for themselves (Bayat 2010: 80/81). The city is divided into various neighbourhoods that differ significantly in their character and history, from upmarket gated communities in New Cairo and gardened villas in al-Maʿadi, to the dilapidated Downtown, and numerous popular areas that house the majority of Cairo's lower-class population. Crossing the often-invisible line between two districts, lifestyle and expected behaviour can differ significantly, and for a newcomer, it takes a while to recognize these lines and codes of behaviour. There is a connection between place and class in Cairo, and one's particular background and performance determine in which part of the city one can feel at home and how one is perceived and treated.

Cairo has been host to various groups of refugees and migrants even before the arrival of Syrians. Iraqis, Somalis, Sudanese, Eritreans and Ethiopians are but some of the communities that have settled in Cairo over the past decades (Fiddian 2006: 296). Living as refugees in Cairo, there is a need to get used to Cairo's sheer size, its transportation system, the long distances, blocked roads, crowds of people, the constant noise and the smell. Its poverty, authoritarian governmental legacy and unstable political climate impact on refugees and make Egypt's capital 'an uneasy refuge', 'a troubled host' and 'a source of anxiety' (Danielson 2015: 15). Furthermore, refugees in Cairo are especially vulnerable to structural violence and are frequently subject to state authorities' round-ups, detentions and deportations (Fiddian 2006: 300).

An ethnography by appointment[8]

The fact that Syrians in Egypt did not live in camps but had settled in various parts of Cairo was one of the aspects that affected my fieldwork to a significant extent. As it is the case with any urban anthropology, there was no clear-cut 'field site' but only a network of Syrian men and women spread across Cairo and 6th of October City that I tried to keep track of by embarking on daily journeys through the city. I took taxis, buses, the metro, and two or three times per week Rafi, a Syrian driver, gave me a ride to 6th of October City. The trip to 6th of October showed Cairo in all its facets: we were passing by deserted areas and took the massive highways with its huge billboards. At some point of the trip, I could spot the pyramids from afar depending on the level of smog in the air. We passed by the outskirts of Cairo with its informally constructed huts built on agrarian land. Before reaching our destinations in 6th of October City, we passed by gated communities, newly built massive malls and luxurious compounds.

Lacking a spatially confined field site meant that I could only meet people when they explicitly invited me and wanted me to be there and take part in their lives. I was not part of a commonly shared social space, where encounters and joint activities might have occurred more 'naturally' and regularly, but rather always a guest, who was welcomed to homes, cafés, offices or communal spaces, but only when the time was right for my contacts. Apart from joining group meetings, visiting families and socializing with people before, during and after English lessons, I met a great number of people individually. I thus mainly conducted an 'ethnography by appointment'. As a visitor, I was occasionally allowed to take part in my contacts' lives. Being in the position of the visitor provides interlocutors with the advantage of knowing that they can control their contact with the researcher. They are thus freer to speak and choose what they want to share in the researcher's presence than in a situation where daily contact is unavoidable. Conversely, however, this meant that I had to deal with the fact that Syrian men and women disconnected from me when they faced troubles and that there was no 'natural' way to share these times with them because of the lack of physical proximity in Cairo. Sometimes, I would not hear from Syrian acquaintances for several months and only once they reached out to me again did I find out that they had been going through a difficult time.

For instance, this was the case with Suhayr, whom I met when teaching in the Syrian nursery. She was married to an Egyptian man and used to invite me regularly to her flat. I had been teaching her three daughters for several months. However, suddenly, she cut her contact with me without explaining why. After six months, she got in touch with me again, asking whether I could teach her daughters during the summer break. When she eventually invited me to her new flat, she told me that she had experienced a divorce in the previous months and had to find a new place for herself and her children. As Suhayr's case illustrates, the lack of regular contact at certain times was not only due to the absence of physical proximity, but similarly grounded in the instability and uncertainty inherent in the lives of Syrian newcomers in Egypt. Like Suhayr, several Syrian contacts of mine would move to new neighbourhoods unexpectedly, would suddenly not attend my classes anymore or would leave Egypt for good, and I could only wait for them to get in touch with me again.

Being a researcher during 'a new era of repression'

When I started my fieldwork in August 2014, the hope for a better Egypt, which was so present during my visits after the uprising in 2011 that had caused the fall of then-President Hosni Mubarak, had vanished. Most of my Egyptian friends who had been on Tahrir Square were depressed and felt betrayed. I remember a conversation in which Ashraf, an Egyptian friend, told me bitterly that he had gone out on to the streets and risked his life for the good of the whole country. Ashraf, who was from a wealthy family, studied at an international university and worked as an engineer, felt that he had not needed the revolution as much as the millions of urban and rural poor in Egypt. He could not believe that he and his friends, who could have simply enjoyed the privileges they had through their social background, had protested against a dictator and his regime, and the outcome was the installation of yet another dictator, Abdelfattah al-Sisi.

Post-revolutionary Cairo in 2014 and 2015 was relatively quiet compared to the preceding years. Nevertheless, I sensed an underlying tension that defined my daily life and dictated my decisions. My fieldwork was embedded with what Hamzawy (2017) describes as a 'new era of repression', which included accusing civil-society activists of treason and foreigners of espionage, depriving citizens of their freedom with legal backing and through police brutality. I felt its presence in conversations with both Egyptians and Syrians, when I read about cases of 'forced disappearances' on social media, and whenever I had to introduce myself and explain why I was in Egypt. Nassif (2017) makes a brilliant argument about the change of self-consciousness and self-perception as a researcher in post-revolutionary Cairo, especially after Giulio Regeni's[9] murder. Even though my official fieldwork ended six months before his killing, the insecurity she describes speaks to the ubiquitous tension, endless worries and self-control that were part of my daily life in Egypt. I constantly surveilled and governed myself, wondering if anything I did could have turned me into a subject of concern for the Egyptian *mukhabarat* (security service). Every three months, when I had to reapply for my tourist visa, I had trouble sleeping and spent the days in brooding anticipation, hoping that it would be extended without any enquiries. Nassif (2017) argues that her fear and insecurity had a thorough impact on her ethnography, since it allowed her to bond and share with her interlocutors who had experienced excessive state control, surveillance and detention as communist students in the 1970s. Similarly, I believe that the environment of mistrust, fear and tension in Egypt alerted me to specific themes, such as Syrian men's perceptions of and relations with the Egyptian and Syrian nation states.

Given the tension, uncertainty and fear of everyday life in Cairo, questions of how to guarantee interlocutors' anonymity played a major role. In this book, I use pseudonyms and give only vague ideas about participants' age and places of origin. In some cases, I also disguised key identifying details such as profession, or information about family background. Even though a few men, mostly younger ones, did not mind the possibility of being identified, the majority wondered nervously who would get to read this book and whether it could somehow affect them, their future or their loved ones. Syrian men and women were initially restrained and cautious when it came to the recording of their voice or the use of their stories if they could be traced back to them. I suggest that their insecurity and worries regarding the sharing of their biographies and political opinions do not only relate to the climate of fear they encountered in Egypt but were also born out of the everyday surveillance and state control they had experienced in Syria, which I analyse in the last chapter.

Researching Syrian refugee men

When preparing to conduct fieldwork in Egypt, I had anticipated to be challenged as a young, unmarried woman who wants to research Syrian men. I was worried to be met with rejection, awkward silences and embarrassment on the part of the men. Indeed, I am certain that the absence of conversations revolving around sexuality was due to my positioning as a woman. Apart from this silence, I felt that my research focus and I (as a person) were generally met with respect and interest. In fact, a young Syrian man working in a community centre congratulated me on having found a relevant research topic, since his work had taught him that Syrian men in their thirties were the 'neglected ones' in current NGO discourses. At the same time, however, my research intent was met with surprise: a Syrian female student and volunteer with an NGO had heard about my research and asked me why I would conduct interviews with her peers. She said that she and her friends were not representative with their ability to travel to Red Sea resorts in Egypt, their high career ambitions and well-known family background. Instead, she urged me to meet the 'poor Syrians' who were in need of NGO support whom she had encountered as part of her volunteering work. She was convinced that they were more suitable for my research.

I chose to get in touch with Syrians by volunteering as a language teacher for English and German in different NGOs and schools. I began teaching in a nursery for Syrian children in Maadi. My classes were frequented by the mothers and older sisters of the children who went to the nursery. In several cases, my contact with my students developed into regular meetings outside the classroom and eventually my students introduced me to their husbands and other relatives. Through my teaching in the nursery I got to know Fadi, whose mother had heard of me. He was a volunteer with the NGO *Fursa* and asked me whether I could imagine teaching two evening classes for NGO volunteers and clients. This is how I got in touch with a vast network of young men and women, some of whom appear in this book. Eventually, I volunteered with an Egyptian NGO dedicated to helping Syrians in 6th of October City. I taught an English class for Syrian teenagers who had dropped out of school upon their arrival in Egypt and wanted to polish their English to get back into the school system. I also volunteered in the main office of this NGO to get a sense of their work and clientele. Moreover, at the very beginning of my fieldwork, I met a couple, Abu and Um Khalid, who described themselves as community leaders and introduced me to several families, among them Mazin's family who I would visit weekly in their small flat in 6th of October City. Then, there was Mahmud, a friend of mine who I had met when studying in Syria in 2009/2010. He held an important role for my research. I would turn to him whenever I did not understand something, be it a reference to Syria's history, the Asad regime, the war or Syrian pre-war society. I also approached him if I wanted to understand certain Syrian idioms, words and phrases with a double meaning. Mu'ayad took over a similar role. I met him through a German contact of mine and began spending a lot of time with him. His insights, explanations and emotional responses to my questions guided my understanding significantly.

The data I collected and present in this research is based on sixty-one semi-structured interviews; countless informal conversations; and daily participant observation when teaching English classes, visiting families and attending events organized by *Fursa* and other NGOs. Most of the interviews were recorded. If interlocutors had concerns with their voices being recorded, I made notes. During interviews, I encouraged my interlocutors to narrate their life stories and would only guide the interview with questions if they asked for it. Most Syrian contacts of mine would eventually agree to recorded interviews after several months of knowing each other, frequent meetings and long hours of informal conversations. The majority of Syrian men did not speak English or were not comfortable using a foreign language. I spoke Egyptian Arabic in my daily encounters, in informal conversations and when conducting semi-structured interviews, trying to adapt slowly to the Syrian dialect. My Syrian acquaintances understood the Egyptian dialect I spoke but predominantly answered in Syrian Arabic (sometimes they would use a muddled form of Egyptian and Syrian Arabic combined). Mu'ayad, Fadi and Mahmud were the only ones who felt comfortable speaking English. With them, the conversations often developed into a mix of Syrian and Egyptian Arabic interwoven with English.

I sensed that older Syrian men often perceived me as a daughter-like figure who needed guidance. They would explain to me how to behave in public and how to talk to Syrian men and women in appropriate ways. This treatment was not exclusive to Syrian men of older generations. Fadi, among others, would often police my language and would explain at length whose hands I could shake and which questions I could ask. I usually followed the instructions I received and avoided trespassing the gendered rules and boundaries. This challenge can be illustrated by one of my meetings with Akram, a volunteer with *Fursa*. He had asked me to come to the office on a Friday morning. Upon my arrival, I realized that we were the only ones there. Akram and I spent an hour talking and drinking coffee but were interrupted by the arrival of a neighbour. Akram introduced me immediately as a German friend. After the neighbour had left, Akram explained himself. He said that it would have not been acceptable for a Syrian woman to spend time alone in an empty office with a man. This rule however would not apply to foreign women which is why he had clarified my background to the neighbour. He wanted to avoid gossip. Another ethnographic vignette captures well how I was perceived and dealt with by the students I met, most of whom were a couple of years younger than me. *Fursa* had organized an event and the group of volunteers wanted to celebrate its success in a restaurant where they ordered *mezze*, soft drinks and later shisha. I was the only woman in the group. A group of young women sat at the only other table that was occupied in the café. The atmosphere at our table was relaxed, the young men cracked jokes and one of them suggested to dance *dabkeh*. His friend who was sitting next to me stopped him, however, pointing with his head to the group of young women at the table in the corner. To my surprise, he had not included me in his definition of women. I realized that I held an ambivalent position vis-à-vis these young men: while I was encouraged to adhere to appropriate gendered behaviour, I was not a woman in its fullest sense, expected to behave and be treated differently from Syrian women my age.

With some of the Syrian men I met, I developed relationships that were defined by mutual trust, and depth. Despite living in a climate of fear and uncertainty, many Syrian men eventually shared deeply personal thoughts and experiences with me, such as their political perceptions, memories of their lives under an authoritarian regime and accounts of their plight in Egypt. This is why the collected narratives of my interlocutors feature strongly in this book. I was very attentive to Syrian men's own theorizing and rely on their words in my analysis. It was one of my main aims to provide space in this book for Syrian men's analyses and interpretations of their situation.

Masculinities during forced displacement

This book attempts to study masculinities in the context of Syrian displacement to the urban milieu in Egypt. What constitutes a man in the eyes of Syrian refugees? Who is involved in the making of Syrian men in Egypt? How does masculinity materialize in the everyday of forced displacement? How are notions of masculinity among Syrian men influenced by growing up under an authoritarian regime? What is the meaning of masculinity when we focus on the reasons that made Syrian men leave their home country?

One of the most-cited and well-known concepts in masculinity studies is Connell's (1995) concept of 'hegemonic masculinity'.[10] In her work, she not only identifies the existence of various forms of masculinities within the male gender, but also describes a hierarchy among them. She argues that masculinity is relational, intersectional and situational and exists in contradistinction from femininity. Hegemonic masculinity refers to the supremacy of one form of masculinity, which, at that space and point in time, has the

> accepted answer to the problem of the legitimacy of patriarchy, which guarantees (or is taken to guarantee) the dominant position of men and the subordination of women. (1995: 77)

This does not mean, however, that many men meet the standards of hegemonic masculinity in a given pattern of gender relations. Complicit men do not oppose this gendered system, since they benefit from the overall advantage of subordinating women (1995: 79). Numerous empirical case studies have been framed with the help of Connell's concept of hegemonic masculinity (e.g. Birenbaum-Carmeli and Inhorn 2009; Ismail 2006; Haugbolle 2012; Jaji 2009; Hafez 2012). They mostly reference Connell to explain culturally dominant ways of being masculine, to describe and categorize marginalized and subordinated groups of men, to reference a competition for domination among men, to analyse women's ability to shake masculinity or to discuss men's reaction to challenges of their masculine identity. The main challenge I see with Connell's concept is its stasis and its difficulty in accounting for incongruities, contradictions and struggles. Moreover, Connell's concept does not seem suited for a situation in which men combine various images of ideal masculinities rather than sticking to a single notion of 'hegemonic masculinity'.[11]

My theorizing of masculinities is deeply inspired by Ghannam's (2013: 7) concept of 'masculine trajectories' which she uses to describe the process of becoming a man and how, during this process that lasts over a lifespan, men identify with various ideals, norms and values. Masculine trajectories do not develop neatly, nor are they fixed in order of their steps, rather they are defined by ambiguity and contradiction. Ghannam's approach takes into account both the ideal version of manhood many men hold on to and the unexpected and often messy reality men are confronted with. Her analysis highlights men's aspiration for approval by their surroundings and their consequent struggle and effort to conform to the norms and expectations of the society they live in. In addition, I find it useful to conceive of masculinities as subjectively and actively constituted (Haywood and Mac an Ghaill 2003), and as composites of various acts, attitudes and relationships available at a given time in a specific context that are woven by the individual into a 'coherent masculine selfhood' (Wentzell 2015: 179). My understanding of gender and masculinities is profoundly influenced by Judith Butler's (2004: 42) argument that the masculine and feminine are performed and naturalized and that (gendered) norms come into being because they are iteratively produced and constantly re-done, even though people are partially unconscious of their continuous involvement in the conditions that structure their lives.[12]

Ghannam's work stems from the field of masculinity studies in the Middle East, which has gained prominence in the past decades. The foci of recent studies are the social and physical changes in men's lives, such as fatherhood and marriage, ageing and disease, and men's various and differing responses to them (Inhorn 2012); the challenge of being a man in heterogeneous, hybrid contexts in which distinctions between 'us' and 'them' are blurred (Monterescu 2006); as well as men's connection with food and the importance of nurturing and providing for their families (Naguib 2015). Another trend in the discipline is an engagement with notions of militarized masculinities (Haugbolle 2012; Jean-Klein 2000; Peteet 1994). All these recent contributions to the study of masculinities in Middle Eastern contexts show how masculinities emerge in and as results of socioeconomic, cultural and political processes. Furthermore, they highlight how being a man follows the logic of the everyday life rather than fixed ideals, norms and values.[13,14]

In this book, I do not apply the concept of 'masculinities in crisis'. Several scholars have described men's confrontation with and responses to challenges by making use of this notion (e.g. Sa'ar and Yahia-Younis 2008; Haywood and Mac an Ghaill 2003; Barnes 2002; Kandiyoti 1994). Even though I recognize the severity of the various issues Syrian men were confronted with, I abstain from using the term 'crisis'. Connell (1995: 84) argues that the term 'crisis' requires a 'coherent system of some kind, which is destroyed or restored by the outcome of the crisis'. However, following Connell's reasoning, masculinity is not a system but rather 'a configuration of practice *within* a system of gender relations' (1995: 84 emphasis in original) and thus, it only makes sense to speak of a disruption or a transformation of this configuration, for example, in the form of attempts to restore a dominant masculinity or conflicts over strategies of legitimation (1995: 85). Instead of speaking of 'masculinity in crisis', I suggest conceiving of masculinities as tensile, elastic and resilient, because of their persistence and adaptability proven in their encounters, negotiations and reconciliation with challenging circumstances. Furthermore, it appears fruitful to apply the adjective 'pragmatic' as suggested by Connell (2013: 56/57). She opposes the assumption that men in contact with weapons, surveillance techniques and legalized authority show violent or extreme masculinities. There is a need to highlight the expediency and resilience of masculinities when being confronted with challenges, such as memories of the uprising and surviving during forced displacement, rather than turning towards dramatic attributions that only reinforce a notion of extreme manhood that requires violent measures to be reinstated.

In some parts of this book, masculinity is described as actively constructed and forged; in other parts, men merely react to being constructed in certain ways. While I study men as agents who actively form and materialize masculinities and pay attention to how men describe and define themselves as men, I do not mean to ignore that masculinities emerge from and often result of socioeconomic, cultural and political processes. Consequently, I also apply masculinity as an analytical lens to understanding their contact with the Egyptian and Syrian nation states, the uprising and the conflict, the workings of sectarianism, etc. Applying masculinity as an analytical lens means listening carefully to Syrian men's narratives, but also paying attention to what they do in their everyday lives, their practices and the situations they create for themselves and their families. As far as practices of masculinization are concerned, a recurring exercise among Syrian men was 'othering'. Kimmel (1994: 128) recognizes practices of 'othering' in his theorization of masculinity. In his eyes, constructing masculinity is a constant fight for recognition and approval by other men. Women are relegated to a 'currency', which men use to improve their ranking on the masculine social scale (1994: 129). In a similar vein, Kleist (2010: 191), analysing a context of forced migration, observed that men distanced themselves from 'other' failed and marginalized men, naturalized certain ideals and tried 'to establish a "traditional" gender baseline' (2010: 200). In order to frame practices of masculinization, I also rely on Goffman's theory of 'presentation of self' which has a strong focus on the 'other'. According to Goffman (1961: 3), people aspire to control how others perceive of them by conveying certain impressions and thus influencing others' interpretation of the respective encounter. There is an effort on the part of the individual to present a polished version of himself as an end-product that conceals sacrifices and compromises being made to conform to the role the individual aspires to hold (1961: 28).

I perceive of masculinities as endeavours and products, their performances dependent on their respective audiences and subject to change if context and audience are altered. Furthermore, I understand masculinities as aspects of men's identity that are protected and shielded. Masculinities are communicated through actions, practices and narratives and need 'others' not only as the audience, but also to serve as an abject prototype, as the 'currency', as a role model or as the controlled. Masculinities are never constant and unchallenged. Rather, they require continuous demonstration and confirmation. I suggest understanding the construction of masculinities as an active process that features the illusion of coherence and the aim to cover incongruities, as well as ongoing assessment and evaluation of accepted and idealized images. The idea of masculinities as put together out of various aspects and notions that are present in a man's social contacts and situations, and the effort it takes to create a coherent masculinity, features strongly in this book.

Belonging to the middle class

In this book, I explore the significance of class, in particular middle-classness. My interest in the meaning of being middle-class aroused because I noticed that belonging to the Syrian middle class was an important and recurring theme in conversations with Syrians living in Egypt. Most of them defined themselves as middle class on the basis of properties, such as a chalet at the beach, or a beautiful house their family owned in Syria. Syrian men and women alike referred to their family's former status and influence and highlighted that middle-classness was dependent on the region one hailed from and on one's upbringing and education. Moreover, middle-classness was based on labour: a man's status was defined based on his income, type of profession, productivity, inventiveness and success. Conversely, a woman could claim middle-classness if she did not have to work. This shows that middle-classness was expressed through certain morals and values and manifested itself in forms of accepted (gendered) behaviour, certain expectations in how one should be seen and treated by others, and in people's dreams and aspirations. Syrians men's use of middle-classness brought me to perceive of it as a marker of identity, an approach to life, as well as a major aspect of their understanding and construction of masculinities and their dealing with forced displacement. Nevertheless, this widespread claim for middle-classness also needs to be problematized: it has to be noted from the onset that being middle-class is a fairly common aspiration and that 'belonging to the middle class' is inherently elusive uniting, as a form of umbrella, various socioeconomic and symbolic positions (Schielke 2012: 36). Despite the reiterated discourse of belonging to the middle class and even though the few reports and assessments that exist describe Syrians in Egypt as stemming predominantly from a middle-class background with work experience and (initially) secure savings (Ayoub 2017; Ayoub and Khallaf 2014), it is important to stress that the group of Syrians that arrived in Egypt after the uprising is not homogenous. While I mostly met people with a similar background, I also got in touch with Syrians who I locate at the margins of middle-classness, such as men who referred to their family possessing huge companies, or others who spoke about their previous work in agriculture in the poor Syrian countryside. Furthermore, several families I met were severely impoverished after they came to Egypt, having lost their savings over the years.

It was in post-independence Syria that a 'new middle class' emerged that was 'attracted to class and national identities that rivalled traditional attachments to family, sect or quarter' contesting the power of the landed-commercial oligarchy (Hinnebusch and Rifai 2015: 108, 110). Following Rabo (2012), class background, ethno-religious identification, region of origin, profession, kin group and political affiliations play equally important roles in Syrians' self-presentation and ways to classify others. Salamandra (2004: 12) advocates the use of Bourdieu's term 'habitus' to properly describe social standing in Syrian society, arguing that religious and class distinctions merge with those relating to region. There is, among other markers, a rural-urban distinction, which serves as a defining characteristic of people. The rural-urban divide as a marker of belonging to the middle class is a major aspect of Anderson's (2018) argument about the commercial bourgeoisie in Aleppo. Furthermore, Salamandra (2004: 41) identifies that the place of residence in Damascus defines one's status and social background. Khaddour and Mazur (2013) stress that sectarian belonging must be analysed in the context of social relations that have emerged in Syria's regions. Rabo (2005: 8) undergirds the importance of the state and its impact on class constructions, since the Syrian state has contributed to the growth of the petty bourgeoisie since the 1970s and 1980s. Another aspect of Syrian social identity was, according to Salamandra (2004: 50), competitive consumption, that is, the ability to buy expensive goods and to present oneself in fashionable venues. This type of consumption was gendered: while Syrian men were image-conscious and showed their status through expensive clothes, jewellery and cars, women were the ones who represent the family's status through their outward appearance. According to Anderson (2018: 260), belonging to Alleppian middle class before the uprising and holding a base in the field of economic, property-owning power did not translate into political power.

While being middle-class was such a central claim among Syrian refugee men in Egypt, attention to social class in the field of refugee studies has been limited. An early ethnographic study shows the importance of refugees' occupation for self-identification, sense of class belonging and adaptation in the host country. Refugees gave their occupation a middle-class image and created class boundaries within the industry they were part of (Finnan 1981). Furthermore, there are a few studies that delineate that a forced migrant remains a 'classed' person (McSpadden 1999: 251; Van Hear 2006), that a middle- or upper-class background can ease the start in a host country, but can also lead to sense of frustration and misrecognition (Kleist 2010: 198), and that a celebrated social status is not always transferrable to the host country (Jansen 2008: 182). The rare combination of an analysis of class, forced migration and masculinity, conducted by McSpadden (1999: 251), shows that class and status affect men's judgement of 'good' and 'bad' lives and that men from a high-class background 'favoured class-congruent life trajectories and at least verbally rejected what they judged to be class inappropriate'. With their interest in transnational contexts, Levitt and Glick Schiller (2004: 1015) highlight that refugees and migrants might 'occupy different gender, racial, and class positions within different states at the same time'. For migration processes, McGregor (2008: 467) argues that class position is established in relation to a variety of aspects: the migrants' workplaces, their neighbourhoods, the social discourse in the host country and the state's legal categories, as well as family networks and social judgements in the homeland. According to Bonjour and Chauvin (2018: 9), motivations and modalities of men's migrations are inherently shaped by classed conceptions of masculinity. Migrants 'navigate and perform gendered and class expectations embedded into receiving-countries' migration and integration policies (Bonjour & Chauvin 2018: 9)'.

Certainly, a focus on class is relevant to embed changes in gender relations: class is dependent on differentiation and gender has always been a way to articulate these differences (Scott 1999: 60). Class and gender mutually create representations, identities as well as social and political practices (Scott 1999: 88). Moreover, one's sense of belonging to the social space is classed and gendered. Thus, these two axes influence the making of masculine (and feminine) subjectivities and define access to opportunities and resources (Ghannam 2013: 165). Concerning middle-class belonging, especially the notion of 'correct' femininity plays a crucial role (Jones 2012: 146). Complementary gender roles are often used to naturalize relations of inequality and function as a form of demarcation from others above and below in the hierarchy (Donner

2015; Vera-Sanso 2016). The images of complementary forms of masculinity and femininity and the idealization of women staying at home are not only prevalent in Syrian men's representation of Syrian traditions, as will be discussed in the following chapters, but can be traced to the rise of the British middle class in the nineteenth century and are deeply engrained in a global culture of middle-classness (Radhakrishnan 2009).

Focusing specifically at the notion of middle class, I perceive of class as related to income, education and profession, but also to dress, comportment and body language (Rizzo 2015: 5).[15] This was already put forward by sociologist Pierre Bourdieu (1987: 5) who argues that one's social stance is both conscious and unconsciously experienced, is inscribed in the body, felt in relation to the positioning of others and 'in the form of personal attraction or revulsion'. Middle-class habitus is predominantly perceived to follow naturally from a person's family background and upbringing (Rizzo 2015: 5). An analysis that pays attention to middle-class belonging needs to deal with it as a category combining aspiration, longing and anxiety (Heiman, Liechty and Freeman 2012: 7). When speaking about middle-classness as a category, I do not mean to use it as a fixed structure. Rather class remains a lived experience and a process that is subject to change. A focus on class means engagement with people's self-perceptions and the decisions they make in their everyday lives regarding their work and consumption. It is about their relations with the state and cultural logics (Heiman, Liechty and Freeman 2012: 9–12). A recurring theme in the literature is the relation of middle-classness with respectability as a marker and standard (Freeman 2012: 86; Skeggs 1997; Strathern 1992). 'Respectability has always been a marker and a burden of class, a standard to which to aspire' (Skeggs 1997: 3). Consequently, respectability is one of the key mechanisms through with groups are 'othered' with respectability containing judgements of class, race and gender (Skeggs 1997: 1). Different groups have different forms of access to generate, resist and display respectability (Skeggs 1997: 2). Schielke (2015: 112) suggests that middle-classness in the context of Egypt means being at the centre of one's society and thus being the 'good, decent people' (2015: 155). Nevertheless, being middle-class is not only an actual position but much more an aspired direction. Middle-classness means living one's life in the future around the aspiration for inclusion in the nation and demarcation from those lower in the hierarchy. Schielke's argument that middle-classness relies on ideas of the future is very insightful in the context of my work, nevertheless I should add a nuance: it was not only the future that was important as a temporality in the context of class among Syrians I met in Egypt, they also engaged the past in their class narratives. The past was revitalized as a proof of their ability to be middle class.

Men and the nation state

Another recurring theme in this book is the relevance of the nation state for constructions of manhood. The state can be described as a centrally organized body of institutions, built with the intention to control including a juridical and repressive apparatus of enforcement at its command and basis (Anthias and Yuval-Davis 1989: 5). Citizenship, as a form of belonging to the state, can create a sense of security and stability: it is a 'substance with heft' because of citizens' economic and cultural rights, their right to enter and live in 'their' territory, as well as their entitlements, duties, and claims to identity (Macklin 2007: 346). Citizenship is shaped by people's contact with the state in the daily practices of government (Thompson 2000: 72). While citizenship means being succumbed to rights and duties, it also translates into feelings of trust, loyalty and identification which are in turn related to the individual's self-respect and dignity (Mendieta 2009: 156/157). Conversely, the loss of connection to the state is similarly burdened with emotions. Parekh (2014: 646), drawing on the work of Hannah Arendt, argues that the loss of citizenship means deprivation of fundamental human qualities, namely, a reduction to bare life, a separation from the realm of humanity and loss of one's ability to act.

For the context of the Middle East, Joseph (1996: 4) argues that the concept of citizenship has presumed the citizen to be male, while women were relegated to second-class membership of the political community. Analysing Syria's personal status law, Van Eijk (2016: 77) writes:

> A woman's status is determined by her relationship to her male family members: until she marries she is connected to her paternal family and, after marriage, her status is connected to that of her husband. Nor is she regarded as a full Syrian citizen.

This implies that Syrian men had several advantages in their relationship to the state by default based on their gender. This relationship also came with expectations in men. In Ba'thist Syria, citizenship has been measured, following Aldoughli (2018), by 'readiness to die for the nation and a commitment to a masculinist conception of national membership based on militarism and chivalry'. Nevertheless, men's position vis-à-vis the nation state did not translate into equally divided access to political power. Only a small elite held an actual locus in the field of state power, while the majority lacked 'a "base" of constitutional citizenship' (Anderson 2018: 256).

I suggest in this book that Syrian men had an ambivalent and paradoxical relationship to their state and as citizens that defined them in their core. On the one hand, the nation state granted them access, rights and duties and was thus a backbone and guarantee of their masculine selfhood. On the other hand, however, the state, its authorities, vast security apparatus and authoritarian regime threatened them as citizens and followed them from their childhood onwards even to their exile in Egypt and thus had an extremely destabilizing effect on their manhood.

Chapter overview

The first chapter challenges the connection between masculinities and armed combat that is often perceived as natural. By engaging with Syrian men's understanding of the army, the militarized upbringing and the use of weapons back in Syria, this chapter manifests that men are critical, sceptical and aware of their expected support of and engagement in armed combat, which they however reject for various articulated reasons. Instead, men search for other accepted masculine roles, such as fatherhood, which they can adopt. Another significant aspect of this chapter is men's responses to and experiences of the uprising.

In the second chapter, I explore encounters and experiences that instilled a sense of refugeeness in Syrians after their arrival in Egypt, among them their contact with UNHCR, insecurity related to identity documents and physical discomfort. The chapter then turns to document strategies Syrian men used to disconnect themselves from the negatively connoted refugee label. This process includes the formation of the prototype of a refugee and one's disassociation from it, by creating distances from those who were found to fit the stereotypical refugee image. The prototype of a refugee was the Syrian man who fled to Europe to seek asylum and Syrian men were invested in clarifying that they were more successful, economically independent and had kept their dignity intact.

Chapter 3 investigates Syrian men's negotiations of paid labour and experiences in the Egyptian labour market. Syrian men in Egypt identified the ideal of Syrian middle-class masculinity through discourses around their own and other men's approaches to work and unemployment. This chapter also illustrates men's engagement with and praise of 'traditional' complementary gender roles, as well as the trouble they experienced when gender relations were subject to change. This is demonstrated through the case of Syrian women who started working in Egypt.

In the fourth chapter, the focus is on Syrian men's positions as bachelors in the marriage market trying to find a Syrian bride. Some young Syrian men realized that their accumulated (economic, symbolic and cultural) capital and status did not travel with them to Egypt. This put them in a situation, in which they had to compete and struggle if they wanted to convince the potential bride and her family that they were a good catch. Other bachelors found that previous class barriers had melted away due to forced migration. Furthermore, Syrian men were confronted with 'their' women marrying Egyptian men.

Chapter 5 engages with various processes of othering. It discusses how sectarianism is an influential marker on Syrian masculine selfhood. Syrian men's ideas of sectarianism were ambiguous: they remembered that conflict with most sects was absent before the uprising. Nevertheless, they recounted the injustice in the country because of the Alawi base of the regime. Moreover, this chapter traces how masculinities are marked by contact with the Egyptians and the consequent establishment of ideal Syrian middle-class manhood vis-à-vis its multiple others.

In the final chapter, I discuss Syrian men's encounters with the Syrian and Egyptian states and their authorities. Despite of being aware of the regime's oppressive methods and injustice, most men had to comply and find a way to live and survive under dictatorial regimes. Furthermore, this chapter sheds light on the omnipresent fear of the Syrian security service and how it did not stop at the borders of Syria but travelled with Syrian men to Egypt and informed their lives there.

Chapter 1

BEING A MAN VIS-À-VIS MILITARIZATION, WAR AND THE UPRISING

If you had asked me whether I was against the regime in the past – no I wasn't. All the Syrians had adapted to the situation. Since we were born, we had Hafez al-Asad and the Ba'th Party ruling us; however, things passed the limits. Now we can't stand the injustice anymore. (Abu Walid)

This chapter traces how Syrian men remembered growing up under an authoritarian regime; how they adapted, struggled and negotiated; and how they eventually experienced the uprising and the civil war. As part of this endeavour, this chapter discusses Syrian men's experiences of militarization and war preparation in Syria. It focuses on the predominantly negative meaning ascribed to the military service and the army. In most narratives, men were critical of the militarization of their lives in Syria and distanced themselves from the army, the regime's war propaganda and the usefulness of the military service, even though they did not have the option to circumvent mandatory military service or military camps in their youth. Most Syrian men I met in Egypt did not identify with aspects of militant masculinity in their past and present, and sought and presented instead other paths to acceptable masculinities. Hence, I contend that literature defining an inherent relation of masculinity and military combat fails to incorporate the experiences of men who do not wish to fight and therefore act accordingly (Cockburn 2009: 163; Segal 2008: 30). After analysing Syrian men's memories of militarization during their childhood, adolescence and military service, this chapter moves on to explore the specific vulnerability of young men, that is, living in a war zone when being of fighting age. Because of the risk of being targeted or forced to fight in the regime's army or opposition forces due to their age and gender, young men were defined in several narratives as the main reason for the whole family deciding to leave Syria. Moreover, several men exposed their vulnerabilities when they described how they experienced the uprising in 2011. They recognized subsequent changes in their feelings and its impact on their life in Egypt. For some men, the uprising felt like a threshold to maturity, while others felt that the experience of the outbreak of the civil war numbed their emotions or evoked a previously unknown sense of fear and anxiety in them. This part of the chapter shows that masculinities are not constructed in a vacuum of ideals. Men were affected by their experiences of the uprising and consequent forced displacement and needed to make sense of them when rethinking themselves as men. Hence, there are elasticity and tensibility in how masculinities are constructed and sustained, adapting to emerging 'unmanly' emotions.

The versions of acceptable manhood Syrian men adopted in exile, namely, being a pacifist, observer or a father, presented at the end of this chapter, show that masculinities are subjectively and actively constructed (Connell 1995; Haywood and Mac an Ghaill 2003) and that men form masculinities by weaving in attitudes, behaviours and practices they find available in their specific social context (Wentzell 2015). Syrian men presented themselves by discursively adopting versions of manhood they considered acceptable and honourable vis-à-vis their current situation as displaced men in Egypt, in which various versions of heroic masculinities were unavailable to them. Ultimately, this chapter is about nuanced responses to violence, military combat and militarization in Syrian men's lives and challenges any direct, homogeneous linkage between masculinities, war and fighting. This chapter exemplifies, on the one hand, that masculinities are consciously created and composed, subject to the specific circumstances in which a man finds himself. In their search for acceptable alternatives to militant masculinity, some Syrian men proved that construction of masculinities meant strategizing and assessing one's options in order to reach a stance that is worthy, accepted and beneficial. On the other hand, however, Syrian men experienced powerlessness, depression and anxiety that could not be incorporated in any form of positive and successful masculine selfhood. In contrast to the other chapters, whose setting switches constantly between Syria and Egypt, this chapter's focus is mostly located within Syria. While touching on the emotional consequences of having experienced the uprising on their lives in Egypt, most of this chapter is dedicated to Syrian men's memories of growing up in Syria, living as (young) men through the beginning of the uprising and deciding to leave Syria eventually.

Growing up with militarization

Laith had baked *khubs al-'aid* (the bread of the feast), a specific type of bread from his home town in the south of Syria. He had invited his friend Mu'ayad and me to share this bread with him. Its taste was slightly sweet. We were sitting in the living room of the small apartment in Nasr City which he shared with three Syrian students. Laith served tea and asked Mu'ayad to prepare *arkile* (water pipe). Laith and Mu'ayad knew each other since primary school. Mu'ayad had left Syria directly after the outbreak of the uprising because of having been injured during the protests. Starting from zero after a hurried decision to flee to Cairo was far from easy. His injuries needed expansive medical care and once back on his feet Mu'ayad needed to find a way to survive financially in an unknown city. Laith had arrived in Egypt in 2012. Despite his background as an engineer, he worked as a driver. When our conversation turned to memories of their home town, I learnt that war was omnipresent when they grew up. Both lived in a village close to the Syrian border with Israel and described how they constantly felt that there was an external threat to their country. Laith described that the conflict with Israel was used in his childhood to make him understand that he and his family could not be rich. He was told that all the extra income a Syrian accumulated should be devoted to the fight against Israel: 'If you are poor you should be fine with that because we are in the state of war.' Mu'ayad nodded in support of this statement. Following Laith, the state of war with Israel could be understood as an omnipresent and permanent national challenge and it was every citizen's responsibility to live their life accordingly, that is, to sacrifice livelihood and individuality, as well as material and financial means for the sake of winning the war.

Syria fought against Israel in 1948, 1967 and 1973 and has lost part of its territory to Israel. Furthermore, Syria's army was active in Lebanon: it entered the neighbouring state in 1976 to 'regulate' its civil war (Rabo 2005: 66). Following Perthes (2000: 151), militarization and war preparation in Syria were not a prelude to actual war making but instead 'an end in itself' that had political, social and domestic benefits. In the discourse of the Syrian government, the preparation for a potential war against Israel had always been given absolute primacy (2000: 151). According to Ziter (2015: 61), who analyses Syrian theatre, the Syrian regime tried to erase the memory of the 1967 defeat and its consequent territorial loss, while the 1973 war was omnipresent and celebrated in textbooks, monuments, war panoramas and government buildings. War was transformed into an 'abstraction' in the background of everyday life in Syria (2015: 57). The conflict with Israel can be furthermore defined as a national trauma and an ongoing fear in Syria's citizens of losing more of their homeland. Theatre plays that followed the 1967 war with Israel illustrate men's suffering because of their defeat in war and their experiences of oppression by the Syrian authorities (2015: 61). War, trauma and self-contempt are thus linked to Israel's victory and to living under a dictatorial regime. Aghacy (2009: 5), approaching the theme from the discipline of comparative literature, considers the war with Israel in 1967 a threat to everything that was assumed to be constant and undisputable. It not only instilled a feeling of constant fear and threat in Syrian citizens, but also caused a male trauma because of men's feeling of incapability to change the outcome of the war. Aghacy (2009: 6) contends that the history of defeats in successive wars in the Levant shook men's self-perception and self-confidence in their dominant role in society.

War and militarization were the background in front of which children in Syria grew up, incorporated ideas, self-consciousness and an adult stand. Abd al-Rahman remembered the influence of the military in his everyday life as a child by referring to the regime's propaganda and the school uniform that had the colours of the military. He had recently got married, lived with his wife Israa in a small flat in Maadi and worked for an NGO supporting the Syrian opposition. His wife and her two sisters were students of mine. Several times I was invited to Israa's flat: for dinner, tea with another student from the English class and a female-only birthday party. During the first invitation, I was introduced to Israa's mother and the youngest siblings. I also met Abd al-Rahman for the first time on that evening. He told me that he came to Egypt to study in 2006, that he had only paid occasional visits to Syria in the time of the uprising and that he worked with an NGO that supported the Syrian opposition. Sitting together in the small living room, Israa's sister Susan asked me about my studies. When I answered that I was interested in gender, it sparked a discussion about masculinity. Susan wanted to know what men were like in Germany. Abd al-Rahman responded to her question by explaining that Western societies were characterized the by absence of religious norms and values and lack of care for each other. Over the course of the evening, Abd al-Rahman engaged me in several discussions about Israel, politics in the region and the Syrian uprising as if he was testing my knowledge and political position. Eventually, he began talking about his life and childhood in Syria. When it came to the topic of military indoctrination, he said:

> We were raised up in Syria in a Ba'thi childhood and the party's childhood. They [the regime] were always saying that we are in the first line of defence against the Israeli enemy. Therefore, the student was always wearing the brown uniform, which has the colour of the soil, so that the child grows up with a military appearance. However, there is something wrong if you look at it from the perspective of humanitarian principles. If I am between five and ten years old, I am still a child. I don't understand what a weapon is. I don't understand the meaning of war. The mentality of the Syrian regime was the mentality of the Ba'th party, which focuses on the topics of militarisation and carrying weapons in order to confront the Zionist enemy or the Israeli enemy. And this is nonsense to start with because for forty years the Syrian Golan has been occupied by the Israelis and not a single bullet was fired.

Abd al-Rahman drew the picture of childhood and youth defined by enforced military upbringing, a direct introduction of military values to the child's everyday life and a normalization of the use of weapons. Shock and cynicism reverberate from his statement about the use of lies to prepare young people to loyally defend their country. Moreover, his memories illustrate the powerlessness of the individual vis-à-vis the authoritarian state: the state enforced militarized education, defined the dominant understanding of masculinity with regard to weapons and the military and the individual was left with little choice but to obey.

Conceptualizing militarization, Macmillan (2011: 63) argues that it does not only mean teaching someone physical skills to participate in war, but to also normalize violence and acquire a disposition to accept killing. Militarization does not only appear in 'war zones', nor is it static and always similarly shaped; instead, militarization should be understood as informing gender relations in various ways and in multiple locations, from factories to police stations and bedrooms (Enloe 1993: 68). As far as militarized masculinity is concerned, Jones (2006: 454) suggests understanding it as inherently extremist 'with a momentum that rapidly pushes it beyond the bound of what would be considered "acceptable" behaviour in societies technically at peace'. Abd al-Rahman's critique of a child who must carry arms in the military camps targets exactly this extremism and the imposition of a radical mindset inherent in militarized masculinities.

Military indoctrination came up as well in one of my discussions with Abu Walid, a short man who was the father of two boys in his thirties. I used to meet Abu Walid in the accessories shop in which he worked. Sitting behind the register with his eyes fixed on the sidewalk of the small street in front of the shop window, his voice slightly louder than the AC behind him, he described what he had experienced in Syria. Like Abd al-Rahman, Abu Walid remembered the military camps he had to attend when growing up.

> Since we were children in the elementary school, there was a camp called 'The children of Ba'th [...] There, they are shouting slogans saying that the president shall live forever. In the intermediate school, there is another camp which is called 'The youth of Ba'th'. You will find a guy who is fifteen or sixteen years old and they bring him to the camp and teach him how to use a gun. It is almost like the system in the army. He is shouting in the same way for the life of the leader. This is what we learned.

Abu Walid's words illustrate how the regime manoeuvred children simultaneously through the process of militarization and glorification of the leader. His statement shows the inevitability of escaping the militarizing campaigns and efforts of the regime.

Serving in the Syrian army

In addition to the relevance of military indoctrination, I realized over the course of my fieldwork the prevalence of references to the army in conversations. The army was described not only as challenging and draining on the soldiers but also as loved and appreciated. The positive perception of the army changed with the beginning of the uprising when many Syrians felt that the army turned against them. Bashar was a student at the medical campus at one of the universities in 6th of October City. I was introduced to him when we both visited Mazin's family. Mazin and Bashar studied at the same campus. Once, when we were talking about the beginning of the uprising in Syria, he underlined his initial sense of the army as a force uniting Syria which however changed with the outbreak of the civil war:

> At the beginning of the revolution, the people had high hopes in the army. They were chanting: 'The people and the army are united!'. The army represents the sons of the homeland. Maybe my friend and my cousin serve in the army or anyone else. You find people from many different ages, so the army represents all of our country. At the beginning, the army was with the people but the problem is that there are people in high positions in the army, but actually, they are not in control. So, the army started to apply their orders. At that time, the army started to lose the support of the people. For each action, you will have a reaction. When the army applied violence, it received the same reaction.

Bashar illustrated how the initially positive connotation of the army had changed and gave place for distrust, disappointment and outright rejection after the outbreak of the civil war.

The army had an important role in Syria. It was the strongest instrument of the Syrian state, since it enabled the regime to monopolize the means of organized violence (Perthes 2000: 155). The militarization of Syrian society and mandatory military service helped to create a spirit of Syrianness beyond loyalty to regional and subnational groups. Instead, this spirit was related to the Syrian post-independence borders (Perthes 2000: 157). In Syria, military service is mandatory for men and lasts more than two years, unless the young man is the family's only son, is incapable of serving in the army due to health issues or has enough money to purchase an exemption. Studying at university or college also means an automatic postponement (Davis 2016: 51). In general, military service had a very bad reputation in Syria and only through payments to the officers was it possible to change the location, treatment, tasks of the conscripts and to ensure a better quality and quantity of food (Rabo 2005: 152). Avoiding military service was however not a solution. Young men who had not completed their military service had, for instance, extreme difficulty obtaining a passport (Rabo 2005: 197). Nevertheless, there were ways and means to avoid conscription. When I asked Mu'ayad whether he did his military service, he explained that he, like other students in university, used to fail in his exams on purpose in order not to officially graduate from university as a strategy to defer military service. Retaining the status of a student meant that they could not be conscripted. Mu'ayad had refused to join the army because of the expected degradation and because of his deep opposition to any form of militarization. When asked why they had tried to avoid the military service, other men told me that they feared humiliation and 'feeling like a slave'.

This stood in sharp contrast with Firas' recollection of his time in the army. Firas was a married man in his mid-thirties who I met through my friend Mahmud. I knew Mahmud since my stay in Syria in 2009/2010. Mahmud used to work as a travel guide back in Syria. He managed to work in this profession in Egypt due to his vast network among independent backpackers, his ability to speak four languages, his knowledge of the Middle East, his presence and advertisement in social media and his self-developed tours and information booklets. He had arrived in Egypt in 2011 and often helped me with various forms of translation. We used to meet almost every week and I frequently asked him for clarification either if I did not understand certain words and phrases or if I wanted to get context for what I had heard during interviews and encounters. Mahmud tried to avoid contact to other Syrians; however, with Firas, he kept a distanced friendship and had invited him one evening to his flat so that he could help me with my research. I arrived a bit early in Mahmud's flat and we prepared the living room together. Mahmud had bought nuts, sweets and lemonade for his visitors. All of a sudden, Mahmud received a call from Firas informing him that he would bring his friend Yasmin along. This required a change of plans. We went downstairs to the café in the street and waited there for Firas and Yasmin. When they arrived, we ordered and I began explaining the focus of my research. Yasmin seemed to feel uncomfortable with the constellation and the purpose of the meeting. She repeatedly asked aloud why she should help me. She was approximately of Firas' age, even though I could only guess because she gave different hints about her situation, marital status and family background throughout our meeting. She and Firas had obviously met only recently. She did not know Firas' actual name and called him 'Ahmad' throughout the conversation. At some point, Yasmin said that she did not want to continue the conversation in the café. Mahmud suggested to go to his flat; however, he urged us not to talk in the staircase because he did not want to give reason to the neighbours and *bawab* (doorman) to gossip about him. In Mahmud's flat over tea and the prepared snacks, Yasmin seemed to warm up and I learned that Yasmin and Firas had met through their mutual search for a trafficker who could bring them across the Mediterranean to Europe, where they were planning to seek asylum. Yasmin became more talkative and willing to take part in the conversation after she had asked countless questions about visa procedures in Germany. She listened carefully to the questions I posed and to the answers Firas gave and began correcting him. After she had asked for a coffee and made sure that Firas would drop her at home, she agreed to stay until the end of the interview. When I asked Firas whether he went to the army, he told us that he managed to complete his military service in the position of the '*sukhra* (service boy) for the colonels'. He seemed proud of having been in this position. Yasmin interrupted him directly in order to point out:

He is of course only talking about himself. Not everyone in the army was privileged like him. In fact, the army is very challenging. Soldiers only get one meal per day and their life is really hard and exhausting.

Responding half-heartedly to Yasmin's interjection, Firas admitted that it was annoying to have lost two and a half years of his life to 'making tea and coffee as a service boy'. When I met Mahmud again a week after this eventful evening, he shared with me his surprise about Firas' feeling of pride to have been a service boy in the army. Mahmud told me that Syrians living outside of Damascus, like himself, looked down upon being a *sukhra* during military service. They preferred suffering regular military service to being in the service of the officers. According to Mahmud, being a *sukhra* could be equated with being a slave and with being available to give the officers sexual services. Since Firas was obviously proud of having found an easy way to survive his military service, this could only mean, Mahmud assumed, that Firas was rich enough to pay for being treated respectfully despite being in the position of the *sukhra*. In fact, Firas was from a rich and influential family and used to brag in front of me and Mahmud about his family's possessions and the luxury of his wedding. Mahmud's reaction to Firas' description of his military service shows that success and respect during military service were defined by one's wealth and social status. The importance of one's socioeconomic background suggests that military masculinity was a class-specific aspiration predominantly related to working-class men. And indeed, it was specifically appealing for young, uneducated and poor villagers to be in the army, since the army represented a chance to leave rural life behind and pursue a career. For them, military service was often the only chance to receive a professional training and climb the social ladder (Perthes 2000: 155; Van Dam 2011: 27).[1] Following the connection of military masculinity with working-classness and rural background, Syrian men, who were critical of the army or had not done military service, proved to come from a class background, in which it was not necessary to pursue a career in the military to demonstrate a form of acceptable and successful masculinity. Obviously, other routes to achieving respectable masculinity were available to these middle- and upper-class men.

While Firas did his military service in the early 2000s, Abu Mazin, who was in his sixties, did his military service during the war with Israel in 1973. I visited Abu Mazin and his family regularly in their apartment. Usually, we ate together before Abu Mazin and I began playing backgammon for several hours. Every now and then, I won a game. Abu Mazin was a determined and thoughtful player and was usually unbeatable. Our eyes focused on the board; we often got involved in conversations about Syria, the news and the situation in Egypt. On one of these afternoons that we spent playing backgammon, I asked him about the Syrian military and Abu Mazin described his experiences in the army in the following way:

> We learned in the army to follow a system and we did sports activities. There were sports as you can see them on TV. So we played sports plus we had exercises with the weapons. [...] For us, the army was an obstacle that stopped the young people, a big obstacle. I mean the person who didn't go to the army cannot do anything. He cannot study or work successfully. As I told you, the army is an obstacle especially for men. [...] Hafez al-Asad destroyed our army. He made it a sectarian place. The army was full of Sunna but the people in power were Alawi. The soldier can't do nothing, everything is decided by the leaders.

Abu Mazin did not only define military service as a hurdle in men's lives, but also drew the picture of a sectarianized hierarchy in the army. And indeed, recruitment and promotions in the Syrian army predominantly favoured Alawites, and thus they occupied most of the dominant positions (see Sluglett 2016; Trombetta 2014: 29). This means that in addition to one's social class and family background, one's sectarian affiliation defined one's experience in the military.

In a similar vein Abu Mazin, Abu Walid, the shop assistant, remembered the privileged treatment that Alawites enjoyed in the army based solely on their sectarian background:

> I went to the army as a normal soldier, but in order to be at ease in the army you should pay the colonel. All the colonels are Alawites. The Alawi sect is the sect of the president. My place in the army was at the Syrian-Iraqi border next to Deir ez-Zor. In order to relax and go to Damascus I used to pay a lot, 10.000 Syrian Lira. It was written that I wasn't a normal soldier but a driver; however, I actually didn't drive for them. I just paid 10.000 SL and I could go to Damascus.

The army is corrupt. With money, everything works. If a soldier cannot pay, he will stay in the barracks and nothing will reach him. Even if the family sends him something, it won't reach him because the colonels will steal it. The soldier has a salary that is not higher than ten dollars a month. However, the Shia and Alawi soldiers were spoiled. The regime treated them well. They got permission for holidays.

Abu Walid's descriptions of the different aspects of life in Syria were often dark and negative. He had experienced arrests, kidnapping and blackmailing and had turned to opposing the regime. His voice was usually quiet and monotone when he shared his memories. He would sit and walk with his shoulders hunched, as if he did not want to attract attention. His memories of military service confirm that not only differing treatment based on sectarianism, but also bribe paying and corruption infiltrated every part of life in Syria. In addition to the presence of sectarian hierarchies, Abu Walid mentioned a certain form of vulnerability, similar to the equation with being a slave that Ihab and Mahmud used, derived from being at the mercy of the officers' ill will. This relates to the 'the utter helplessness in the face of total, arbitrary authority, where each man will have been controlled by the whims of another man' (Kandiyoti 1994: 206). In the context of Syria, this sense of powerlessness vis-à-vis the hierarchies within the army was intertwined with sectarianism and being ruled by a corrupt, authoritarian regime and thus affected men in the army differently depending on their social status.

Akram was a primary school teacher at the beginning of his thirties who fled to Egypt because he did not want to do military service. He was a religious man who often engaged me in discussions about how he imagined his marriage, which expectations he had in his future wife and his complementary responsibilities. Our friendship was defined by my admiration of his skills as an *oud* player and once I asked him to help me find an *oud*. He agreed and we met on a Saturday afternoon in 6th of October City to roam the music shops in search for an *oud* for beginners. After our successful purchase of an *oud*, we sat down in a café where Akram helped me to add the strings to the frame. Our chitchat eventually reached the level of a deep conversation during which he described how the conscription transformed into a choice between life and potential death after the uprising in 2011.

We had something that we called military service. However, if we go and do the military service we will probably die, maybe by the hands of the people who are fighting the army or by people with whom we refuse to collaborate. [...] They started to take the young people from the checkpoints. They stopped you and asked you to show your ID. For example, you are travelling and they stop you and they see your name. Then, they tell you: 'please come with us!'. Then, they obligate you to go to the military service and they accuse you because you didn't want to do the military service in the first place. With all this trouble and horrible things, we used to say that we live but we live like animals that only survive to eat. Animals just eat and sleep and follow their desires, but enjoying life and being happy – no!.

Akram compared the situation back in Syria to the life of animals, reduced to basic instincts and survival. What made him feel like an animal was the inability to refuse to follow what the dictatorial system expected of him.

In her analysis of Syria, Davis (2016: 51) defines conscription 'as not a huge issue of concern for most Syrian men'. Contrary to her statement, I found an alternative reality present among Syrian men in Egypt: some expressed the feeling of having wasted a significant amount of their lives or of being obstructed in their personal development due to military service. Others remembered military service as a time of humiliation and unfair favouritism based on sectarian belonging and social status. Tracing Syrian men's memories of growing up in Syria in a system of militarism and state indoctrination and their experiences in the Syrian army shows that their time as conscripts defines a break with militarization inculcated from early age onwards. Syrian men's lived experiences in the army do not reaffirm the ideologies they were exposed to during their childhood and adolescence and leave most of them critical of militarization and the regime. Hence, in contrast to Davis' view, conscription was an issue of concern for Syrian men which does not mean however that it was a marker of adult manhood. The presented plethora of experiences within and views on the army shows that the perceptions of conscription and the military were highly ambivalent but mostly connoted with negative feelings and predominantly not used as a tool to reach a form of respected and successful masculinity.

Being young, male and vulnerable

Mandatory military service was one of the reasons why complete families decided to leave Syria. Especially young men had been in danger of being recruited into al-Asad's army, arrested, kidnapped or killed. In any situation of war, the most vulnerable and constantly targeted population group is non-combatant men of 'battle age', since they are perceived as a threat to the conquering force (Jones 2006: 452). This group is also most likely to have the repressive apparatus of the state directed against them. Syrian men, even if they do not carry weapons, are assumed at the very least to be willing to fight and are consequently viewed either as an asset or as a threat to the regime or the opposition movement (Davis et al. 2014: 35). Since the conflict began, even men who have already completed their military service have been called up to serve again until the age of forty-two (Davis et al. 2014). While it used to be possible to pay 7,500 US dollars to be exempted from service, the regime raised the fee to 15,000 US dollars in 2013. Since 2012, it is not only men who have not completed their military service who are banned from leaving Syria, but all men between the ages of eighteen and forty-two are prohibited from travelling without prior authorization (Davis et al. 2014: 36). It thus became almost impossible for men of fighting age to avoid serving in the army or to leave the country legally.

Describing leaving Syria from a parent's perspective, Um Marwan, a mother of two adolescent boys, remembered the moment when the fleeing family was stopped at the Syrian border because the border guards were suspicious of her younger son's age. She was a well-known, elderly woman in her neighbourhood in 6th of October City. Several women I had got to know recommended to meet her if I had any questions. Um Marwan took pride in her reputation and knowledge of the conditions in Egypt. She enjoyed giving advices to other Syrian women during female-only gatherings. When being stopped at the Syrian border, Um Marwan told the soldiers that her son was only seventeen-and-a-half years old and consequently he had six more months before he had to present himself available for the military service. Before she and her family left Syria, she had made sure that her older son, who had just finished his military service, escaped, since she was extremely worried that he would be recruited. When I first met Um Marwan, her sons were already in Sweden, and she was proud of how they were doing and was relieved to know that they were safe. Sitting in her classily furnished living room, she showed me videos on her mobile and called her sons via Skype to talk to me.

In a similar vein to Um Marwan, Um Basim, a mother of three children, decided that her eldest son had to leave Syria immediately when the revolution broke out. Once, when I visited her in her small, cramped apartment in need of renovation, we came to speak about her decision to leave Syria. She told me that her son had had an accident before the beginning of the uprising and both his legs were broken. Um Basim was worried that the regime would suspect that he had participated in the demonstrations and had been injured there. She thus sent him to a relative living in Cairo. When her son wanted to come back after seven months, she did not allow him to return because she still feared he could be arrested.

The mothers' memories of deciding to flee from Syria can be complemented by turning to the perspectives of sons. Abd al-Rahman and Bashar were among the young men who were impelled by their parents to leave Syria at the beginning of the uprising against their explicit wishes to stay. Their parents feared their arrest or wanted their sons to continue without interruption with their studies. The young men eventually complied. Nevertheless, Bashar clarified that he and his family did not 'decide to leave' but were 'forced by the conditions' to flee. And Abd al-Rahman remembered that his father told him to leave because of his age, gender and because of being talkative and outspoken. In the context of deciding to flee, Ghassan, a shy student in his last year of high school aspiring to study pharmacy, said that his family decided to leave because of his parents' concern for their sons.

> We lived in an area that was not very safe. My uncle had some problems. They arrested him in this area. There were some people who brought the security service to my cousins only to arrest them as well.

Young men and their families realized that young men were in the scope of the Syrian regime and in danger to be arrested because of their age and gender. Being visible in the streets became dangerous which was why Fadi and his family left Syria abruptly after he was seen in the demonstrations. Upon arriving in Egypt, Fadi remembered his despair:

'I was shocked. I didn't want to leave my country but my father forced me to go with the family. I couldn't believe that I had left my country. I was so sad.'

Fadi and I used to meet to prepare English classes together. Once we were done with the lessons, we would often go to a café to have *arkile* and tea. Fadi was a diligent student who had to interrupt his studies to support his family by earning money. He also helped his father in the corner shop which he owned. In his little free time, Fadi volunteered with *Fursa*. Part of his volunteering was to organize language classes that members of the NGO could attend for free.

Even if several young men described their parents as the main decision-makers and the ones who pushed them to leave Syria while they had opposed this decision, this experience cannot be applied throughout. Mu'ayad, for instance, was shot in Syria while protesting in the first days of the revolution and when the wound did not heal, he decided to leave Syria for Egypt. In Syria, he could not get medical help, since the secret service was checking hospitals for patients with bullet wounds, which they took as proof of their participation in demonstrations. Patients with bullet wounds had to fear arrest and death, Mu'ayad said. He also knew that a bullet wound in a young man's body would not only put him in danger but would also be a safety risk for his family and friends. The longer he stayed in Syria and was hiding in different places, the more people knew about him and his injury, and the clearer it became that, sooner or later, his family and the people who offered him shelter would get into trouble with the regime. Hence, Mu'ayad decided to leave Syria. He did not tell his family that he was planning to escape to Egypt but only informed them that he would stay in Damascus until his wound healed. Mu'ayad had wanted to change his country to the better. He had participated in demonstrations, had wanted to inform the world through videos and pictures about what was going on in Syria, and had wanted to press for changes. Once, he showed me the extensive number of videos and pictures of the demonstrations he took in his hometown with his mobile phone in the days before he was injured. He told me that he would only allow me to watch this material, if I agreed to keep the tone muted at all time and so we watched in silence the horrifying testimonials of exceptional violence in the streets of his hometown. Nevertheless, Mu'ayad had to accept that he was powerless apropos the authoritarian state and for the sake of his family and in order to save his own life, he fled from Syria.

There was a specific vulnerability to being young and male in Syria after the outbreak of the uprising in 2011. This vulnerability had its roots in military indoctrination from early childhood onwards and the inability to avoid its impact on one's life. The omnipresence of militarized values, the difficulty in avoiding conscription and the visibility as a man of battle age created a condition that left little room for young men to stay in Syria. Not only do these memories prove young men's specific vulnerability in Syria, they also show the love and care for each other and the cohesion and utmost importance of the nuclear family. What reverberates from all the accounts and statements is that decisions are not made individually but rather in a 'connective' and 'relational' (Joseph 1994: 55) way, proving 'the primacy of the family over the person and society' (Joseph 1994: 56).

The theme of ultimate love and care for the family should thus be understood as a defining marker of lives, relationships, decisions and understandings of gender roles. Constructions of masculinities were reactive to their surroundings and dependent on immediate others. Men's compliance with their families' wishes was thus, on the one hand, a form of accepting defeat in a country that could not offer them safety anymore and, on the other hand, a form of respect paid to their immediate families. Even though several young Syrian men expressed in front of me that they opposed their families' decisions, they might have benefited to an extent from complying with the families' wishes. Complying meant that they did not have to take an active stance about their involvement in the war but could 'outsource' the responsibility of taking over or rejecting military masculinity.

Experiencing the Syrian uprising

Fleeing from Syria was for Syrian men an end to the immediate exposure to the Syrian uprising and its violent aftermath. Nevertheless, Syrian men carried the memories of having experienced the uprising to Egypt. Inspired by Nordstrom (2004: 59) who asks in her ground-breaking ethnography on war: 'And how does violence feel?' suggesting that it feels like hopelessness, loss of future and existential crisis, the following paragraphs discuss how violence and death affected the Syrian men I met in Egypt.

The Syrian uprising began in 2011 with several small events and protests throughout the country. In March 2011, children sprayed a wall in the southern town of Deraa with the slogan: 'the people want the downfall of the regime'. The local governor responded with extreme brutality, ordering the boys to be thrown in jail where they were tortured. Townspeople and the boys' families reacted with repeated demonstrations over the following weeks (Stacher 2012: 16). The regime countered with violent crackdowns and a siege of the city until May 2011 (Ziter 2015: 1). Eventually, protests and rallies spread throughout Syria, demanding freedom and the end of the rule of the security services. Further demands of the protestors were: the release of all political detainees, the removal of the state of emergency, and constitutional changes that would terminate the monopoly of the Ba'th Party in government institutions (Ismail 2011: 539). Outrage over the regime's actions in Deraa – the torture of the children; the disrespect shown to the elders, who attempted to negotiate with the regime; and the lack of accountability of the regime officials who had tortured the children – added to dissatisfaction with corruption, authoritarian caprice and the government's ignorance about its people's circumstances (Wedeen 2013: 856). At the beginning of the uprising, activists and members of the opposition tried to maintain peaceful and nonviolent resistance. However, from its early days, the army quashed the protest movement with violent crackdowns on public demonstrations, arrests, imprisonment and torture in custody, which was in turn met with further resistance from the population (Ismail 2011: 539). Moreover, the regime provoked sectarian strife by dividing the people according to their religions and regions, and by promoting the arming of the pro-government Alawi population (Sawah and Kawakibi 2014: 154). Since 2012, the conflict in Syria can be viewed as a civil war between the government and rebel forces. Over time, the war started to develop sectarian undertones with clashes between Sunni, Shia and Alawite sects and jihadist groups, such as ISIS (Deardorff Miller 2017: 4). The conflict eventually became fully sectarianized and the multiple oppositions forces increasingly engaged in combat against one another (Lawson 2016: 13/14). In 2013, Syria saw an acute escalation in armed conflict as the government intensified its attacks and began using increasingly deadly and indiscriminate weapons, including a chemical weapons attack on the Damascus countryside in August that year (Human Rights Watch [HRW] 2013). Eventually, the conflict became a proxy war involving Iran, Russia, Hezbollah (supporting al-Asad) and Turkey, Saudi Arabia, Qatar, Jordan and the United States (supporting Sunni rebel factions) (Deardorff Miller 2017: 5). By 2018, the death toll had risen to 511,000; 6.6 million Syrians were internally displaced and 5.6 million were seeking refuge abroad (HRW 2019). Since 2011, 117,000 people have been detained or have disappeared. By mid-2016, an estimated one million people lived in besieged areas (HRW 2017).

The uprising changed Syrian men's lives in various ways. Most of them described a change in their emotional state and a new perspective on life due to the uprising and their life in exile. Akram, for instance, who fled Syria with his father in 2012, described a long-lasting and previously unknown encounter with fear and anxiety.

> During the last two years in Syria I was afraid of sleeping and waking up only to find someone arresting me and taking me to I don't know where. Maybe a bomb or a missile will fall on me and kill me. This fear put a heavy weight on our shoulders. When I arrived in Egypt and I heard any fireworks, I was afraid. I thought that there were bombs and attacks. [...] Even if we are young people and we have a big capacity to stand these situations, we really became exhausted. It took me the whole first year to forget all these noises of bombs and explosions. When I see certain types of cars, I still get scared. When I see a pickup, I get afraid because the army used these cars. There were many things that I used to get afraid of.

Akram felt that he was supposed to tolerate and endure fear easily. However, he had to realize the burden of constant insecurity, distress and anxiety that he described as a feeling of being pulled down by a weight put on his shoulders. Anxiety haunts him and occurs unexpectedly in his daily life in Egypt. He is confronted with an 'unreal reality' (Gampel 2000: 50) that is incompatible with anything experienced before. It creates an overwhelming feeling of 'uncanniness', anxiety of one's imagination and loss of trust in one's senses (Gampel 2000: 55).

In contrast to Akram, who described his hitherto unknown experiences of anxiety, Ihab, who came to Egypt in 2012, referred to a loss of emotions and deadening of his feelings. He was a construction worker in his early twenties. We met at the activities of *Fursa*, in which he both volunteered and attended language classes. Ihab was the entertainer no matter in which group setting I met him.

I never saw him with a sad face; he usually smiled and made jokes. Only once, his face turned pale and his eyes were teary: it was when he told me about the dog he used to have back in Syria and that he had to leave behind. This contrasts sharply with his recollection of how he experienced the civil war.

> The bad thing is that I lost feelings. Even if I hear a lot that my friends died or that my relatives died, I don't have any feelings. The feelings died and this is the bad thing. In Syria, when someone died, we cried for him, but now it became normal and we don't cry anymore. We got used to it. In Syria, bombs flew over your head and there were bullets in the air, but now it's normal. We became used to it. The violence planted in us toughness. There are no more tears and nothing else.

Ihab finds no emotions or tears in himself to adequately mourn the multiple deaths of loved ones around him. There is nothing in him that can respond to the catastrophe he experienced. Arbitrary and untimely death 'can neither be construed as the consummation of a journey nor the conclusion of a story' (Jackson 2002: 92). And thus, death occurs as a fact without significance. The inability to make sense of the arbitrary and unexplainable death around him transformed Ihab's emotions and evoked a feeling of incomprehension, emptiness and eventual normalization of the killing in Syria.

In addition to feelings of overwhelming anxiety, liminality and insecurity affected Syrian men during their forced displacement. Mazin, for instance, arrived in Egypt in 2011 on his own before his parents joined him in Egypt several months later. He described the painful situation of not knowing whether his family back in Syria was safe and the consequent emotional turmoil he felt.

> The first month was chaotic and during the first five months I wasn't sure what I wanted to do. Will I leave? Will I continue with my studies in Egypt? Will I go back to Syria? Will I stay? The situation was confusing and difficult. Many times, we didn't have connection to our families in Syria. And we are here and hear that there are problems, bombs and attacks in our areas but couldn't contact our families. The first five months were really very difficult but thanks God at the end it worked out.

In Mazin's account, one senses not only the emotional distress of not knowing whether one's family is well but also the struggle of liminality and insecurity that defines his state of being in Egypt. Refugeeness is often described in Victor Turner's (1967: 93) words as a liminal phase of being 'betwixt and between' and of being in an 'interstructural situation'. Simon Turner (1999: 7), who analysed the situation of young Burundian men in a Tanzanian refugee camp, used this definition and extended it by declaring that 'refugees are neither here nor there, neither this nor that, they cannot be classified as boys or men'. Being displaced often introduces a phase of complete insecurity, instability, perplexity and precarity and surviving this phase challenges men in their identity, masculine being and belonging. For

Mazin, this liminality and insecurity were present in a deeply painful way, when he was separated from his elderly parents, unable to be the responsible son he aspired to be and utterly in doubt about his present and future.

Refusing to know

The uprising and the emotions it triggered had to be incorporated in the everyday life upon forced displacement in Egypt. Syrian men's reactions and strategies to deal with their memories and the accompanying emotions proved the elasticity of masculinities. There was, for instance, Hani's ambivalent reactions to and handling of information he received from Syria. Hani was a friend of Bashar and Mazin. He studied at the medical faculty like the other two young men and often spent time with them.

> I am here for three years now and my soul is completely destroyed. I am very influenced by what's happening in Syria. Sometimes one or two months pass and I don't care about the news. I am not following the news. Sometimes they bombard the areas where my family and friends stay and I don't know about it. The areas of some of my relatives in the countryside were bombarded and I didn't know about it. It is a negative thing. Also, my friends here in Egypt, who have families in Syria, do not follow the news anymore like they used to before.

Hani described not only being unable to follow the news but also a strategy of refusing to know and be aware of the dramatic developments in Syria in order to endure daily life in Egypt. This decision served as a coping mechanism and helped Hani to survive in Egypt. At the same time, it shows a strong sense of depression, anxiety and a consequent conscious deadening of his emotions. Mu'ayad had found a similar coping mechanism: he had family back in Syria and avoided any conscious confrontation with daily news about the war. He feared that they would leave him heartbroken, utterly worried and unable to continue with his daily routines. Consequently, Mu'ayad abruptly and almost rudely interrupted conversations with friends and acquaintances, as soon as they turned to the news from Syria. If someone asked him about his opinion on recent developments in his home country, he said categorically and firmly: 'I don't know. I don't follow the news.' He also told me once that he did not want any of his friends to use WhatsApp as a way of communication, since he had received devastating news, such as the death of friends in Syria, via this messenger. The notification signal of WhatsApp on his phone made him worried and stressed.

   In order to pursue their lives during forced displacement, Hani and Mu'ayad tried to control their emotions by rejecting a daily engagement with the war in Syria. Refusing to know what was going on in their home country helped them avoid unknown, irrepressible and overwhelming emotions being triggered. This meant that they could retain an image of being in control and could move on with their lives and responsibilities. In a similar vein to the anxiety and the deadening of emotions, the practice of refusing to know what was going on in Syria illustrates the effect the uprising had on Syrian men and proves that it had become a significant part on their everyday life and constructions of the self in Egypt.

Becoming mature

Yet another response to the experiences of the uprising, the subsequent civil war and forced displacement was young men's feeling of growing up fast and losing a sense of normalcy in their lives. Hani and Mazin shared with me the changes they observed in their approach to life since the outbreak of the uprising and their consequent flight on a hot day in summer. The fan was running on high speed in Um Mazin's living room where we were treated with cold lemonade and self-made cookies. Hani compared the ideas he had had before the outbreak of the revolution and his current attitude to life.

> The events changed many things. It changed my mentality, my way of thinking. I learned more about life. Life taught me many things. When we were in Syria, we were thinking in an easy way about life. But really, life is difficult and it needs effort. Life became difficult and the Syrian starts to compare death with death in order to find a country where he can live a good life. We thought about a good job, a car, a house, a nice position in the social class background in Syria. I remember that a long time ago there was hardly anyone who went by the sea to Europe, but now there are many. [...] These people risk their lives. They either die or arrive.

The uprising taught Hani to see the hardship in life and to assume responsibility rather than to take life easily. Life after the revolution during displacement is defined as full of dilemmas, dangers and devastation and people's decision to risk their lives to live in safety is generated out of this condition. People's options are confined and limited to a choice between two paths and at the end of both paths lies potential death. Mazin, who sat silently next to Hani while he was talking, picked up on the topic of growing up and described the uprising and its consequences for his life as a lesson for him to act responsibly and have a mature outlook on life.

> I think that I grew up faster. I feel that I am more mature and more responsible here. When I left Syria, I was 21 years old and now I am 25 years old. I grew older and understand more now. When I graduated, I started to think about what I should do. At the end of Ramadan in 2011, two of my friends died as martyrs. The first one died on the first day of Ramadan, the second one died on the 15th of Ramadan. They were living in the same house. They died in the demonstrations. I was here in Egypt. Now, I am older and I understand more. In Syria, I never thought about all these things. My life was normal. I thought about having a job, a house, a family, but now it is different. Here I think about my future, my situation, my family, where I should go and what I should do.

Mazin defined his experience of hardship during the uprising as a transition to maturity. Knowledge, experiencing the death of loved ones, confronting worries and attempting to make sense of an uncertain future are the characteristics that have made him more mature and sensible and have a deeper understanding. Mazin juxtaposed his absence from the conflict in Syria and his friends' death in his narrative suggesting that his consciousness of this contrast added another layer of maturity and an urge to make something meaningful out of his life. And indeed, Mazin did not only talk about responsibility and maturity but also acted accordingly. In the late summer of 2015, he decided to travel via Turkey to Germany after he had been trying unsuccessfully to obtain a visa at the German embassy in Egypt. Knowing that his elderly parents depended on him, he took them with him on his two-week long journey to Germany where he began to attend language courses in order to be able to work in his profession as a dentist to provide for himself, his parents and his new wife.

Becoming active

The strategies of avoiding information and acting responsibly were reactions to surfacing emotions which had their roots in men's experiences of the uprising. I read these strategies as attempts to control these emotions. The strategies imply passivity because they are in the first place tactics of adaptation in order to keep being in control of one's life. These men held specific roles they needed to fulfil during their forced displacement, such as being a caring son or being the (partial) breadwinner for the family. In order to keep functioning, they found coping mechanisms in their everyday life in Egypt.

For Abd al-Rahman and Abu Walid, however, strategies of dealing with their emotions included activism. For them, the arrival in Egypt, the inability to (continue to) engage in the Syrian uprising and do anything for their family and friends back in Syria, and the feeling of powerlessness translated into actions. During one of my visits to his family, after Israa and her sisters had served food, Abd al-Rahman described the devastating helplessness he felt when he could not reach out to his family back in Syria.

> They were writing about heavy bombing in [his hometown] and about dozens of people who got killed there. My family was still there and there was no communication so I couldn't check on them. I always imagined, when I heard the word bombing, that it was raining bombs and bullets from the sky and all I thought about was death and blood. We decided here in Egypt that we should make a stand to show to the world what was going on in Syria and that it was wrong. We contacted our friends and we arranged the stand in front of the embassy. We were attacked there. Many thugs came out of the embassy and attacked us. [...] The demonstrations in Syria took place in [his hometown]. I was angry because it was my home city and I couldn't control my anger and

I started chanting: 'Down with the regime and down with Bashar al-Asad!'. This might have been the first time I said it in public.

Abd al-Rahman stressed how the unfamiliar fright and rage he experienced, when demonstrations took place in his home city and he had no opportunity to participate in the protests or check on his family, transformed into new forms of bravery, courage and resistance which he canalized into activism in Egypt.

Likewise, Abu Walid remembered that upon his arrival in Egypt his 'psychological state wasn't good'. We were sitting in the corner of a small café next to the shop in which he worked. He had closed the shop for a bit so that we could chat without interruption. After his arrival in Egypt, Abu Walid felt that he wanted to become active again, after having been involved in weapon transfer in Syria, and so contacted some people in Syria who put him in touch with activists in Egypt involved in support of the opposition.

I wanted to participate in something. I talked to some people in Syria and they said that there were some people in Egypt. [...] I went out of a place where there was a revolution so I should continue with the same work that I used to do. So, I talked to some people and the line of Egypt, Libya and Turkey was working. There were money transfers taking place. Even though the Muslim Brotherhood was in power in Libya, Egypt and Turkey, these things weren't official. They left for us things to do in secret, like using bank accounts of someone. When Muhammad Morsi fell and al-Sisi came to power, the security service stopped these things because they knew who was helping in this situation.

Since its beginning, Abu Walid had been involved together with his family and friends in the revolution in Syria. Eventually, he had to flee due to his activism after having been exposed to acute danger in Syria. He felt restless in Egypt and sensed that he could not give up his activism for the uprising during his forced displacement.

The various ways in which the experiences of the uprising had an ongoing effect on Syrian men's lives during their forced displacement in Egypt call for an analysis of masculinities which is sensitive to emotions, vulnerabilities and memories that have ingrained themselves in men and have become a marker of their self. Being a displaced man, who fled civil war and violence, involved dealing with traumatizing experiences that had a lasting effect on the self and included incorporating and accepting them. Memories of the civil war determined differing actions and motivated various decisions: from complete refusal to know what was going on in Syria to angry activism in Egypt; from a deadening of feelings to barely controllable fear. This shows the elasticity and tensibility of masculinities especially in the context of forced displacement from a war-torn country. Describing masculinities as elastic and tensile means that versions of manhood that were sustainable in Egypt had to be able to incorporate certain characteristics that were not associated with ideal images of masculinities, such as anxiety, sadness, incomprehension of what was going on around them, passivity and helplessness. Being a man from Syria in Egypt meant to reconstruct the self around unknown emotions and to create an acceptable version of manhood that could exist alongside traumatizing memories.

Defending the home country?

Among the reactions and responses to the uprising, one trajectory was missing: I rarely heard that a man wanted to go back to Syria to fight in the ongoing civil war. I realized the absence of this narrative after I paid a visit to Yussif, an Egyptian acquaintance of mine, and his family. Yussif's aunt – a middle-aged, resolute woman – who enjoyed discussing Egyptian politics with me, was present during this visit. I had known her and other members of Yussif's family for a while and she had questioned me repeatedly about my research. She was a supporter of Morsi and the Muslim Brotherhood in Egypt and also supported the Syrian opposition. While having tea with Yussif's family, she asked me why Syrian men came to Egypt instead of staying in Syria and defending their country. She could not understand why they escaped from their country leaving the stage open for the regime and ISIS.

In fact, I rarely heard of men who returned to Syria in order to fight. A Syrian woman I met when I volunteered in an NGO told me that her son had recently completed his studies in Egypt and had just returned to Syria in order to fight with the Free Syrian Army (FSA). She said that he was guided by the wish to fight for freedom and a new government. She also told me that he was initially against the use of weapons and that his original idea was to help the people in Syria. When I took a short break from fieldwork to spend Christmas with my family in Germany, I heard another account of wishing to return. One of my students had urged me to get in touch with her brother who had just arrived in Germany and was in a desperate mental state. This is how I met Abbas, who was in his early twenties and whose hand got injured in Syria. He wished to go back to take up arms, unable to stand the fact that so many of his friends were dying in Syria while he was safe in Germany. Abbas was religious and believed that Syrian men would be held accountable on the Day of Judgement for having left Syria. They would be punished for having fled, while Syrian women were still and continuously being tortured in Syrian prisons. Abbas believed in a 'natural' connection between fighting and manhood, expecting punishment because of having fled from his responsibility to fight. He had told me when we first met in the winter of 2014 that he was injured during the demonstrations in Syria; however, the longer we knew each other the more openly he talked to me culminating in his confession that he had lied to me at the beginning and that in fact he had been injured while fighting against the regime. Since our first encounter, he kept mentioning that he wanted to return to Syria to participate in the fighting again. The only thing that seemed to stop him was his parents, who were still in Syria, begging him to stay in Germany, in safety.

In contrast to Abbas, when I asked Syrian men in Egypt what importance they ascribed to going back to Syria in order to take up arms and engage in the armed conflict, I often heard that they did not see any sense in fighting. They were against carrying weapons, violence, bloodshed and killing. Ihab, for instance, the young man who had to leave his dog behind in Syria and had bought a hamster in Egypt that he brought to *Fursa*'s office rooms, described a sense of disillusion and hopelessness when thinking about fighting.

> Who shall I defend? Both are fighting each other. This one is killing in the name of God and that other one is also killing in the name of God. With whom shall I side? He is killing and you are killing, so whom will I support? And now there are even more groups that are killing each other and each one has its army. At the beginning, there was the FSA and the regime's army only, but now you don't know anymore. Now there are too many militant groups.

Ihab was not able to see the bigger cause for which the various groups in the Syrian war were fighting. None of the groups convinced him and thus, their actions could be boiled down to useless killings that made them all the same. He could not find a position in this conflict for himself. I sensed a feeling of impotence and helplessness when he continued to explain who the beneficiaries of the revolution were.

> No one got benefits from the revolution. There are people who died and there are people who sold their property. Some people got benefits like thieves and the people who work in weapon trade and the big traders who are controlling the prices. These are people who don't care if the FSA or the regime might get destroyed – they don't care about these things, the ones who control the prices.

Directing the focus to the bigger picture of the proxy war and its economy that had developed in Syria, Ihab describes the loss of touch with the beginning of the uprising in which people went to the streets with ideals and hope for changes. This war had lost its meaning and held no place for him.

The feeling of being utterly unimportant to those holding the reins in the Syrian civil war came up when I discussed with Muhannad the meaning of fighting. Muhannad was the head of *Fursa* – the NGO for Syrian students in which Ihab and Fadi volunteered. Upon his attempts to enrol in an Egyptian university, Muhannad had realized that it involved difficulties and challenges and founded *Fursa* to ease the path to enrolment in Egyptian universities for other Syrian students. *Fursa* offered to process students' university registration and gave free consultancy for foreign students. Muhannad was a skinny man who was always busy. His eyes had dark circles because he rarely slept. Being a student of dentistry, he dedicated his entire free time to the expansion of *Fursa*.

> In the first demonstration, I went out with my friend. [...] But now, after four years, I don't know who I am with anymore. Frankly, no one cares for us. Everyone

only wants his benefit. Now there are many groups. That's why I somehow agree with the neutrals. What will happen? What's the end of this? At the beginning, I was hoping for a civilised society, civilised people, civilised leaders. Now we are refugees with all this destruction.

A prominent theme in Ihab's and Muhannad's perceptions is the inability to find meaning and a position for oneself in this conflict and the unwillingness to take up arms for one side. In contrast to the several young men who told me that they initially fought with their parents to be able to stay in Syria upon their parents' decision that they had to flee, these two young men willingly retreated to the role of external observers.

There was also Abu Muhammad who refrained from an active engagement in the war. Abu Muhammad was the father of a student of mine. He had heard of 'the German teacher' and wanted to meet me in order to learn about German habits and practices. He was chosen by UNHCR to be resettled with his family to Germany. During our first meeting, Abu Muhammad asked me a plethora of questions: how was he supposed to raise his children in Germany? Did he have to silently accept harassment in the streets? How should a man act in Germany? We had agreed that I could ask questions about Syria in return. When I enquired how he had experienced the uprising, what caused his decision to flee and what he thought about fighting, he responded: 'I don't want to be one of the people who are destroying the country by being on one side or the other.' Abu Muhammad was a self-confident man in his fifties, who engaged in all sorts of activities and had managed to buy and sustain a corner shop in a wealthy neighbourhood of Cairo. In Syria, he had experienced that his involvement and activism in the uprising had only caused problems and dilemmas. He felt that his participation, his donations and voluntary activities were misused for reasons and ends he did not support and eventually he decided to refrain from any engagement in the Syrian conflict and made sure that his adolescent son would not get involved in supporting any group.

Men are often self-evidently associated with the rhetoric of domination, the use of coercion, toughness, assertiveness, stoicism, obedience and heroism (Segal 2008: 30). Women are instead perceived to be more passive during war and are attributed with roles, such as the caregiver to family members, the mourner for kin and the potential victim of war crimes (see Toivanen and Baser 2016: 299; Gentry 2009: 244). The dichotomous categorization of women as victims and men as militia fighters does not pay attention to men who are 'marginalized, silenced, or injured' in times of conflict (Enloe 2004: 104). And thus, it needs to be noted that there is a significant difference between representation and practice: while men are represented in a generalizing and essentializing way to be courageous fighters, there are men in all wars who are frightened, reluctant to fight and unwilling to kill (Cockburn 2009: 163). With several Syrian men expressing their scepticism about the civil war and participation in it, a 'natural' connection between men, war and fighting is challenged. Instead of striving to conform to a form of militant masculinity, several Syrian men took up a critical position regarding the use of violence and involvement in the war. They could not find for themselves a role in the civil war in which they believed. And thus, they presented themselves as unwilling to fight based on their own informed judgement and decision.

The use of weapons in Syria

In addition to feeling that there was no position in the Syrian conflict in which they could believe, several Syrian men expressed reluctance to make use of arms. One day, when we were sitting after class in the rooms of *Fursa* chatting and playing with the hamster he bought, we came to talk about pre-war Syria and I asked Ihab about the use of weapons. He informed me that being armed was not common among Syrians in their everyday life before the uprising. If someone carried a gun, it marked him as influential, dominant and powerful, connected to the regime and, for this reason, above the law.

- Magdalena: Were weapons normal in Syria?
- Ihab: No, weapons were forbidden. It's not like in Upper Egypt. In Syria, it's prohibited. No one can carry them. It's even forbidden to have a knife. If someone fights with a knife, he will be imprisoned for several months.
- Magdalena: So, it wasn't normal at all?
- Ihab: No, not at all. A person who carries a weapon is either supported through *wasta* (connections) or is an official in the government.

Ihab's description clarifies that being armed was not a signifier of every man's masculinity in pre-war Syria, but rather a display of a powerful position within Syrian society that only a few men held.

In a similar vein to Ihab, Bashar, the student of medicine, highlighted that carrying guns was not common on pre-war Syria. He remembered the time of the uprising as a moment of degradation. His comfortable life in Syria became gradually less accessible and was threatened by insecurity and danger:

At the beginning, we lost the safety in the countryside and by time we also lost it in the cities until it reached friends and family and eventually it reached you.

He stressed that in Syria the majority of men neither carried nor used weapons.

There are some people who want to go back [to Syria] to carry weapons. However, carrying guns can bring a disaster. In Syria, we were not used to the culture of guns. We were like a civil country and most of us were civilians. No one was thinking about having guns. And the regime considered having guns a big thing! When we started the revolution, it was peaceful. Then, with time, having guns was like a reaction. The people who brought the weapons to the revolution stayed, the ones who didn't use weapons left. The problem is that the people started to get used to the life with guns. With time, it started to become normal. Now the people who have guns are showing off. It's like: 'look, I have a gun!'.

Bashar described a gradual normalization of the use of weapons. In a society in which bearing arms was not common before the uprising, he observed that weapons had become a status symbol. Bashar's friend Hani who had nodded in agreement to Bashar's description added that he had 'no clue' about how to use weapons, let alone how to kill someone. He said that he was not raised this way and for this reason it did not occur to him to participate in the fighting in Syria. While Ihab clarified that the possession of weapons signified one's belonging to the ruling class, Hani brought in the notion of upbringing and education. Weapons are usually considered integral to the context of violence, war and militarization and are furthermore frequently described as symbolizing manhood (see Jaji 2009; Maringira et al. 2015; Sa'ar and Yahia-Younis 2008). Carrying weapons is predominantly perceived as natural and as part of a particular notion of masculinity that equates manliness with the accepted and authorized use of violence (Myrttinen 2003: 37). Weapons are used as status symbols, as instruments to acquire economic and social advances, and as a way to apply power over unarmed men and women. Through the display of a weapon in public, a man exhibits his masculinity and his role in society (Myrttinen 2003: 38). In a context of everyday violence, wearing a gun becomes an integral aspect of hegemonic masculinity, and men who flee from violence and from men who carry guns can only exist on the periphery of this masculinity (Jaji 2009: 181). The absence of arms during combat can easily represent a profound failure and rejection of masculinity (Jones 2006: 455). Syrian men's memories of the use of weapons before and during the uprising show their reading of their own society through a class lens. Their rejection of the use of weapons and the denial of weapons as a symbol of manhood have a class component and are part of a discourse that several Syrian men used to describe themselves, while not belonging to the ruling class, as too educated and cultivated to make use of weapons.

Refusing to kill

Syrian men did not only remember the absence of arms in Syrian society before the uprising, but went as far as rejecting the use of weapons completely. Akram, the primary school teacher with whom I often discussed religious rules and how they ought to have their significance in married life, refused to bear arms and fight because he could not reconcile killing with his morals and ethics.

> I was peaceful in the revolution. Like for any guy in Syria, it would have been possible for me to get weapons during the revolution, however, I used to refuse it because of the issue of killing another person. No matter if he is my friend or my enemy I refuse to kill a person. Some people got used to it and started to kill others. My attitude is like the attitude of everyone who is waiting for someone to give us back some kind of dignity.

Based on his moral code that tells him not to kill, Akram chose to be passive. This attitude aligns with the religious standards Akram pursued. What is expressed here is a form of manhood that is based on pacifism and passivity. Akram put himself in the position of someone who prefers to 'wait' and rather takes pride in refusing to kill others. His description implies distance to the civil war and a sense of being above and in control of feelings of revenge vis-à-vis enemies.

Not only Akram's self-description was guided by the ideal of not using violence, in fact, many Syrian men perceived the use of weapons as the main reason for the escalation of the conflict and as having brought evil to Syria. In contrast to the common association of weapons with masculinity, they did not regard them as tools of protection or markers of their manhood. Rather, to them, arms indicated the opposite, namely uproar, illegitimate possession and use of power, and a guarantee of conflicts. Hani, for instance, who emphasized that it had not been part of his upbringing to deal with weapons, described weapons as instruments that transformed people into killers and destroyers.

> The people who participated in the revolution were educated people and they weren't extremists. However, when the weapons arrived many people took up arms even though they were still thinking about freedom and the goals of the revolution. They used arms, but, at the same time, they continued thinking about all these goals.

Hani's account can be read as a classed description of the development of the uprising: 'Educated people' eventually radicalized, arguably when less educated people got involved in the conflict, and the use of guns was normalized and employed to press for their visions of a better Syria. His account implies an initial distance between educated people – the group he considered himself to belong to – and the use of weapons. In a conversation with Abu Muhammad, the father of four who would soon move to Germany with his family, he voiced a similar explanation for the escalation of the Syrian uprising:

> Starting with weapons and using bullets were the main reasons why the problems grew bigger. It was the wrong decision. You shouldn't use weapons! You can use other ways to claim your rights and apply pressure.

This distancing from any form of combat masculinity shows that, in the context of war, the use of violence remains merely one means to achieve masculinity among several other ones, rather than an integral component of manhood (Dolan 2003: 78). Nevertheless, consciously choosing an alternative to combat masculinity includes an effort on the part of the men to explain themselves and justify their decisions. In a similar vein to Akram, Abu Muhammad put himself above and at a distance to the immediate, acute and pressing feelings of revenge and hate that can well up in people and create readiness to kill. As if he was an outsider, Abu Muhammad judged and despised the fighting in his homeland. He, like several other Syrian men I met, engaged in a process of condemning the use of weapons and the people who had picked up arms during the uprising in order to make his line of argumentation plausible. This discourse culminated in the creation of 'the educated pacifist' and 'the informed observer who is unwilling to fight' as two versions of acceptable manhood during forced displacement. Another version of acceptable manhood that appeared was the 'committed father'.

Helping in a 'human way'

There was not only a strong condemnation of the use of arms at the beginning of the uprising, but also a strive to be able to be involved in the conflict without being forced to use weapons, as Abu Muhammad argued:

> I had some money at that time and I told them: 'I want to help in a human way. I want to help the old and the sick. I don't want to give money to support the militias'. I refused it because if I paid for weapons the people would use them against each other. If a problem appears between the owner of the weapons and one of his friends, he will use the weapons and the government will not understand this. In such a situation, I would have helped in killing people rather than in solving and helping. I personally want to participate in building Syria. I want to help humanity. I am not into the topic of weapons.

The role Abu Muhammad preferred for himself in the Syrian civil war was not the one of the fighter, but rather the one of the educated pacifist who is guided by his moral compass. He presented himself as someone who managed to foresee the devastating consequences of armed involvement in the uprising and refused to be part of a chain of reactions that culminates in the death of people. Similarly, Fadi, who felt forced to comply with his father's wish to leave Syria even though he had wished to stay to support the uprising, laid out to me his vision of taking part in the conflict:

> I don't want to be with the FSA. I only want to fight if I have to in order to save other people's lives and to defend them. It is not because I like to carry guns. I only want to fight to help people. I don't want to fight innocent people. Ideally, I would want to demonstrate in Syria and to volunteer in hospitals. I want to help people rather than killing them.

Fadi displayed a pacifist attitude and the urge to engage in peaceful activism for his homeland. He accepts involvement in fighting only as a means to defend people and prefers peaceful activism over participation in the war. I argue that it was one of several strategies among Syrian men who lived as refugees in Egypt to articulate a form of non-aggressive, non-violent masculinity. In light of the inaccessibility of combat masculinity outside of Syria, their distanced pacifism was one path to reaching an acceptable notion of manhood. In the context of conflict, non-combatant men's ability to achieve key elements that confirm the normative model of masculinity in which they have been socialized is severely reduced (Dolan 2003: 67; Jaji 2009). And thus, I argue that men like Abu Muhammad, Akram and Fadi managed to stabilize themselves through the verbal adoption of the role of the informed, passive, pacifist and distant, non-violent observer. Articulating how they opted out of violence helped these men to present themselves as educated and belonging to the middle-class – an endeavour, in which Syrian men generally invested a lot of energy.

Being a father

Another strategy of constructing an acceptable version of masculinity I observed among some Syrian men with children was to define themselves as sacrificing fathers. Among the Syrian men who had children, Abu Muhammad was the one who spoke at length with me about his responsibilities and fears as a father. He described in great deal how he had tried to prevent his son from joining the armed groups in Syria.

> There is the problem that people take advantage of the enthusiasm of the young people. I told him [his son]: 'I will stay here [in Egypt] and I will work in the field of helping people, but if you want to go back I won't stop you. Do what you want. It is your choice. But I will stay here.' He answered: 'You are more experienced than I am and you know more than me so I will stay with you and the family.' So, he decided to stay. I told him that in case something happens to me he has to continue with my job. To be honest, I would have not let him leave, however, I brought it to him in this way, as if he had a choice. I used this way in order to impose it on him to stay. I wouldn't have let him leave, even if I had to force him back then to come here because I know that anyone can do anything with him. So, I told him: 'You have two options: either you leave or you help me in my work.' I used this way to convince him.

Abu Muhammad displayed a form of patriarchal manhood retreating to the position of the experienced provider and head of the family to assert himself with his son. Exposing his strategies of convincing his son shows calculus and awareness of the respect that family members pay to his opinion. He urges his son not to forget his manly responsibilities including taking over his father's position in case of his death. Abu Muhammad continued explaining:

> Since the beginning of the uprising, when we were still in Syria, I was trying to protect my children from the psychological pressure of the uprising. Thank God, I was able to do that until now. I consider this one of the achievements I made for my family. The achievement is that I protected them from the incidents physically and mentally so they didn't influence them. If my son had been influenced by the incidents, he would have gone back to Syria to take revenge for his father in case something had happened to me. Now he might do nothing, but maybe in ten years he would go. We decided that we don't want to be with any group. We are just observers. All the sides make mistakes and we don't want to be a part of them. If you need any help from humans, yes, we help, but use

the correct way to ask for it. Our country is dear to us but now we cannot do anything for it because the allies entered into this question. The best thing that I did in these years was to make my children avoid this kind of problems.

Avoidance and pulling back are described as the most feasible and reasonable, if not most heroic decisions. Abu Muhammad takes pride in not doing mistakes and describes this endeavour as a valuable goal in and of itself. Love for the family trumps love for the homeland. Consequently, he retreats to protecting his children when a meaningful, pacifist and infallible position for himself from which he can protect his country remains unavailable. Throughout our discussion, Abu Muhammad argued that the loss of financial and economic resources became a problem during the uprising and that this was another reason when choosing between providing for one's family or joining the uprising. He said: 'Imagine you demonstrate, you are with the revolution and you lose your job, so how can you feed your children?' His statement reinforces that a man must choose between his responsibility to stand up against an unjust regime and his responsibility to his family and offspring. He had to weigh two versions of himself against each other. He could have been engaged in protecting his country; however, he came to the conclusion that he was unable to defend it in accordance with his morals and values, namely in a 'human way'. Instead, he turned to fatherhood and put all his efforts into protecting his family, especially his son, from harm. He repeated his commitment to his family, and especially to his children, several times throughout our various conversations.

In 2015, UNHCR offered Abu Muhammad and his family the chance to resettle to Germany. His children, he emphasized, were the main reason why he decided to accept the resettlement. He was convinced that he would be able to give them security, safety and good education in Germany. When contrasting his life in Egypt with his children's future in Germany, he said:

> I cannot live my life like this working twenty-four hours. I go home and sleep and wake up and work. It's impossible. At the same time, I don't want to be unemployed. Also, there are problems in education and health care [in Egypt]. There are also problems in many other fields. I think about them even when I am asleep. I don't want my children to live this way. That's why I will sacrifice my life, everything, in order to make them not live my life without shopping, without relaxation and anything to enjoy themselves. The other thing is: if they live and study in Egypt, which future do they have? When I came from Syria I hardly managed to have a good situation here. It will be difficult for them. [...] The most important thing in my life are my children and once I said to me wife: 'We already lived a good life. We used to go out a lot – so it's okay now!'.

Abu Muhammad clarified through this statement that he spoke from a middle-class perspective that defined a good life as one that provides time for shopping, relaxation and pleasure. Describing the sacrifices he made for his children, Abu Muhammad managed to define himself as the caring and devoted father whose main focus in life was the well-being of his children. He succeeded in modelling himself as a respectable father and dedicated head of household – a role that is traditionally regarded positively and an ideal that is defined as worth pursuing in Syria (see Rabo 2005). Abu Muhammad turned to fatherhood at a time when other ideals of manhood, such as the defender of one's country, were, even if available, not appealing and viable to him. He himself benefited from the sacrifice he described as being willing to make for his children, because being a father, provider and head of family granted him legitimacy, authority and approval.

The theme of sacrifice for one's children, mentioned by Abu Muhammad, occurred in several of the Syrian fathers' narratives. Firas, the father of two daughters who used to work in his father's factory in Syria but did not manage to find work in Egypt and prepared himself for his trip to Europe, repeated many times that he wanted to go to Germany via the Mediterranean Sea for the sake of his children. Firas kept hinting to his privileged class background in every possible way, by referring to his family's wealth, his former profession or the amount of money he was able to pay for his wedding. Concerning his decision to leave for Europe, he explained:

I am not travelling for myself, I am travelling for my children. I don't care for myself, I can live here, but they won't adapt to this country.

To my question why there was no future in Egypt, he answered:

The education is very bad and if you want to give them [the children] good education it is very expensive. There are no possibilities. And if they don't study in an excellent way there is no future. […] The Egyptians themselves don't have a future here. So how can Syrians, the refugees, have a future here?

When Firas put the sacrifice for his children to the fore, he managed to hide behind the valuable role of the caring father the many other reasons that might have influenced his decision to travel to Europe, such as his unemployment and lack of perspective in Egypt. In my encounters with Firas and Abu Muhammad, I sometimes felt that they benefitted themselves from emphasizing the sacrificing father role they claimed to have adopted. The role of the 'sacrificing father' was prestigious, respected and appreciated. And thus, I argue that Abu Muhammad and Firas could use fatherhood as a protective shield to boost their manhood. In addition to highlighting that masculinities are tensile and elastic, the adoption of available forms of masculinity, such as the sacrificing father, shows the effort that has to be made on the part of the men. Moreover, it implies that finding, adopting and appropriating an acceptable version of manhood can cover the self and keep it charged and agentive.

Conclusion

This chapter has illustrated men's perceptions and critiques of having grown up with little opportunity to avoid enforced adaptation to a radical, militarized mindset.

The state's interference in Syrian men's everyday lives from early childhood onwards is described as a painful, omnipresent and inescapable experience. Several Syrian men were critical of the state indoctrination and militarization enforced on them and did not want to conform to a form of 'natural' connection between manhood, fighting and violence. Syrian men's specific vulnerabilities that resulted from their visibility, age and gender in Syria become part of their constructions of masculinities during their forced displacement in Egypt. The uprising caused for many Syrian men a new, and so far unimaginable, confrontation with fear for their lives and those of their loved ones. Various emotions are new companions in the everyday that are experienced as a heavy burden that continuously affects them. Hence, this chapter shows that conceptualizations of masculinities in contexts of forced displacement, in which individuals have experienced war and violence, need to pay attention to the ways in which men deal with shock, trauma, despair and depression. Ultimately, masculinities should be understood as challenged, shaken and questioned by experiences of forced displacement from a war-torn country, but, at the same time, as tensile and able to incorporate men's extreme emotions and memories. Disagreeing with the literature using the term 'masculinity in crisis', I prefer to highlight the elasticity of masculinities. Syrian men proved to be pragmatic when they recreated themselves as men integrating their traumatizing memories and consequent 'unmanly' emotions and reactions into new forms of acceptable manhood. Moreover, this chapter has shown that most Syrian men struggled with finding their place during and in the aftermath of the uprising – they did not know how to reconcile their values and expectations with military masculinity. Hence, several men expressed other version of being proper men, namely, through pacifism, a rejection of violence and a glorification of fatherhood. The expression of various non-violent forms of ideal masculinity proves Syrian men's conscious effort to create an acceptable version of masculinity using what is available in their current context. Ultimately, this chapter highlights both men's vulnerabilities during war and their agency and efforts to reformulate their masculinities and put them back on stable ground after it was shaken by their flight from Syria.

Chapter 2

BECOMING AND 'UN-BECOMING' REFUGEES

At the beginning of my fieldwork, I got in touch with Um and Abu Khalid, community leaders in 6th of October, and parents of two teenagers. Their family was one of the first that had arrived in 6th of October City back in 2011, they said. A Canadian contact of mine who used to collect donations for refugees had given me Um Khalid's phone number. After introducing myself on the phone, I was asked to come to Husari mosque, a huge mosque in the centre of 6th of October City, where Abu Khalid waited for me. He entered the taxi that had taken me to 6th of October City and guided the driver through the small streets of the neighbourhood until we reached the family's flat. It was interesting to follow the conversation of the Egyptian driver and Abu Khalid. They spoke about the alleged participation of Syrian refugees in the demonstrations on Rabaa Square. The Egyptian driver firmly believed that foreigners should not interfere in Egyptian interior politics. Abu Khalid avoided any confrontation with the driver and only emphasized on the difficulties Syrians faced in Egypt. Abu Khalid told the driver to drop us in front of a modern building and led me into a spacious flat that was nicely furnished. Um Khalid welcomed me together with her children Khalid and Munira. I was invited to sit down and was served *mana'eesh* (flatbread with different toppings) from a shop nearby and self-made *ouzi* (filo-wrapped rice). Um Khalid informed me that they were activists and received donations in order to share them among their broad network of Syrian families. They had become known as community leaders who were approachable for NGOs, foreigners and Egyptians in case they wanted to donate to Syrian refugees. As if he wanted to prove his wife's words, Abu Khalid showed me a long, hand-written list of names and addresses of Syrian families living in 6th of October City. He said that all of them were in need and that he was trying to get for them what they lacked, for instance, medication and furniture. Then, he excused himself and left me with Um Khalid and their son and daughter. Um Khalid explained the situation faced by her own family and all the Syrian families they supported. They had arrived with savings since both of them had worked back in Syria. However, their savings had decreased over the years and almost

An earlier version of this chapter was published under the title 'Becoming and "Unbecoming" Refugees: Making Sense of Masculinity and refugeness among Syrian Refugee Men in Egypt', in *Men & Masculinities* 21(3), 2018.

nothing was left. While her son prepared fresh grape juice, Um Khalid opened the topic of treatment by UNHCR. She complained bitterly calling UNHCR staff corrupted and liars accusing them of nepotism. Her anger then turned to the food vouchers which were distributed among Syrian families in Egypt by the World Food Programme under the supervision of UNHCR.[1] Each person received a voucher of 200 LE per month and had to redeem it in a well-known supermarket chain. She exclaimed sarcastically: 'Refugees are not allowed to eat chocolate', referring to the restrictions on items Syrians could get for these vouchers. Apart from chocolate, they could not use them to buy soap and other household items, she explained. Um Khalid felt that her personal freedom to choose which food was best for her was constrained by the rules set out by the agency: 'They think they know better', she said bitterly.

The first part of this chapter engages with encounters and experiences, similar to the one narrated by Um Khalid, that instilled a sense of refugeeness in Syrians I met. Among these experiences and encounters were disappointment in UNHCR policies, worries about identity documents and papers, enduring absence of legal protection in Egypt and physical discomfort. The second part of the chapter traces Syrian men's strategies of distancing themselves from the refugee label. These strategies included process of othering, in which Syrian refugees in Europe were defined as the ultimate failure. With the 'real' refugee in Europe defined as the abject other, Syrian men in Egypt could establish a hierarchy, in which they were ranked more highly. In order to stabilize this hierarchy, they emphasized on their self-ascribed economic success and independence from government support. By calling the first part of this chapter 'becoming refugees', I do not mean to imply that this process is one-directional, linear and all-encompassing. Rather, I suggest that 'becoming refugees' is a situational transformation that can be reversed, challenged, actively confronted and rejected, as discussed in the second part of the chapter.

'Becoming' a refugee: The encounter with the UNHCR

Um Khalid's criticism of UNHCR policies is loaded with meanings: she disapproved of how UNHCR and the World Food Programme drew the line between what was considered a necessity and what was merely an item of luxury. She criticized how the agency had taken away her ability to choose what was best for her. Her critique is testimony of a middle-class lifestyle she had adapted to but had to give up in Egypt, which defined itself through consumption and modest luxury. Not only was Um Khalid upset about the agency's definitions of necessary items for refugees, she accused UNHCR of nepotism, favouritism, lying and accepting bribes. She told me that her husband and her son had written a letter of complaint in December 2013 about the UNHCR regional office in Cairo addressed to the UNHCR headquarters in Geneva that was signed by several Syrian families. The statement criticized the head of the UNHCR regional office in Egypt for publicly stating that UNHCR would provide Syrians in Egypt with a large amount of money, which, according to the writers and signatories of the complaint, was not only false but also led to a decline in financial support by other donors. Khalid showed me pictures of a small gathering in front of the UNHCR office in November 2013. Some of the protesters held posters with one of them saying: 'No one is responsible for the Syrian refugees except UNHCR.' Um Khalid told me that even though the group received a formal response from the UNHCR office, nothing changed and their demands were not met. The statement printed on the poster addressing neither Egypt nor Syria, but demanding UNHCR's protection for Syrian refugees, signifies both a belief in UNHCR as the entity legitimately responsible for Syrian refugees and their identification with this category. The protesters' reasoning brings to mind Arendt's (1973) analysis of the refugee as a 'rightless' person vis-à-vis the nation state who has to seek protection elsewhere. Being excluded by the host country because of their status as non-citizens, refugees continue to exist in relation to entities other than the state, such as UNHCR or NGOs, in order to satisfy their material needs and to have an identity (Parekh 2014: 654). That the group of Syrians made the effort to protest in front of the UNHCR office and that they filed a complaint show that there was an initial trust in the agency, which Um Khalid and the signatories, however, lost when the response by UNHCR was unsatisfactory and did not result in any action.[2]

Um Mazin, who was introduced to me by Um Khalid, was also dependent on support from UNHCR and the World Food Programme. She belonged to one of the families whose address was on Abu Khalid's list because her husband could not find work in Cairo due to his advanced age and poor health. Neither of their two children could support their elderly parents: their daughter had moved to Spain with her husband ten years earlier, where they were facing a constant challenge to provide for their three daughters; and their son Mazin, who lived with them in Egypt, was still a student of dentistry managing to continue his studies because he had found a sponsor. I used to visit the family almost every week in their modestly furnished flat in a calm neighbourhood in 6th of October City. There were almost no personal items in the flat. Um Mazin described how UNHCR staff had come to their flat to conduct a needs assessment and asked her if and how often she and her family brushed their teeth, if they ate fruits regularly and if they had a garbage bin. She was appalled by the humiliating nature of the questions and by their implications. She also showed me the food vouchers, stored safely in a shelf of the cupboard in the living room, which she could use to buy basic groceries, such as rice, pasta, oil and sugar. However, she complained that she was not allowed to buy detergents, shampoo or body lotion with them. Um Mazin who always stressed that they had lived a luxurious life in Syria felt restricted by the food vouchers, even though she was dependent on them. The food voucher policy implied to her that she could not make reasonable food choices, could not buy what she perceived as necessary and did not know what was best for her and her family.

Once, I accompanied Um Mazin to a large hospital in Cairo funded by UNHCR dedicated to helping Syrians (see Davis et al. 2017: 30), since her gum was inflamed and she needed dental treatment urgently. Together with Mazin we took the long journey from 6th of October to a neighbourhood in Cairo's city centre. The ride took a long time, it was hot and the streets were crowded, blocked, the air full of exhaust gases. At the hospital, Syrians could receive medical treatment subsidized by UNHCR, which had an office right next to the hospital's entrance. According to information Um Mazin had heard, UNHCR or Caritas would cover most of the cost for medical treatment in the hospital. However, in the UNHCR office that was only identifiable by a hand-written sign saying UN, she was told that UNHCR would only contribute 100 LE to the treatment she needed and that Caritas only operated in Alexandria. After asking her son's opinion, Um Mazin decided to go back to 6th of October City, where she hoped to find a Syrian dentist who would be able to treat her and accept payment in small instalments.

A couple of weeks later, the family intended to approach UNHCR for another reason. I went with Mazin to the UNHCR office in Zamalek, where he sought to register as an asylum seeker. He and his family had the right to reside in Egypt because he was enrolled as a student at an Egyptian university. However, since he was close to graduation, their residency would expire soon. If he wanted to work as a dentist in Egypt, he needed to be a specialist registrar for a year. His university offered this training; however, he would need to pay 200 US dollars per month and his prospects of practising in Egypt afterwards were not promising. Hence, he hoped that through applying for asylum with UNHCR, he would have the chance to be resettled and to conduct the training abroad. The legal status of Mazin and his family was in question and decisions needed to be made to gain back a sense of security and stability. When we approached the office, a security guard stepped in our way refusing to let us enter. He said that Mazin would need to call the office's hotline first to request an appointment. This was in contradiction to what Mazin had heard, namely, that registration for asylum seeking did not require an appointment. In addition, there was a display case next to the office door, in which documents in English and Arabic explained the procedures. One of the documents clearly stated that 'new registration for asylum seeking' was possible at the office without requesting an appointment in advance. The security guard explained coldly that procedures had changed and that, according to the new rules, Mazin would need to call the hotline first. Eventually, a UNHCR caseworker left the office to speak to Mazin and other people, who had gathered in front of the door because they had been denied entrance by the security guard, explaining that the new rules required everyone to make an appointment via the hotline. When Mazin tried to call the hotline, his call remained unanswered. After this experience, Mazin did not speak about seeking asylum anymore thinking instead of alternatives to leave Egypt for a third country.

Both encounters with UNHCR left Mazin and his family feeling helpless, ignored and humiliated. Rules and procedures were changing constantly which led the family to feel that UNHCR was unreliable and indifferent to their situation. In both cases, the family sought alternative solutions for their problems, that is, dental treatment by a Syrian dentist in 6th of October City whom they could pay in instalments, and an eventual trip to Germany via the Balkan Route. Refugeeness meant for Mazin's family that they had become a faceless part of a bigger group that could be judged and managed according to stereotypes created about them

(Zetter 1991: 144). It meant being unable to access aid at the non-state entities designated for refugees, to be treated coldly and unfairly, and to be obliged to accept this treatment. The encounter with UNHCR does not only show the individual's position outside of the state-citizen relationship facing a condition of uncertainty and insecurity, it also expands on feelings of mistrust in structures that seemed to work against the best interest of the individual.

Lack of protection through documents

Apart from unpleasant encounters with UNHCR, refugeeness meant for many Syrians I met in Egypt constant worry about their papers and whether the Egyptian authorities would accept them. They were concerned about various kinds of papers: the documents they needed to enrol their children at school, their Syrian driver's licence and whether it would be recognized by the Egyptian police, and their Syrian identity documents in case they were about to expire. Documents are affectively loaded phenomena (see Navaro-Yashin 2007) and produced an imagination, experience and (unwanted) relationship with both the Syrian and Egyptian state apparatuses. Anxiety was exacerbated by the fact that the only establishment that could provide Syrians with these documents, in case they had not migrated with their owners from Syria to Egypt, was the Syrian embassy. The Syrian embassy had a very bad reputation among Syrians and most of them tried to avoid going there, if they could. It was perceived as the long arm of the regime and many horrible stories grew around it, such as arrests of Syrian visitors and forced returns to Syria. Several men expressed their fear to approach the embassy once their passport would be expired. They worried about the regime's response to their request.

Whenever Abd al-Rahman mentioned the topic of identity documents, he got angry and raised his voice. On the evening we talked about expired passports, he was the only man in the sparsely furnished room with his wife Israa, his mother- and sisters-in-law, and myself seated around him. The occasion for the meeting was a sad one: Israa had decided to embark on the trip via the Mediterranean Sea to Europe. Her destination was Holland and even though she was silent, teary, scared and intimidated on this evening, she was determined to travel. A little backpack, filled to the brim, was sitting in the corner of the room. Israa's brother had managed to arrive in Holland a year ago when he was thirteen years old, had received refugee status and could, as a minor, apply for family reunion. His parents and siblings would soon be allowed to travel legally to Holland. This was not the case for Israa, though, because she was married and above eighteen years old. Israa could not imagine to stay in Cairo with her husband but without her siblings and parents. For this reason, she wanted to travel and bring Abd al-Rahman through family reunion to Holland once she received refugee protection. Abd al-Rahman said that he was against the dangerous journey and that he did not want to live in Europe. If Israa managed to apply for family reunion, he muttered, he would go for a visit, wait for an official legal status in the Netherlands, only to go back to

Egypt. Not only Abd al-Rahman seemed distanced and emotionally uninvolved, but also Israa's sisters and mother did not express their sadness and fear regarding Israa's trip in front of me. The evening went by just like others that had preceded this one: there was food, tea and eventually a discussion in which Abd al-Rahman took centre stage with Israa, her sisters, their mother and myself becoming the audience. After food, served by Israa's sisters, Abd al-Rahman lit a cigarette, took a sip from the tea that had just been served by his in-laws and began explaining to me the issues Syrians were facing in Egypt. The tone of his voice became increasingly aggressive, he would not listen to any interruptions, and his monologue felt like a lecture. He expressed his fear of expiring passports in the following way:

> We are afraid here in Egypt of being stopped at any checkpoint, and if they checked our passports they would find that they are expired. We said that even if the passport was expired that doesn't mean that my identity is expired, too. The name is written in the passport and the passport has the code. Only the date is expired in the passport, so my identity shouldn't be expired, too. We demand that even in the case of an expired passport, the holder of the passport should be treated like a human being.

His voice trembling with anger, he continued:

> Imagine that your passport is expired and you were not able to renew it, imagine they told you that you were not Magdalena and that you were a problem. No, I am not a problem! I am not a disaster! I am a human being and a human being has the right to live wherever he wants in the world!

Documents are not neutral (Navaro-Yashin 2007: 88) and have specific relations with people to whom they belong. They have the potential to provoke multiple effects in them, such as fear, insecurity or nervousness. Documents are especially prone to engender fear and uncertainty when they are absent or useless, that is, when bureaucracies leave people and things undocumented or routinely contest the validity of the existing documents (Hull 2012: 258). This is the case for Abd al-Rahman who expresses loss of trust in the documents that used to provide him with an identity and humanity.

In a similar vein to Abd al-Rahman, Akram struggled with the loss of meaning of his documents. It was a desperate moment for Akram in Egypt – his father who was his only relative in Egypt had passed away, he struggled with getting married and he did not seem to find his life in Egypt liveable anymore. We were sitting in a café and Akram asked me whether there was a legal way to access Germany. Despite his wish to leave Egypt for Europe, he was certain that he did not want to become a refugee and neither did he want to get a German passport:

> I don't want a German passport. I have neither become a worse nor a better human being only because the circumstances have made my Syrian passport useless. The passport doesn't say anything about me.

Repeatedly, he expressed that he did not want to become a refugee in Europe; at the same time, however, he could not imagine a future in Egypt at this moment in time. Akram eventually stayed in Egypt, got married and had a daughter.

The struggle with papers is clearly not exclusive to refugees; in fact, Syrians did not have an easy relationship with documents back in their home country. They were pricey, difficult to get and often Syrians had to use their contacts to influential people if they needed specific documents. Syrians shared memories of checkpoints where they had to produce identity papers that could easily be invalidated. Abu Muhammad remembered how, after the beginning of the uprising, people were taken to prison and forced to sign documents that they would not join the demonstrations again, even if the person had never demonstrated before and even if the officers confirmed that they knew. The struggle with papers and documents was thus part of their lives in an authoritarian state and was exacerbated by the uprising. Nevertheless, it seems that being a refugee could still intensify the disputes with the authorities and increased the amount of paperwork.

It was not only the expression of critique and worries about expiring documents that alluded to the heightened relevance of papers in the context of refugeeness, but also the procedure of filling in documents that I witnessed a few times. Several Syrian families I met were constantly thinking about solutions for their situation and were filling in various applications for scholarships, resettlement or family reunions. I sensed that the effort to manage bureaucratic hurdles often evoked uncertainty, unrealistic hope and fear, which were all related to the question of whether the effort would be rewarded. Once, for instance, I helped Layla, a widowed mother of two children and the cousin of Abu Muhammad, to fill in documents to apply for family reunion with her son who had managed to gain asylum in Sweden. Layla felt extremely vulnerable with no male provider and protector in the household. She had tried to find work as a secretary in Egypt but was not working at the time I met her. She was worried about her daughter, who was studying sociology and had experienced sexual harassment several times on Cairo's streets. Abu Muhammad and his family, who were her closest contacts and support in Cairo, had been accepted for resettlement to Germany and were about to leave. Hence, Layla's situation was about to worsen. Despite the hardship she faced, the chances that the family reunion would be successful were minimal given that her son was over eighteen years old. Nevertheless, we filled in the documents required by the Swedish embassy meticulously, as if this alone could convince the authorities. I was seated on the couch with a fan directed at my face and Layla, who did not speak English, sat next to me looking over my shoulder all the time I was writing, trying to control how I filled in the papers and making sure that I did not lose focus. She did not allow her daughter, who spoke basic English, to fill in the documents, but at the same time she had difficulty trusting me with this important task. Possession and production of documents played an important role in the everyday life of Syrians in Egypt. They were deeply entangled with a sense of refugeeness and could create sentiments of insecurity, uncertainty, loss of dignity, fear and anger.

The troubling contact to the state

Closely related to their tensed relationship with (expiring) documents was Syrian men's sense of losing proper contact to the Syrian and Egyptian state. Having talked about identity documents, Abd al-Rahman took up another theme: the right to have rights based on his humanity, which he described in the following way:

> We have the right as people and from the principle of humanity to be treated with respect in any country in the world, to be provided with a living, a place to live and to be provided with a good life. An Egyptian official might say: 'I can't provide these things to my own people!' This is alright, but at least provide me with what you provide your people. You give your people an identity card and a passport. You protect your people, so why don't you protect me too?

Abd al-Rahman's words resonate with Salih's (2013: 83) observation that Palestinian refugees in Lebanon called into question that rights were only accessible for those who were citizens of the country they lived in. Criticizing this restricted access to rights, they expressed a different political imagination in which their humanity, and not their belonging to a nation state, granted them access to full rights and to political life (2013; 2018). Abd al-Rahman's experience of refugeeness leaves him critical of the political order, in which he, as a refugee, does not find a place for himself that grants him dignity and protection. Refugeeness holds the potential to shake the core of one's (legally recognized) being and the risk of loss of contact to the state. Forced migration leads to the inability to approach the state to claim basic rights, for example, the renewal of an expired passport, and consequently threatens one's ability to build self-confidence on the fact that one has the right to exist and to claim political subjectivity. I could not be certain as to why Abd al-Rahman picked these topics on the day before his wife's departure. It might have been his worries and inability to change what was about to happen. I had asked Israa, when we were alone in class a couple of days before her farewell evening, why Abd al-Rahman would not take the dangerous journey via the Mediterranean Sea to the Netherlands. She said that she did not want to stay in Egypt all by herself once her siblings and parents had left and wait for her own family reunion. She seemed determined and convinced that her trip to the Netherlands was the only reasonable decision in her situation. A couple of weeks later, I would hear from Israa's sisters during English class that Israa had arrived in a refugee camp in Italy.

Abd al-Rahman was not the only one who bemoaned the loss of dignified and human treatment since having become a refugee as well as the loss of one's former position as citizen. Bashar, Mazin's friend, discussed with me the situation of newcomers to Germany and asked:

> Is a civil servant working in the ministry able to live on the street for one week without water and a toilet? No! So why do I have to live on the streets if I come to Germany as a refugee? Because I am now a second-class human being.

Bashar referred to the news from Germany which went viral in the summer of 2015, when hundreds of new arrivals waited for many hours and even slept in front of LaGeSo (the State Office for Health and Social Affairs) in Berlin in order to submit their asylum applications (see Eddy and Johannsen 2015; Murray 2015).

Once, I met Mu'ayad for tea and shisha right after he had tried to renew his visa in the crowded *Mugamma*. He told me that he felt that his chest was about to explode. He hugged himself tightly, saying that he felt pain inside because of the problems that the Egyptian authorities and their bureaucracies caused him. He was not a talkative man and rarely shared thoughts and sentiments with people; however, the encounter with the Egyptian authorities had agitated him to an extent that he could not keep in his bodily and emotional pain. Being a refugee can thus not be reduced to a legal category, but is, at the same time, an emotional state directly related to bodily responses and reactions.

In addition to loss of contact to the state being experienced as lack of protection and becoming a second-class human, the need for making and analysing the connection between the state and the individual's worth is furthered by Dawud. He was a man in his mid-thirties who had found work as a consultant in an Egyptian organization and had just got engaged when I met him. After his arrival in Egypt, right after the beginning of the Syrian uprising, he used to travel back and forth between Syria and Egypt. He said that his stay in Egypt back then was of a 'touristic' nature, relaxing, and that he went for sightseeing trips to Alexandria. Dawud had influential contacts both in Syria and in Egypt and was in a privileged position. He thought about applying for expensive master programmes abroad. After Morsi's ousting, when visa restrictions were imposed for Syrians, Dawud began to feel troubled in Egypt. He said that perceptions of Syrians changed and that bureaucratic procedures became complicated. Not only did it become impossible to leave and re-enter Egypt, he also had to renew his visa regularly, faced difficulties obtaining a work contract and received a rejection when he tried to bring a family member from Syria to Egypt. Given the constraints he faced in Egypt since 2013, he said:

> If something happens, I hope not, then maybe I will go back to Syria. Once I went back from Egypt to Syria to see my family and frankly if I will go again, I won't come back because in your own country you feel your value, you feel that you are important among your family and friends and that is a nice thing.

Dawud's sense of lacking worth due to being outside of his homeland, far away from family and loved ones, reminds of an argument put forward by Gabiam (2015: 488) who conducted research among Palestinians in France. She stresses that statelessness evokes a sense of non-existence, lack of recognition, vulnerability to injustice and oppression, while statehood is related to belonging, control over one's life and rootedness. Bashar, Dawud and Abd al-Rahman associate a functioning contact to the state to stability and value for themselves. Again and again in this book, the topic of a man's relation with the state and his position as a citizen comes up. The just-presented narratives are the first implications of the intimate connection that exists between men and their state and the aggressive effort that is required to reconfirm one's identity if this core relationship is disturbed.

The encounter with the Egyptian authorities

For Abu Walid being in Egypt as a refugee meant not having legal assistance and being excluded from the right to be protected from crime. The father of two boys was regularly picked up at his workplace by an Egyptian police officer. Abu Walid had come to the attention of the police officer when he had tried to open a sweetshop in the area and the police regularly came to check if he had the required licences. In fact, Abu Walid could only show proof of his children's school registrations that granted the family a one-year residence permit. However, he did not hold a work permit. This is how the police officer figured out that Abu Walid was victim to his ill will. This led to several visits to Abu Walid's workplace, where the officer entered in civilian clothes and took him to the police station. There, the officer applied different strategies, accusing him of being a terrorist or a criminal and eventually settling on the fact that Abu Walid had no official work permit. Any attempt to counter the blackmail was useless, since the policeman threatened that if he did not pay the bribe he would be thrown out of Egypt. The visits became more frequent and Abu Walid became more afraid that one day he would not be able to pay the bribe and the police officer would then take him to the Syrian embassy, where he would be sent back to Syria and killed. When Abu Walid asked a lawyer at UNHCR to help him, the lawyer requested the number of Abu Walid's file at the police station. Obviously, there was no file because the blackmail happened on an individual, arbitrary basis. When Abu Walid tried to ask for international protection through the UN by calling the agency's hotline, he could not reach anyone in the relevant office. Then, Abu Walid got in touch with a lawyer working for a Syrian NGO who told him to call him the next time he was taken by the police officer. However, when this happened, the lawyer did not show up, presumably out of fear of getting into trouble himself. When Abu Walid tried to involve an international NGO, he was told that his problem with the officer was of a personal nature. The NGO caseworker was worried that if the officer was asked by the NGO law department to stop abusing Abu Walid, he would seek revenge. Even though the caseworker tried his best to help Abu Walid, he felt helpless vis-à-vis the comprehensive power of the police officer. The only advice the caseworker could give him was to find a job in another area of Cairo, where the police officer could not find him.

The experience of being victim to a police officer's malevolence and the lack of legal support were surely not exclusive to Syrians in Egypt. Indeed, large numbers of Egyptians themselves have been regularly subjected to police violence, arbitrary arrests and forced disappearances (see Hamzawy 2017; Abdelrahman 2015; HRW 2015; Ismail 2006). However, Abu Walid's specific vulnerability lies in his extreme fear of being sent to the Syrian embassy or back to Syria – an outcome of his status as a refugee, in addition to the financial and personal pressure applied by the police officer.

Refusing the categorization as refugee

Refugeeness had various facets among Syrians I met in Egypt. It created humiliation, worries and insecurity, dependence on non-governmental institutions and entities, inability to form one's future, despair and hopelessness, and pain and embarrassment. In the words of Khalid, refugeeness was like 'an injury inside' that was rarely openly discussed. In a climate in which identity needs to redevelop around and adapt to these experiences of refugeeness, I suggest that masculine identity can easily be damaged and requires active and conscious effort to be reinvented. Syrian men managed to cope with their refugeeness by applying various strategies, such as active refusal of the category and by defining who was a 'real' refugee.

The longer I spent time in Egypt and got in touch with Syrians, the more I realized that there had been an initial refusal to register with UNHCR. Several caseworkers in NGOs offering services for Syrian refugees said when asked about this phenomenon that Syrians needed time to adapt to and accept their new situation, in which they had to bear the refugee title. Khalil, for instance, a young Syrian man who worked with an Egyptian NGO offering psychosocial support to refugees, described the Syrian people as 'proud and rich'. Before the Syrian uprising, it was unthinkable for a Syrian to ask for help, he explained. Consequently, Syrians in exile needed time to accept their new status that was defined externally by need and poverty. Qutayba, who came to Egypt as a student together with his family but soon after his arrival managed to find work in an international cultural institute as an IT specialist, assumed that it was due to the sudden change in their life that Syrians were reluctant to apply for refugee status. I had met him at the party of a friend and there we had agreed to meet again for coffee. Most Syrians who came to Egypt had a good life before the outbreak of the civil war and had yet to come to terms with the abrupt transformation of their lifestyle, he said. Without intention, he gave another reason why the association with the refugee category was painful. It was when he told me about a meeting with an American female friend and how offended and embarrassed he was when she wanted to pay for their drinks giving the explanation that 'he was a refugee'. Even when he recalled the situation, I could feel his unease about being considered poor because of the association of his nationality with refugeeness and of refugeeness with poverty. This seemed to be a painful form of misrecognition for someone who earned 1,000 US dollar per months, as he proudly mentioned, and who had decided to donate a fifth of his monthly income to Syria.

There are certain attributes associated with the 'genuine refugee', such as pacifism, morality, trauma, victimhood and femininity (Griffiths 2015: 472; Pupavac 2008: 272). Other associations with the refugee are neediness, lack of competence and helplessness (Szczepanikova 2010: 466/470). The reluctance of most Syrians in Egypt to publicly admit one's need and poverty and to being associated with these attributes shows the difficulties Syrians had with interiorizing their identity as refugees.

Another reason for rejecting the association with refugeeness was put forward by Abu Muhannad, who had successfully opened a cosmetics shop in 6th of October City and could pay the fees at a private university for his two eldest sons. Everything in his shop and his office, from the giant leather seat to the selection of items, alluded to his privileged background. Sitting in his office, Abu Muhannad recounted how life in Syria became dangerous, how he and his wife decided to come to Cairo where his children could study in safety, and how he got the 'yellow card' recently. He described Syrians as 'a people without a country, like the Palestinians'. Yet, he strongly opposed the stigmatizing refugee label because of its incompatibility with Syria's perceived wealth and history:

> Refugee is a difficult word for me. It doesn't fit the Syrian people. We are from a rich country and we had everything. We have never been refugees before.

He assured me emphatically that he would not accept being called a refugee by an Egyptian:

> I would kill the Egyptian who says to me that I am a refugee. We have developed 6th of October City to what it is today. There was nothing here before. It is only through the Syrians that 6th of October City has become such a good place.

In fact, several neighbourhoods in 6th of October had visibly changed because of the arrival of Syrians who had opened restaurants, bakeries, retail shops and hair salons there. Abu Muhannad refused the attributes associated with refugeeness for himself and the Syrian people and the rage and firmness with which he expressed his argument showed that refugeeness was a threat to his sense of dignity and pride as a Syrian man. My encounter with Abu Muhannad is furthermore evocative of the relationship to the state. I heard the comparison of Syrians with the Palestinians – a people without a state – several times over the course of my fieldwork and read it as an expression of the feeling of severe loss of a recognized nation state as one's backbone that deeply concerned and affected Syrian men.

In a similar vein, Abu Muhannad's son, who had taken me to his father's shop and had introduced me, opposed the stigmatizing refugee label. Muhannad repeatedly mentioned that he perceived it as his mission to transform the picture of the needy, poor, victimized Syrian refugee in Egyptian society. On the desk of his office, he had put a golden name plate with his name preceded by the title 'Doctor', which, in fact, he did not hold. He had given the advice to his colleagues and volunteers to attend every event they organized for *Fursa* or were invited to in white button-down shirts and jackets. Muhannad explained to me that he did not only aim to prove the image of the active, self-confident young Syrian outwardly to the Egyptian host population, but also wanted to instil self-esteem in the young Syrian volunteers who had to cope with their new, externally imposed status as refugees. This included a mission to move on from 'old ideas and practices'.

Muhannad prohibited political talks among *Fursa*'s staff and volunteers and taught them constantly that they were representing 'all of Syria'.

Majd, a student of economics in his early twenties who worked while studying and participated in some of the events organized by *Fursa*, had high ambitions for the future. He stressed his initial reluctance to go to the UNHCR office and explained that he and his mother did not want to have refugee status because of their notable family background. Majd was a short man with a deep voice and brimmed with self-confidence. Regularly, I saw him on stage, performing songs or giving lectures to high school graduates as part of *Fursa*'s events. At our first meeting, when he helped me to organize an English class, he told me that his great-grandfather used to hold a key role on the political stage before Hafez al-Asad's rule. Because of being from a family of 'influential politicians and investors', as he called it, in whose footsteps he wanted to follow, he did not find it easy to reconcile his lineage with claiming asylum. What changed his mind eventually was the increasing insecurity of living in Egypt without a proper residence permit. Because of his initial enrolment in school and being granted a student residency, Majd and his mother could eventually stay in Egypt. However, for a while, it was uncertain whether he could continue his studies at one of the Egyptian universities and thus Majd decided that it was safer to go to UNHCR and apply for refugee status. In order to justify his decision, he said:

> I don't like the idea of asylum, however, this card [the yellow card] is like a guarantee for the future, so if in the future I need to seek asylum, I should have this card with me in order to get a visa.

Majd was guided by pragmatism and the hope that registration with UNHCR could be useful in an uncertain future after his initial rejection. In a similar vein, Ghassan, the high school student who wanted to pursue a career as a pharmacist, justified his registration and use of the 'yellow card':

> Yes, I went to UNHCR and I have the yellow card. At the beginning, we didn't want it, however, for four months we have it now. At the end, this yellow card can be useful if the father or mother dies and the children become orphans. Maybe then the UN can help them. If you have a legal problem, the UN lawyer can defend you, especially if they arrest you and they want to send you back to Syria. In this situation, it is useful.

It was pragmatism and a sense of being prepared through registration for unforeseen problems and circumstances that motivated Ghassan to go to UNHCR.

Even though many Syrian men I met rejected the refugee category for themselves and tried to distance themselves from it in their narratives, almost all of them had eventually registered with UNHCR. Their action thus stood in contrast to their narratives. Ayoub and Khallaf's (2014: 22) study of Syrian refugees in Egypt stresses that most Syrians eventually registered with UNHCR because of the changing political situation in the summer of 2013 and the consequent heightened need for protection and assistance. This rejection of the refugee marker for various reasons and simultaneous acceptance of the refugee status to guarantee one's security in Egypt reverberate with Peteet's (2005: 209) argument that the meaning of legal refugee status among Palestinians in Lebanon was not constant over time but shifted in accordance with the power and persistence of the Palestinian resistance movement. At times when they were empowered by the resistance movement, the Palestinians in Lebanon rejected any self-reference as refugees. However, belonging to the category eventually became a necessity in order to receive services from United Nations Relief and Works Agency for Palestinian Refugees in the Near East (UNRWA) (2005: 210). In a similar vein, Ludwig (2013: 13) and Malkki (1995a: 158/159) in their respective fields of study observed changing uses of the refugee status over time. The early years of displacement were related to social hardship, poverty and acknowledgement of being a refugee, while leaving refugee status behind became a marker of success at a later point in time. In contrast to both scholars who found that refugeeness was primarily linked to early years in the host country, most Syrians I met strictly refused any identification with refugeeness when they first arrived in Egypt and only recognized and reluctantly accepted its usefulness and necessity at a later stage of their stay in exile. The initial reluctance followed by an eventual acceptation of the refugee status relates to the specificity of the Syrian case in terms of its uncertain outcome: when I conducted fieldwork, Syrians in Egypt had been displaced for no more than two or three years and the civil war in Syria was ongoing. Their mindset, thinking and planning still had one foot in Syria and they were in a position of absolute liminality, not knowing if they could return to Syria or would continue with their journey in exile. Since they had experienced a worsening of their situation in Egypt over time, it comes as no surprise that Majd and Ghassan, like many others, opted for a pragmatic solution expecting potential further deterioration of the circumstances in Egypt.

Creating distance from the refugee label

Having discussed why most of the Syrians I met rejected the refugee definition for themselves for as long as possible, this chapter now turns to the strategies applied by several of the Syrian men to actively distance themselves from this category. I found the use of these strategies especially prominent among Syrian men who were relatively well off in Egypt, having found work and being able to live a relatively comfortable life. When I asked tour guide Mahmud, whom I had first met back in Damascus and whom I used to meet regularly in Cairo, whether he felt like a refugee he answered:

> On the one hand, we can say refugee because I am afraid of going back to Syria, so I can be considered a refugee. At the same time, however, I am working and I sometimes help if I can, and in this case, I don't feel like a refugee.

Mahmud did not only speak about helping, but often donated parts of his income to Syrian families in need in 6th of October City. The ability to work and provide for oneself as a marker of incompatibility with refugee status is even more pronounced in Hani's narrative. The student of dentistry made it clear that he had nothing in common with what he perceived as the prototype of a refugee.

> I don't feel like a refugee because the government doesn't pay for me and there is a difference between someone who is supported by the government and someone who doesn't receive anything. I am not like this. I am working and I pay the rent and I pay for my life. I don't need the government to help me.

Hani's account suggests that being an independent agent, who can lead and control his life, is incompatible with the 'genuine refugee'. Both Syrian men actively created their identity by referring to what they were not, namely beneficiaries of governmental support, purposeless and unable to ensure their own survival. A similar line of thought was present in many other conversations: accepting external help was generally conflated with being a refugee and hence rejected for as long as possible. Creation of distance was one of the prominent strategies applied by well-off Syrian men to clarify their non-belonging to the refugee category. They highlighted how and why their personality, background and lifestyle had nothing in common with the prototype of a refugee. 'Masculinity is defined more by what one is not rather than who one is' (Kimmel 1994: 126) and following a similar line of argumentation Syrian men made sure that they were positioned as the opposite, namely, active, independent and in charge of their lives. Syrian men made use of resources and strategies that were available to them in their position as refugees experiencing various challenges to their identities once taken for granted.

The importance of destination and transportation

Besides the significance of work and independence from support, Mahmud's and Hani's statements include another aspect that was taken as a proof of their personal incompatibility with the title of the refugee: they had a purpose in life. Mahmud worked as a tour guide and Hani was a university student. Likewise, Ghassan's statement asserts that having a purpose in life could not be aligned with refugeeness:

> The people who are going by boats to Europe can be considered refugees, but if you are a student and you want to study, I think that they will accept you as a student. Then, you will work hard and you will be useful for their country.

Ghassan created a hierarchy between the people who migrated by boat, who could not easily escape the refugee definition over time, and a student, who would eventually be useful to the host country. In addition, he relates refugeeness to migration to Europe via the Mediterranean Sea. This needs to be placed in context: all the Syrians I met in Cairo had travelled to Egypt by plane. This clearly related to their class background and the timing of their trip: they had left Syria early after the outbreak of the uprising when there were no visa requirements for Syrians and had had the financial capability to pay for a ticket for themselves and their families. Their trip had been direct and relatively safe, mainly departing from Damascus airport and arriving without further interruption in Cairo. Ghassan disparages Syrians in Europe because of the means of transportation they used to travel to the host country, which indicates despair and the inability to choose a safer option for oneself and one's family. In a similar vein, Mahmud once told me:

> Now you can read on Facebook that Syrians differentiate based on how they came to Europe. They say: 'You came by boat but we came by plane!'

The classification he refers to is most likely based on the fact that travelling to Europe via plane was only possible if one had a visa in advance or was chosen to resettle by UNHCR. The judgement of the individual's means of transportation thus seems to relate to one's legality in the host country and the legality of one's journey.[3]

The strategic importance of stressing one's independence from government support, one's success in the Egyptian labour market and the emphasis of one's incompatibility with the refugee definition explain why those Syrian men who were in a good economic position in Egypt often immediately clarified what brought them to Cairo during our first encounter. They mentioned that they came to Egypt for economic reasons, like businessman Faris who stressed that he was sent by his boss in Syria to become the supervisor of a local branch of the company in Egypt. Others mentioned immediately that they came to study. Correspondingly, Syrian men with work and relative security in Cairo stated that they would only go to Europe to pursue education or a specific career. Dawud, for instance, described what would have motivated him to go to Europe:

> I tried to go to Europe through scholarships and I tried to apply with some organisations like the UN but I got rejected. There are ideas that you can improve and develop in order to use them later to return to the homeland, as generations, as governments, as society. I wanted to study conflicts that happened around the world during a master's programme.

The focus in Dawud's narrative is on a legal entry into Europe and a purpose for his stay that would even benefit Syrian society in the post-conflict era. He also clarifies his privileged position as someone who would only go to Europe to pursue masters.

The discussion revolving around one's personal incompatibility with the refugee label because of one's educational aspiration or background reiterates the model of the modern middle-class man, which emerged at the beginning of the twentieth century in the Eastern Mediterranean (Watenpaugh 2006: 89). The modern, middle-class man was in the first place defined by his intellectual action and stood out by his political, social and commercial achievements in the public sphere. Being a modern middle-class man or woman meant reaching out for education, cultural and social improvement as well as political awareness (Watenpaugh 2006: 90/91). These attributes still resonate with prominent characterizations of middle-classness in Syria and Egypt. Conducting research among Aleppian traders, Anderson (2018: 258) argues that being middle class is defined by its claim to order, culture, civility and intellectuality. As for Egypt, middle-classness means being educated and acquainted with modern institutions and enjoying a 'clean' life at a distance from the Egyptian working class (see de Koning 2009: 12). The focus on one's incompatibility with the refugee label based on one's profession, educational aspirations, achievements and hard work thus suggests a form of masculinity based on a middle-class consciousness.

Refugees in Europe

Based on the idea that being a refugee was contradictory to successful participation in the labour market, many Syrians, who were in a privileged situation, additionally stated that only the economically successful Syrian newcomers stayed in Egypt, while those who could not settle and make ends meet left for Europe. Syrians in Europe were described by Abu Muhannad as coming 'from a lower-class background', and by Muhannad as 'a burden on society' and 'lazy'. In contrast, Syrians who stayed in Egypt were defined by Faris as 'rich and hardworking'. With these narratives conveying a sense of arrogance and pretension, Syrian men not only created distance from, but also identified themselves as superior to, refugees in Europe based on their attributed hard work, class background and wealth. They actively de-classed refugees in Europe and reclaimed their own middle-class belonging.

Over the course of my fieldwork, I realized that Europe occupied an ambivalent status. Most Syrians I met believed that life in Europe for Syrians arriving as refugees was good and certainly better than the treatment Syrians experienced in Egypt and the wider Middle East. Often, I heard idealized assumptions which were clearly based on rumours and speculations. Abu Ali an elderly man who came with his wife to seek support from an NGO in which I volunteered on that day, said:

> As refugees in Europe our situation would be much better. Here, we don't get anything as refugees. In Europe, there is money, they give you houses and 300 dollars [*sic*]. The Syrians in Europe are refugees just like we are, but we are underprivileged. No one knows how to deal with us. They don't care for us.

In addition to the widespread belief that Europe treated refugees well, Syrians talked frequently about the stable political and economic situation they believed they would find in Europe and about its considerable development, wealth and progress.

In contrast to these assumptions, I also heard that European countries were perceived as the countries of the unbelievers, where morals and values were degraded and people did not care for each other. Europe was associated with sexual relationships before or outside marriage, promiscuity, sexual laxity, and a lack of morals and code of ethics. Frequently, I was asked by Syrians who had relatives in Europe or planned on going to Europe themselves, if and how the governments in Europe would interfere in the nuclear family's life: Would the child be taken away by the state authorities, if it was beaten once? How much parental authority was acceptable? Do the voice and signature of a woman as wife and mother count as much or more than the husband's or father's? Can a woman decide family-related issues on her own without consulting her husband? Can she travel on her own? Abu Muhammad, who was preparing himself and his family for resettlement to Germany, had several questions and concerns regarding his prospective life there and told me the following:

> If you go to Europe you should assimilate and accept new things. You will need to spend at least one year studying the language. You will waste one year only for getting a language certificate. I wasted years of my life just because of this. It's better to study German in Syria and then go to Germany immediately. It's better than staying in Germany for two years doing nothing but studying the language. I am really upset that I will go to Germany and lose two years of my life.

Here, living in Europe is clearly associated with a standstill in one's personal development and with giving up autonomy over one's personal plans and preferences in exchange for asylum and the obligations that come with it.

Likewise, Qays, the founder of an aid organization for Syrians in Cairo, was critical of the idea of leaving the Middle East for Europe. I met him in his office which was located directly next to the rooms of *Fursa*. Muhannad had introduced Qays to me and had invited Qays to talk to me about his work. Sitting in his newly opened office behind a huge desk in an otherwise empty room under cold neon light, Qays seemed eager to promote the NGO's mission and engaged in lengthy monologues. He only spoke in Modern Standard Arabic to me, presumably to make his words sound more sophisticated, educated and convincing:

> In Germany, there are Syrians who prefer to just take money, so they don't need to worry about anything. The Egyptian society is close to the Syrian society. It's better that the Syrian stays in societies that are close to our societies. Western society for us is a strange and different society. Europe and the US are strange for us. They are different from Middle Eastern societies. Many Syrians left and went to Europe. I find it strange. It means that there is a social problem. I don't remember that the Germans left Germany after the war. I didn't hear anything like that. And even if the German left the country, he decided to come back to rebuild Germany.

Qays juxtaposes the proximity of Egyptian and Syrian culture with the alienating 'other' culture of the West. Even though he was at times critical of the Egyptian host population, in this specific context he made use of the notion of the uniting, border-crossing Arab culture. The refugee who seeks asylum outside of the Middle East is looked down upon because he is only after the social benefits he will receive, giving up for financial support the geographic and 'cultural' proximity to the Middle East.

While Europe was associated with progress, stability, wealth and provision of financial support for refugees, it was similarly connoted with an unlikeable value system, standstill, enforced adaptation and assimilation as well as acceptance of state inference in family life. Europe's ambiguous status played a role in the creation of the image of people who sought asylum there.

Developing new masculine hierarchies

Muhannad was not against going abroad. In fact, several times we filled in scholarship applications together because he wanted to attend summer school in the United States or a conference or a language course in Europe. However, he disagreed with the rising trend of Syrians leaving for Europe via the Mediterranean Sea or the Balkan route.

> When the guy cannot find a job, cannot study and cannot find anything [in Egypt], he will think about going to Europe. In Europe, he will drink, he will eat and he will sleep. Should this be the reason to make me leave? Why? Here, I am going out, I am working, I am meeting people and I am getting new experiences. There, I will just stay at home and I will be a burden on society.

Muhannad describes a man who is in Europe to satisfy his basic instincts, while being unable to meet his manly responsibilities, which consequently turns him into a burden for the family and society. Furthermore, he was critical of the illegality of actions people accepted in order to enter Europe:

> Why do you travel to Europe via the sea? You can apply for a scholarship and you can travel the legal way!

This echoes the theme of legality or 'illegality' that was brought up by Ghassan in relation to the means of transportation from Syria to Europe. Furthermore, it displays Muhannad's privileged position as a student at a private university and potential recipient of scholarships unable to imagine the plight that forced others to risk their lives by crossing the Mediterranean.

In a similar vein, Mahmud said in one of our conversations that Syrians in Europe had opted for an undignified treatment only to receive financial support in return.

They must feel like beggars in Europe since they are dependent on money from the government. No one admits it, but it really does something to the people. No one would have ever accepted such support in Syria. This goes against one's dignity.

Just like Muhannad, Mahmud had thought more than once about travelling to Europe, weighing his options and trying to estimate which place could guarantee him most security, well-being and a meaningful future. He then decided that staying in Egypt was his best option. In Cairo, he could continue working and would not need to interrupt it or find a new profession while waiting for his legal status determination in a European refugee camp. By comparing them with beggars, Mahmud created the image of Syrians in Europe as people who should be pitied and looked down upon, positioned at the bottom of society. The beggar is often associated with a physical handicap and consequent dependence. A person who is physically whole and still begs is thus considered shameful and can only be ridiculed (McSpadden and Moussa 1993: 210). Following this perception, Mahmud described Syrians in Europe as the ones who had lost their former status and became the ones who were the lowest in the hierarchy, left without agency and totally dependent on help from outside. Mahmud thus strips refugees in Europe of their agency and dignity.

Even though Mahmud was convinced that travelling to Europe was not feasible for him, he kept complaining about his life in Egypt. He told me how he once got in trouble with an Egyptian doorman when he wanted to withdraw money from his bank account. The Egyptian doorman, when he had found out that Mahmud was from Syria, made a joke about Syrian women working as prostitutes in Egypt. Angrily, Mahmud told him:

If a war breaks out in your country, you will hear stories worse than this about your people. In any place in the world, if there is a war, you will even find men working in prostitution. The war makes people this way. If there was a war in Egypt, you will find more Egyptians than Syrians travelling to Europe!

The doorman answered that he could not imagine that Egyptians would ever leave their beloved country. Outraged, Mahmud responded:

Yes, you will leave your country! We said the same. We said that we would never leave Syria and now we are spread all over the world!

This conversation is revealing because it brings in the urgency and despair of forced displacement from a war-torn country that ultimately changes those affected by it. Leaving one's country is used here to define the individual's failure and functions as a humiliating insult. The underlying theme is a man's responsibility vis-à-vis his home country. A hierarchy is established based on a man's decision to stay put in one's homeland and the undignified option to flee.

Finding work, a purpose in life and independence from government support were the resources several Syrian men used to create markers of successful manhood. They used the currency of managing one's life upon displacement to create a hierarchy between themselves and others, labelling those, who in their perception were the least successful, namely the one who takes a boat to Europe, as refugee. The refugee in Europe is then described in the most unmanly way: as the 'useless burden' and the 'beggar' who gives up dignity to satisfy basic needs. He does not meet manly responsibilities of staying and rebuilding one's home country and chooses external feeding over work. The outcome of this process was the creation of a hierarchy in which Syrian men in Egypt, no matter if they were successful in their strivings or not, could still make themselves and others believe that they were more of a man than refugees in Europe.

Conclusion

This chapter described situations and encounters in Egypt that made Syrians feel like belonging to the refugee category, such as encounters with UNHCR or the Egyptian authorities. Refugeeness informed most Syrians' lives in one way or another: it was experienced as feelings of insecurity, uncertainty, helplessness, as well as anger and frustration, when men felt that their dignity was challenged. Some Syrian men sensed that their identity was in question and that they were subject to others' ill will. They felt the need to reconfirm themselves and did this aggressively. Being identified as a refugee led to furious disentanglement of one's self from the ascribed label and its consequences. By distancing themselves from the refugee category, Syrian men tried to keep their dignity and pride intact. Another underlying emotion was arrogance that came to the surface when men engaged in the demarcation of those who were perceived to stand lower in the hierarchy. The prototype of a refugee that Syrian men created was the refugee in Europe – an emasculated phantom. Syrian men in Egypt created a hierarchy by downplaying this 'other' Syrian, who sought refuge in Europe. The discussion about the 'other's' refugeeness not only is a way to prove one's incompatibility with the refugee label, but simultaneously establishes proper middle-class manhood. Syrian men I met actively erected boundaries and a hierarchy based on their self-ascribed moral and economic superiority and stern discipline in contrast to the Syrian refugee's assumed laziness in Europe, and based on their loyalty to the Arab world, in contrast to the Syrian refugee's willingness to compromise their autonomy and lifestyle in return for governmental support in Europe.

Chapter 3

CLAIMING SUCCESSFUL MIDDLE-CLASS MASCULINITY THROUGH WORK

Having discussed what instilled a sense of refugeeness in Syrian men and how men found ways to disconnect themselves from the label and from other people associated with that label, this chapter turns to Syrian men's experiences in the Egyptian labour market and how they claimed successful middle-class masculinities through their engagement in paid labour. Scholars dealing with men and masculinities have long recognized and theorized about the connection between employment and masculinities (see Connell 1995; Edwards 2006; Collinson and Hearn 2005; Morgan 1992). Particularly in the context of migration and forced displacement, scholarly attention has focused on men's ability to work and remain as provider for the family. This literature suggests that men are likely to experience a crisis when they can no longer uphold their status as provider, and especially if women take over increased economic responsibilities (see Kabachnik et al. 2013; Donaldson and Howson 2009; Jaji 2009; Schrijvers 1999). Another recurrent focus in the literature targets the question of whether men and women's changing economic responsibilities and daily practices during displacement lead to the transformation of gender relations (see Brun 2000; Turner 2000). Charsley and Wray (2015: 407) argue that (forced) migration can challenge gendered domestic relations of power and that these challenges are especially tough on men leading frequently to conflict and frustration.

Discussions with Syrian men about their work conditions and their perceptions of Syrian working women suggest that they identified an ideal of Syrian middle-class masculinity through narratives about their own and other men's and women's work. They idealized complementary gender roles: on the one hand, there was the man as provider and breadwinner; on the other hand, there was the woman who was in the privileged position, because of her male kin's work, to stay at home. Despite this verbal idealization, most Syrian men in Egypt were not in the position to confidently claim for themselves success in being providers and in allowing their female kin to stay at home. In fact, most Syrian men I met faced various challenges as participants in the Egyptian labour market and in several families Syrian women had picked up work in Egypt. The fact that Syrian men were in Egypt as refugees often aggravated their working conditions, and at the same time, it seemed to enforce a stricter version of middle-class masculinity and stern identification with this ideal. Thus, two contradictory narratives were prevalent and persisted despite their incompatibility: the discourse of the providing man and his female kin who has the luxury to stay at home, and the accounts dealing with challenges in the Egyptian labour market that enforced on Syrian men to work for low salary, under challenging conditions and in professions they considered inferior to their education and status. Being faced with these challenges, some Syrian men highlighted their qualities as entrepreneurs. The narratives and worries revolving around the challenges in the Egyptian labour market differed depending on a man's position within the family, whether he was a young man or a father. Focusing on men who were at different stages of their lives, I show in this chapter that it is important for an analysis of masculinities to take into consideration men's age, position in the family and specific social context. Furthermore, this chapter analyses women's roles and stakes in negotiations and constructions of masculinities. I show in this chapter how women held various positions: in men's narratives, they were relegated to the household to complement a system in which Syrian men could define themselves as the provider for the family. They were the ones against which Syrian men masculinized when they were described as 'weak' and 'unable' to deal with the consequences of forced displacement. However, at the same time, Syrian men had to acknowledge reluctantly that women were indeed active in the labour market and had begun to change their lifestyles and perceptions accordingly. In some cases, women came to a man's rescue, when they downplayed their own contributions to the household income or when they defended a man who did not live up to common expectations in public.

Syrians in the Egyptian labour market

Syrians coming to Egypt encounter a saturated, overcrowded and unstable labour market and live in an overall climate of precarity. Over the past decades, the Egyptian government liberalized its economy, reducing public services and subsidies, selling off a significant share of the public sector and decreasing government employment (Singerman 2013: 4). In this process of liberalization, Mubarak's government launched legal reforms to guarantee 'flexible' employment, privatized agriculture, removed trade barriers and put the interests of capital above all else (Abdelrahman 2015: 7). The gradual removal of the welfare structure and state subsidies on food, education and housing sectors had a major effect on the economic well-being of the rural and urban poor (Ali 2003: 323). Deboulet (2009: 202) identifies a 'generation of neoliberal modernity' that lives predominantly in informal neighbourhoods, consisting of deprived families who do not receive any security from the state because of the unavailability of subsidized goods and services as well as the scarcity of jobs and low wages. Sixty per cent of all workers in Egypt are employed in the informal economy, which means that most of them lack minimum wage protection, health insurance, pensions, sick leave, paid vacations, maternity benefits and trade union protection

(Singerman 2013: 1). Furthermore, a significant number of Egyptians are either unemployed or underemployed, and even those with higher education often have to work in the informal sector (Grabska 2006: 15).

Compared to other refugee groups living in Egypt, Syrians are considered advantaged in the Egyptian labour market because of their reputation as experienced and hard-working employees and entrepreneurs[1] with outstanding skills in the food industry (Ayoub 2017; Ayoub and Khallaf 2014: 25).[2] In fact, the Syrian presence in Egypt is demonstrable through the proliferation of Syrian restaurants, food shops and bakeries, and their increasing visibility in the Egyptian food sector has attracted national and international media attention (e.g. Kingsley 2013; Primo 2015; Shahine 2016). Nevertheless, despite the reported success of a few Syrian restaurant managers and company owners in Egypt, the majority of Syrians work informally, having changed their occupation and taken up less-skilled jobs (Ayoub and Khallaf 2014: 27; International Labour Organisation 2015: 20).[3] There is no doubt that the economic situation of most Syrians in Egypt worsened over the years with decreasing support available from UNHCR, loss of savings and because of their alleged association with and support for the Muslim Brotherhood in the Egyptian public (Ayoub 2017).

The variety of work experiences that Syrian men in Egypt faced was reflected in their occupations. Over the course of my fieldwork, I met a chef in a Syrian fast-food restaurant, a dentist, numerous case workers in NGOs, several shop assistants, a shop manager, a housekeeper, a young man employed in IT support, primary school and language teachers, taxi drivers and shop owners. Some had received or 'bought', as Dawud put it, permission to work; however, most of them worked informally. Apart from Abu Walid, who was threatened and blackmailed by a police officer because he had no work permit, most Syrian men I met assured me that they could work in Egypt with no fear of interference by the state. Nevertheless, even if the state seemed to turn a blind eye to Syrians' informal labour, their work conditions were mostly far from satisfactory.

Claiming middle-class masculinity through complementary gender roles

When talking with Syrian men about work, I heard frequently quite general statements referring to traditions, customs and habits that were considered 'Syrian'. These statements established a framework of acceptable divisions of labour within the family, ideal gender roles and relations. This gendered framework was static and in most cases unrelated to the lived experiences and challenges Syrians faced both back in Syria and in Egypt. Through the reference to Syrian traditions, customs and habits, Syrian men showed the enormous value they ascribed to the ideal of provider masculinity. Majd, the student of economics who worked while studying, had invited me home. He and his widowed mother lived in an upcoming area of Cairo in a spacious flat on the ground floor. Majd's mother, a resolute woman, had furnished and decorated the flat. They could not bring any belongings from Syria, she told me. 'Even our clothes are new', Majd explained. Then, he and his mother began to show me pictures of friends, family, their property and a wedding back in their hometown. While going through the pictures and images saved on their mobile phones and laptop, Majd's mother mentioned repeatedly that they were from an influential family. Several family members used to be prominent politicians before Hafez al-Asad became president. Um Majd described how she spent her days while her son was out to study and volunteer. She said that she would not meet other Syrians. Instead, she would often go to a mall in neighbourhood to drink a coffee, smoke and dwell on her thoughts. Occasionally, she worked from home as a tailor, sewing prayer garments which she sent to her relatives in Saudi Arabia who sold them for her. She prepared a simple meal, *mujaderra* (a bulgur and lentil dish) and *laban be kheyar* (joghurt with cucumbers), for us while Majd engaged in lengthy analyses of the political situation back in Syria. When turning to the topic of the Syrian community in Egypt and how they stayed true to their traditions, which differed from those in Egyptian society, he said:

> In our tradition, it's shameful if the woman is responsible for providing money for the house. This is shameful for the man. If she wants to work because she wants to go out and get to know people, it's okay. However, if she has to pay for the flat – no, if she has to buy the house – no, if she has to pay for her clothes – no, if she has to pay for her gold – no. This is the man's responsibility.

Majd identified and idealized 'traditional' gender relations in a system that naturalized men in the provider position and women in the position of the weak and privileged in need of manly protection. According to the rules of this gendered regime, women's options in the labour market were clearly demarcated and limited. Shame and loss of respectability await the man who cannot uphold the ideal of provider masculinity.

In a conversation I had with Samir, a middle-aged director of the Syrian programme in an influential NGO providing support for refugees who lived in a middle-class neighbourhood in Cairo together with his parents, he presented a similar idea of women's roles and appreciated contributions. We met in a crowded café enjoying the evening breeze after a hot day in June drinking cocktails made from different fruit juices. Samir had agreed to talk with me about his work in the NGO. Over the course of our three-hour long conversation, Samir emphasized several times that in his family all men were working. He was convinced that most Syrian men would rather work for twelve hours a day than accepting support from NGOs. In order to clarify his position vis-à-vis working women, Samir described a situation he had faced in the context of his work. He recalled how a Western donor organization suggested an approach directed at Syrian women, which he strongly condemned. The donor organization had announced that it would support Syrian women who submitted ideas for business plans aimed at earning an income for the family. Indignantly, Samir said:

> It is as if you asked a child to hold 100 kg. If you ask a man to hold 100 kg, he will find it hard, but a child will not be able to do it at all. In Syria, women took care

of their husbands and children only and now they are supposed to come up with business ideas. In Syria, it's not appreciated to have a wife that works.

In an essentializing and homogenizing manner, Samir explained that Syrian women were not able to stand up to the responsibility of earning an income because they had not been exposed to work in Syria. The ability to work is, in his account, comparable to bodily strength that women simply lack. He portrayed women's labour as impossible and additionally unappreciated. Samir stressed that back in Syria only 5 per cent of all women would work while 95 per cent would stay at home. If women worked, they would have worked as doctors or teachers, he said, but never as cleaners. This image is far from representing the reality. In fact, many households in Syria depended on women's participation in the labour market (Shaaban 1998; Rabo 1996). However, it proves Samir's classed perspective on Syrian society.

For Muhannad, the student and founder of *Fursa* who emphasized several times that he came from a conservative town in Syria where it was uncommon to see women in the streets who were not veiled, the incompatibility of Syrianness and female labour was a unifying aspect, a way the Syrian community came to imagine itself. I asked him, while we were sitting in a fast-food restaurant in 6th of October City and I watched him eating a burger in between meetings and while taking several phone calls, whether there was a new form of responsibility put on the shoulders of men during forced displacement. He told me:

> For us as Syrian society, the common thing is that the girl doesn't work. In the Egyptian society, the majority of the girls work. In Syria, however, the girl is *sitt al-bayt* (the queen of the house). The potential jobs for the girls are usually employee or assistant. There are the possible professions. Other jobs are usually not an option. It is very very rare. Even if there is only one guy in the family usually he is the one responsible for all of them.

He created an imagined Syrian communality based on the idea that women's participation in the labour market used to be uncommon. He continued:

> I told you that a high percentage of Syrians don't like, even if he is about to die from hunger, to ask his wife or sister to go to work. He finds it difficult to request money from her or her family. For us, it is a big shame, if I don't spend for the family. Even if I am dying from hunger, I rather choose to die. Likewise, if I receive a guest, I should be generous with him even if I don't have anything. Poverty is not a shame, but the mistakes are a shame.

Muhannad masculinized the notion of responsibility and spoke in idealized terms about men's obligation to provide. His descriptions were permeated by notions of respectability and the threat to lose respect if women work at all (or in specific professions) and if men do not make all the effort to shoulder provision for their kin. Describing women's contribution to the household as disgrace and failure, the notion of shame looms on the horizon and applies to the man who cannot provide for his family. Muhannad had not experienced poverty and spoke from a privileged position.

The presented narratives suggest that the speakers remained on a meta level and were thus a testimony of the speakers' aloofness and inability to relate to a form of precarity in which each member of the household needs to labour. Majd, Muhannad and Samir all referred to some form of 'tradition', past, culture or life back in Syria to define men's and women's position in Syrian society and to put their claims on stable grounds. There are several motives why men made such strong cases about Syrian traditions and men's and women's roles: by turning to terms such as tradition and culture, they were able to gain credibility and give their statements weight. They could create 'images of timelessness and subjection' (Tétreault 2000: 75) implying that Syrian men's and women's positions in life were determined by certain essential qualities. It's not uncommon that men make use of the notion of tradition to guarantee and preserve their dominant position over women (see Ratele 2013; Kleist 2010; Sideris 2004; Carrigan, Connell and Lee 1985). Syrian men seemed to need such language and rhetoric in order to protect their self-worth and self-image and in order to clarify their personal incompatibility with the shameful position of not being a providing man. Several Syrian men were in fact in precarious positions in the Egyptian labour market und struggled to make ends meet for themselves and their families. Another reason for valuing the ideal of complementary gender roles relates to Syrian men's aim to claim for themselves forms of successful and respectable middle-class masculinities.

Challenges in the Egyptian labour market

Syrian men's presentations of complementary gender roles and the idealization of men's position as the provider stood in sharp contrast to the accounts of what they experienced as participants in the Egyptian labour market. Once, I asked Dawud about the challenges Syrians in Egypt faced. It was an evening in Ramadan and he and his sister Nur had invited me to their flat for *iftar* (evening meal during Ramadan). After food, we watched TV and I had the change to discuss with Dawud what it meant to work in Egypt. He said:

> The situation is difficult because of the visa. The people say that the work situation is normal by now and that you can find work. Sometimes they say that the Egyptian worker is demanding but that's not true because at least he doesn't need the things that people from another nationality require. You need documents from the ministry of social affairs and you also need health insurance and a visa. These are the necessary things for the non-Egyptian workers.

Since arriving in Egypt, Dawud had worked as a consultant for several Egyptian organizations and could thus be considered to be in a fortunate, privileged position. The siblings' flat was spacious and luxuriously furnished. Several times, I met them in a branch of an international café chain close to their home that was foremost frequented by foreigners and middle- and upper-class Egyptians. Concerning the work conditions for Syrians in Egypt, he continued:

> There are some Egyptians who give work to Syrians but without contracts. Additionally, they make them work longer hours than the Egyptians. Their salary is low and I don't want to say that Egyptian employers are 'taking advantage', but I see that the Syrians are better workers than the Egyptians. [...] Some people opened restaurants and some people opened clothes shops. They are working in these fields because they already have experiences. You cannot work in something that you don't know. A restaurant or a sweet shop or clothes shop, these types of shops are the main jobs that the Syrians do.

Dawud emphasized on Syrians' energy, sense of entrepreneurship and imported knowledge, despite the hardship they faced as non-Egyptians seeking work in Egypt. His sister Nur who had a well-paying job added, her eyes fixed on the TV screen, that she and her brother saw that Syrians were preferred by Egyptian employers because they would work more efficiently for the same payment, had a better education and would not disagree with their employers. When I asked her why Syrians would not protest, Nur simply answered: 'because they cannot complain'. Nur had found work in an Egyptian ministry and said that this situation was 'a little bit rare' among Syrians in Egypt. In the siblings' accounts, it was Syrians' experiences, commitment and knowledge combined with being disadvantaged vis-à-vis Egyptian workers because of their precarious position as foreigners in Egypt that defined their work conditions. Nevertheless, Dawud and Nur did not miss to convey a sense of pride in Syrians' work ethics, while they acknowledged the shame and unease related to being helpless vis-à-vis exploitation and abuse on the part of the Egyptian employers.

In contrast to Dawud and Nur's perspective, which was defined by their relative privileges in the labour market, Abu Walid did not manage to bring in a notion of pride when speaking about his challenges of being informally employed in Egypt. The first time I met Abu Walid in the accessories shop, where he was a shop assistant, was on the Egyptian national holiday *sham al-nassim* (Egyptian Spring Festival). The shop consisted of one main room packed with fashion jewellery, cosmetics, false eyelashes, scarves and stockings. To my surprised question as to why he had to work on a public holiday, he answered, 'I have to work because I am Syrian.' He explained that his boss was Egyptian and demanded his presence on public holidays, that he had to work long hours and could not ask for any vacation. According to Abu Walid, his boss knew that he, as a Syrian, could not complain. Hence, he worked thirteen hours a day for 1,500 LE per month (in 2015 this amounted to approximately 170 US dollars).[4] Because he and his family could not live off this income due to a monthly rent of 1,000 LE (approx. 115 US dollars), he started offering body-piercing services in the shop and had begun attending a course in the evenings after his thirteen-hour shift. He opened a drawer in a corner of the shop to show me his piercing instruments and pointed at a discreet sign in the shop window written in English that referred to the piercing services offered.

I had to promise him not to tell his wife about his second profession, since Abu Walid was sure that she would disapprove. He explained:

> I was obligated to do another job about which my wife doesn't know. For my age and my situation, it is shame to do this work. My wife doesn't know my workplace because I am working as a piercer. My wife thinks that I work with accessories only. I get a percentage for this work because I introduced it to this shop.

Abu Walid refers to shame in the context of his profession, similarly to Muhannad and Majd when they described appropriate gendered behaviour. At the same time, Abu Walid could not abstain from doing work that was shameful in his eyes, while Muhannad and Majd were in the privileged position of not being in need to negotiate their values and gendered ideals. As for Abu Walid, he constantly repeated throughout our various conversations that there was no future in Egypt – neither for him and his family nor for the Egyptians. He felt overwhelmed by the fact that he could not afford education in a private school for his children and that even though both he and his wife were working, the family could barely make ends meet. He felt that he could not rely on anyone's help, saying that he 'stopped going to the UN' because he never 'had an advantage through the UN' and that he had 'never got used to asking people for help'. Powerlessness and depression accompany his sense of shame of being unable to provide for his family in accordance with his personal standards and work in a respectful profession.

Working in less prestigious professions

Even though many of the Syrians I met had found work, most of them did not work in the profession they had held in Syria and their new job lacked the prestige of the previous one. An old woman, whom I met in an NGO in 6th of October City providing aid for Syrians, told me that her son used to be a trader and had his own office in Syria, while in Egypt he was employed as the office boy in an engineering company preparing tea and coffee for the other employees. Her son's inability to find a well-paying job in the profession he had learned and mastered in Syria caused the family's impoverishment and was one of the reasons why the old woman was queuing for food baskets in the NGO. Another woman, who used the services of the NGO, shared with me that her husband was currently unemployed, but had worked as a waiter for a while and was desperate and ready to accept any kind of work in Egypt. In Syria, he used to be an accountant.

The loss of prestigious work and the inability to find a suitable job following forced displacement were themes I also discussed with Abd al-Rahman. He explained:

> The situation in Egypt is more comfortable [than in Jordan], since it is possible for the man to work and go out, but unfortunately the salary is low. The Syrian teacher couldn't find work when he came to Egypt. His wife also couldn't find

work, while they used to have a solid income in Syria, which they spend partially and partially saved, and they had their own house there. [...] As you can see here in Egypt, there are many people, who have university degrees but they work as drivers. [...] Any man who has a family and left Syria for any other country suffers a lot because there are no jobs but there is the responsibility. He was comfortable in Syria. His big family was close to him and when he needed money he asked his brother or his friend. Now, I am in Egypt and a friend of mine is in Jordan and another one is in Libya. There was no suffering before, but now there is a huge suffering.

He describes that in Syria, working held the promise of consumption, possession and ease of life, creating linearity between a person's education, social status plus network and the guarantee of a comfortable middle-class life. However, in times of forced displacement in Egypt it is an accumulation of loss of prestige, network, income and savings, living in a country with a high unemployment rate, and especially a man's responsibility for his family, which causes a man's suffering. Similarly, Samir mentioned, drawing on his encounters with Syrian families as part of his work in an NGO, how Syrians in Egypt had to accept the loss of status, income and economic chances. He described settling and finding work as severe challenges in a context without network and an established diaspora. He said: 'When Syrians came in 2012, it was their first experience abroad as refugees and they had to discover everything.' Learning to cope with forced displacement is described here as a crucial, defining aspect of Syrians' work conditions.

The problem of not finding a job in one's former profession was also experienced by Rafi, a father of three children in his late thirties. He had learned to be a carpenter from his father and later opened a clothes shop in Syria. In Egypt, Rafi initially tried to work as a carpenter and decorator but was often not paid by his clients. Consequently, he decided to work as a driver by renting an old car from an Egyptian for which he had to pay a high lease. Nevertheless, the car was not air-conditioned, could not go faster than 80 km per hour and used a lot of petrol. The car was always meticulously clean on the inside as well as on the outside, and in order to protect the occupants from the burning sun Rafi had put black curtains at each window. Rafi had advertised his service as a driver via a Facebook Group called 'Syrians in Maadi' and relied on word of mouth and recommendations from satisfied clients. The first time Rafi drove me in his car to 6th of October City, he immediately drew my attention to the car's condition, which he had improved by himself because, as he said, he was a hardworking man: 'I love to work. All the Syrians are hardworking people.' Then, Rafi reiterated that he decided to work as a driver because it was the most reliable way to get money in Egypt. Nevertheless, being a driver was not an easy occupation for Rafi. He had difficulties memorizing street names, routes and easily got lost in Cairo. He had clients who left him waiting at the agreed meeting point in his car without an AC in the middle of the day, not telling him that they would be late and not answering their phones. However, when comparing this kind of work to staying at home unemployed, Rafi said that he preferred hard work and tough working conditions; being at home without work would make him distressed and depressed. On one of our regular trips to 6th of October City, he joked that his children would be happy not to have him at home unemployed, because, feeling anxious and unsettled, he would be very strict with them and would compel them to study all day. Rafi was even available during Ramadan and the time of *iftar*. He told me he would take a bottle of water and a sandwich with him in case he was booked at the time of sunset. His strict work schedule, his availability at any time even in Ramadan and the determination with which he practised street names and tried to memorize routes in Cairo made it clear to me that it was far from easy for a man with a completely different career background to make a living in Egypt. Despite all the challenges he faced starting from the scratch, Rafi was full of new business ideas. He wanted to rent a car with an AC and in better condition to attract more passengers and he eventually managed to find an Egyptian car owner who agreed to give him a newer car with an AC, albeit for a higher rent than the old one. The first time Rafi picked me up with his new car, he was not only full of pride but also showed me his newest service: on getting into the car, I was offered water and biscuits. Rafi believed that this service was a unique business idea that would improve the clients' overall comfort during the journey.

Rafi used the discourses of the hard-working Syrian people and his personal love to work hard reconfirming his pride and dignity. Assuring me that it was his desire to work constantly could hide the fact that he had no other option but to labour in this way in order to earn enough money. Despite his creativity, diligence and ingenuity, he was always on the edge of being unable to provide for his family. Often, he would ask me whether someone in my circle of international and Egyptian friends would need a driver. Rafi practised with rigour the role of the aspiring, ambitious, self-making neoliberal subject, who tries to conceive himself as an enterprise (Dardot and Laval 2013: 3 in Cornwall 2016: 9; Walkers and Roberts 2018). Ideals of entrepreneurship, such as self-discipline, autonomy, drive for success, are predominantly associated with being male (in addition to being white and able bodied) (Knight 2013: 346; Turner 2019: 6). Moreover, entrepreneurship is associated with the 'outside', that is the public sphere, a traditionally male context in which women struggle to maintain middle-class feminine respectability (Freeman 2012: 94) Furthermore, Rafi's aim for achievement through hard work echoes Schielke's (2012) argument that aspiration, success and advancement are significant aspects of middle-classness and important markers upon which the individual's class belonging is judged. By adopting the role of the entrepreneur, Rafi could foreground some characteristics that elevated him and brought him closer to the ideal of middle-class masculinity. Yet, his entrepreneurship was born out of impoverishment and the dire need to provide for his family.

Being young: Working and studying at the same time

Several young men faced a specific challenge in Egypt: they had to interrupt school or university studies or worked and studied at the same time in order to support their family. The temporal context of their current position defined their specific challenges and negotiations of masculinity. They were at a specific intersection in which their age, gender, social status and forced displacement in Egypt played a role and defined their constructions of masculinities.

This was the case with Fadi, who should have been in his first year of university but had had to interrupt his education to support his family upon their arrival in Egypt. By the time I met him, his family was in better conditions. Thus, he could reduce his workload and only worked occasionally. He intended to go back to school in order to finalize his high school degree and had to prepare for his final school exams. Once, he took me to his workplace, a lingerie shop owned by a distant relative of his. While Fadi showed me around, a female customer interrupted our conversation in the shop asking for the best body-shaping underwear. In a professional tone and manner, he recommended one model and then referred her to his female colleague. Afterwards, while we were smoking shisha and playing backgammon, he told me:

> It is not my dream job. I would like to become a programming engineer. I find it embarrassing to work in this job because the girls who shop there flirt with me.

He described that coping with work while also studying for his final exams in high school made him feel 'older' than his peers, 'impatient' and 'depressed', sensing that this double burden distinguished him from others. He said: 'I feel that I am not supposed to handle of all of this.' Fadi's sense of feeling aged and more mature than his peers makes sense when comparing his situation to others of his age cohort. There are certain privileges to the phase of being young: relative freedom of mobility and spending that are accepted by parents as an important learning aspect of growing up.[5] Fadi, however, had only a little time to spare. Usually, he was roaming the city with an explicit reason, for example, to volunteer and to meet someone to study together. This did not mean that Fadi could not meet his friends at all; he usually spent some time with them after he had volunteered, studied or worked. Nevertheless, as far as most of his time was concerned, it was expected of Fadi to behave like a 'responsible, serious and productive individual who abides by social norms and fulfils his family's demands' (Ghannam 2013: 71). As a partial provider for his family, Fadi was not only frustrated about his reduced ability to enjoy the privileges of being young, he was certainly also proud to manage work and studying at the same time. Having described his frustration, he added:

> Men should be strong. They are stronger than women. They should support the family. I work and study at the same time. This makes us men. We stand more than we can.

In an environment with limited resources available, Fadi spoke with pride of the burden of simultaneous work and study as a threshold to manhood. He transformed the heavy workload he was facing on a day-to-day basis into a sign of masculinity and proof that he had transcended from boyhood to manhood. His definition of manhood did not match traditional perceptions: he had not completed his education, did not have a professional career, did not have the means to get married and build a family and had not accumulated social knowledge.[6] Fadi's take on being an adult and a man is an 'articulated composite' (Johnson-Hanks 2002: 868) and a carefully composed version of masculinity from the material that was accessible at that point in time (Wentzell 2015: 179).[7]

Over the years, Fadi continued supporting his family through work in the corner shop his father bought in an affluent neighbourhood in Cairo, while at the same time studying. Once, at the end of 2016, when I had been back in the UK for a while, we chatted about his workload via a social media messenger.

- Fadi: I am now in my second year at university studying engineering and I am working too. This is how I am spending my life.
- Magdalena: You are working a lot!
- Fadi: Yes, really, Magdalena, I am tired but this is life. We need to exhaust ourselves in order to reach what we want.

What reverberates from Fadi's account is the neoliberal maxim of self-improvement at all costs as well as the need of constant hard work to reach security, stability and fulfilment that Schielke (2012; 2015) describes as a major aspect of being middle class and living one's life in the future tense. As a young man and part of a family who is forcibly displaced, it is expected of Fadi that he exhausts himself. Hard work, sacrifice and a focus on the future are what define Fadi's take on life as a young man.

I also discussed young men's responsibilities with Muhannad. He was always busy studying for his exams in medical school or involved in organizing events, planning future activities and raising funds for *Fursa*. Muhannad's family enjoyed very good living conditions in Cairo with his father being able to pay the high tuition fees at private universities for his children. Thus, Muhannad neither needed to work nor was he forced to interrupt his studies which defined his perception of work:

I don't work because I need money; I work because I feel that it is necessary that I work. As an adult guy, one should be able to take care of one's family. Also, I should not remain a problem for my family. There are people who are spoiled and they are against working while studying.

Similarly to Fadi, Muhannad described work as a necessity of adult manhood. Like Fadi, he took for granted the ideal of provider masculinity and consequently not working as a grown-up male could only be condemned and looked down upon. Understanding masculine adulthood as a composition that is dependent on one's current social situation and surrounding helps to make sense of Fadi's and Muhannad's accounts in which they describe themselves as men in a specific social context, namely, when comparing themselves to other young Syrian men, who were not working and studying simultaneously. Their perceptions of being adult men clearly show the importance of paid work and labour as part of masculine maturity and reiterate ideals of middle-class masculinity and breadwinner masculinity. Finally, Fadi's and Muhannad's negotiations of who defines as adult men show the importance of an intersectional analysis that takes into account men's position within their masculine trajectories. Their social, temporal and spatial contexts define their specific positionalities which cause their concrete struggle and consequent negotiations of masculinities.

Being a father during forced displacement

While I used to spend a lot of time with Syrian male students, mostly in their early twenties, I also got to meet men who were fathers. After having met and talked to Abu Muhammad about his negotiations of fatherhood in the context of involvement in the uprising and the decision to flee, I became interested in fathers' specific position and the impact of fatherhood on their experiences and constructions of masculinities during forced displacement.[8] Generally, Syrians I met talked about fathers with respect and with appreciation. In their eyes, fathers were the ones who did the right things for the families, supported their children for as long as possible and were in most situations the backbone of the family. In several accounts I collected, fathers were the heroes who overcame challenges in Syria, who were decisive and knew what should be done during difficult situations, who managed to preserve their integrity vis-à-vis the oppressive Syrian state and who solved difficulties for their children. Layla, Abu Mohammad's cousin, whose husband passed away when their children were adolescents, said the following about fathers from the perspective of a mother and wife:

> Nadim [her husband], may God grant rest to his soul, passed away and it became very difficult for me because I had a doubled responsibility. Whenever I think of anything, I wonder what he would have done if he was still alive. The father is very important in the house. It is a real mercy for the family to have a father. You can give half of the decisions to him. [...] My son felt, after his father passed away, that a pyramid collapsed in front of him.

Layla presented herself as strong, independent and autonomous. She told me that she had never shown her feelings in front of anyone back in Syria and did not intend to lose her reputation as being resilient in Egypt. Only when she talked about the loss of her husband, she expressed her insecurity, deep grief and worries to make ends meet for her children. Her husband had been essential for the stability of the family, had functioned as the backbone, and in his role as the caring father he had been deeply respected by her and her children.

Muhannad, who was the oldest of four siblings, described the changes he perceived among Syrian fathers in Egypt from the perspective of a son:

> Back in Syria the family was more confident with their son. If I had trouble I was sure that they would help me. This is not the case here. They tell you here: 'if

there is a ten-percent chance that something will cause problems, then stay away from it. We don't need problems.' Families changed and started to put pressure on their sons. In the past, they were more relaxed. There was more security in the family. The worst feeling is if the son has a problem and his father has to watch him struggle and cannot do anything for him, or if the father has to force his children to leave school in order to help the family. From inside the father's heart will be cut in pain. [...] There are many actions [fathers] had to take and they didn't want to do it.

There are two emergent themes in Muhannad's narrative. On the one hand, he voiced a feeling of loss of safety and security because the family, and especially the father, broke away as his mainstay and protector in times of problems and trouble. In the context of his own family and when being in contact with all the volunteers and students he met through *Fursa*, he recognized a shift in the position of the father during forced displacement, describing that fathers could not fill their traditional place and tasks in the family anymore. This affected him as a son of young age who used to rely on the strength of his father and family. On the other hand, he articulated compassion for fathers who had to observe their children struggling without being able to support them or who even had to make their children's life and future more challenging.[9] Muhannad recognized that the liminality, insecurity and uncertainty which define forced displacement had entered the relationship to his father in the form of decline of support and an urge to take distance from risky decisions. His father's dominant and, at the same time, reassuring position shook since their forced displacement.

Not only sons but also fathers recognized the changes that found their way into forcibly displaced families. Abu Walid, the father of two boys in primary school, stressed that the life he had to live in Egypt did not allow him to be the father he aspired to be, namely, the provider and protector. He suffered from the feeling of being unable to shield his children. He told me that his son's teacher wanted to be paid for giving him good marks and that she used to beat his son. Abu Walid felt that he could not complain, comply or protect his son from his teacher because he had no name, financial means or network to rely on and no support to turn to in Egypt. He was driven by the fear that his inability to provide his children with what they asked for would harm their well-being:

I am working sixteen hours a day so that I can live in this country in a reasonable situation. [...] If my children ask for something and I can't provide them with it, it will cause them psychological damage. I am trying to answer their needs so that they don't feel that they are missing anything.

Abu Walid was mostly worried about his children's future and their education. He felt that it was his failure as a father that he could not afford to send them to better schools:

I know that they won't improve because I cannot afford to let them go to private schools.

Abu Walid's inability to be the father he aspired to be evoked sentiments, such as shame, resignation and depression in him.[10] Because of his economically unstable situation, the poverty he lived in and the constant blackmailing he experienced, he could not juggle with different registers of masculinity. While Abu Muhannad and Firas, when talking about their decisions to leave Syria and move to Germany, used their role as fathers strategically as an acceptable and respectable version of manhood when other forms of masculinities, such as militant masculinity, were not available to them (see Chapter 1), this was not option for Abu Walid. He could not invent for himself a strategy or rhetoric that made him look or sound more manly. He was unable to use fatherhood as a strategy or a protective shield to boost his manhood. Instead, his inability to be the father he wanted to be was a hugely negative factor in his life during forced displacement that made him feel depressed, guilty and inadequate. Challenges he faced as a refugee from Syria in Egypt defined his position as a father by determining the present and future he could offer to his children and by informing his relationship with his children as well as his emotions, inner life and sense of guilt.

Syrian working women

Despite Syrian men's attempts to ignore and downplay women's participation in the Egyptian labour market, Syrian women were visibly engaging in different forms of employment in Egypt. I met Syrian women who worked as primary school and kindergarten teachers, social workers, hairdressers and secretaries, and I got in touch with several women selling home-cooked food on the street on a daily basis. In some areas, Syrian women were also begging in the streets. Syrian women in Egypt were not only visibly working in Cairo's streets, NGOs and schools, they also described themselves and others as working women. When talking with Syrian women who attended my English classes or when I was invited to a women's gathering, there were frequent discussions about work that altered the picture presented to me by most Syrian men. Some Syrian women told me that they were indeed working for the first time in Cairo and would have not started working had their family's economic conditions not forced them to do so. Others had held jobs as teachers, accountants or secretaries in Syria. Most women agreed that in Syria a woman would not be seen cleaning the streets or working in a shop, which reflected their middle-class backgrounds. Nevertheless, they indicated that there was nothing unusual about the notion of working women in and of itself.

Existing literature (that is mostly outdated) on women in the Syrian labour market points to the importance of taking into consideration a woman's class background. According to official numbers summarized by Shaaban (1998: 111), women made up 21 per cent of employees working for the Syrian government and constituted a third of the labour force in the agricultural sector in the 1990s. However, Shaaban (1998: 112) doubts the latter number assuming that women constituted 50 per cent of the workforce in rural areas but were neither officially recognized, nor had access to the attendant benefits, such as independent income, pension or a role in management. Rabo (1996: 162) goes as far as to call rural women in most Syrian regions the backbone of the labour force. Furthermore, she highlights that it was well known and accepted that poor, uneducated women worked as house cleaners or engaged in work from home, which was usually low-paid, and mainly textile-related, farmed-out work (Rabo 2005). For women from the Syrian upper class, however, work was a way to see and be seen. Young, single, upper-class women rarely worked to become self-sufficient and to set up an independent household; work was rather a venue for display with the aim to secure a successful future as a married woman (Salamandra 2004: 52). For married women, work functioned as an opportunity to gain social contacts and exhibit their husbands' affection and economic status through their outward appearance (Salamandra 2004).

Layla, the widow and mother of two teenagers, who often stressed her family's middle-class background, said the following with regard to women's position in the family and in the labour market in Syria. Layla had cooked dinner for her daughter and me. After food, Layla and I sat down on the small balcony of her apartment looking down on the busy street by night and Layla talked about growing up in a middle-class family and what it was like to get married to an older man when she was still a student:

> The woman in Syria was very precious [...]. The woman only works if she wants to and only in a good job. According to our traditions, the woman is allowed to work and can go out and do whatever she wants, but all of that was optional for her. If she wants to work then she works, if she wants to practise her hobbies or teach, she can do that. She had the freedom to do whatever she wants, but her role here in Egypt of course has changed.

Taking a sip from her tea, her eyes fixed on the street in front of her house, she continued:

> The woman in our homeland is honoured. The husband does everything. Everything is done by the husband or the brother or the son. The girl at her family's house gets whatever she wants.

Layla reiterated what most Syrian men I met said: she referred to the Syrian tradition, the order of the Syrian middle class that guaranteed women's precious, valued and honoured position in Syrian society. She used to fit into the role of the stay-at-home mother back in Syria where she had quit university after getting married and once she found out that she was pregnant and stayed with her children at home to raise them. Her statement shows that women can be compliant in creating acceptable versions of masculinities, in this case, middle-class masculinity.[11] The ideal of middle-class masculinity depends on a complementary notion of femininity, that is, the woman who happily accepts to stay at home with the children. At the same time, however, Layla had picked up work in Egypt. Her son's job did not provide with enough income so that the family could pay the rent for their flat. Hence, she began working in an Egyptian company for eight hours per day for a modest salary. After a while she quit and tried to find another job which turned out to be extremely difficult. Layla was clear that she did not want her daughter to work because she feared that she could be sexually harassed on the streets. When asked whether the Syrian women who came to Egypt changed, she responded impulsively:

> I know many Syrian women who work from their houses. They cook *Kebbeh* or do any kind of decorations, or they make desserts to help their husbands. For sure, the woman has changed since the revolution. Women have tried their best to help their men in life. Honestly, they stood by them either by raising the children or by supporting them financially.

With a solid idea of how Syrian male-female relationships ought to be, Layla did not deny the changes that came with the uprising. During forced displacement, especially if it was accompanied by the family's impoverishment, gender relations undergo change for the sake of the family. While the narratives about gender roles in Syria remain static, idealized and coherent, narratives and people's action in the here and now of forced displacement are flexible, inconsistent and in the first place responsive to the needs of the family.

Making sense of Syrian working women

While most Syrian men's description of women working in Syria was rigid, static and clear, some of them reluctantly acknowledged that women's situation had changed and that some women were indeed engaged in work in Egypt. Rafi, for instance, proposed on one of our trips to 6th of October City that his wife could cook Syrian dishes for me. He explained that she would cook for Egyptian clients occasionally and justified this by saying that she would simply love to work, just as all the Syrian people would love to work. He also mentioned that she could keep the money for herself, while he was in charge of providing for her and the children. Interestingly, the narrative he used resonates with Stolleis' (2004: 30) analysis of middle- and upper-class working women in Syria. Rafi uses the same line of argumentation as the women Stolleis met in Damascus, who commonly underlined that they were not forced to work, that their husbands had a good income and that they could keep their income for personal expenses, knowing that it could damage their reputation if they confessed that their husbands did not earn enough to provide for the family. Rafi's way of introducing his wife's work did not only seem to protect his wife's reputation but also his own, assuring me that it was his wife's will, personal freedom and love for work that made her start cooking, while he was still in charge of providing for her and his three children. At the same time, however, Rafi reluctantly admitted in direct and indirect ways that his family struggled financially and that he was not yet established as a private driver.

Qutayba, the IT specialist, acknowledged women's participation in the labour market, as well. He told me that he recognized women's presence as street vendors in Cairo's streets, which was a sharp contrast to women's labour in his home town. There, women rarely worked and if they did, they worked as teachers. Qutayba said that he had a hard time accepting seeing Syrian women working in the street. Once, he saw a teenage girl from his home town selling food in the streets. While he remembered that her family used to have a good standard of living back in Syria, here, she had to carry her wares and surely had to endure sexual harassment from Egyptian men. He also believed that Egyptian men would consider her to be a prostitute. I sensed shame and humiliation when he talked about her visible and enacted poverty. The girl's poverty was a painful reminder of the omnipresent risk of downward social mobility that many Syrians in Egypt had to experience.

In a similar vein to Qutayba, Muhannad described the changes induced by forced displacement which caused women's participation in the labour market.

> Some changes took place and now some women are obligated to work. So women's paid labour became somehow acceptable here in Egypt. It is not like before. It was something totally unacceptable back in Syria, even if the wife was a doctor. However, then her husband tells her: 'Stay at home, I don't want you to work!' This is the difference between Egypt and Syria. The biggest responsibility remains on the young boys.

There is a strong sense of before versus after, of Syria versus Egypt, of a system in place versus unforeseeable changes. A woman's participation in the labour market is a strong marker of the family's social degradation and what is implicit is the loss of manly authority and control.

Only a few Syrian men, among them Abu Walid, whose wife worked as a kindergarten teacher, expressed a positive perception of the developments that made more and more Syrian women start working in Egypt.

> Women became stronger. What happened in the country made them rely on themselves. My wife didn't use to buy anything on her own. I used to buy everything for her. In Syrian society, a woman can work, she can be employed, she can go to university, but according to the majority of the people, the man should provide for everything. He should buy everything for her. Any time she goes out, the husband should pay for it and in addition to that, she sometimes doesn't know the names of the streets. But this situation here obligates women to rely on themselves. So, they started to go out by themselves and make decisions. The whole thing helped them in general. They were tortured by the situation but it made them stronger, so they started to figure out how to make a decision. Speaking about my wife and my sister and the people around me, they all changed 180 degrees. They became stronger.

Again, there is a sense of the 'before and after forced displacement' and the description of an intact system guided by what people said and thought about working women back in Syria versus a new, unprecedented system of gender roles in Egypt. While Qutayba and Muhannad gave the phenomenon of working women a negative connotation relating it to men's loss of control, Abu Walid emphasized the opposite side of the same coin by highlighting the burden on men's shoulders if women stayed at home in Syria and how it changed women and gave them increased autonomy and self-confidence when they began working in Egypt.

What does it tell us about forced displacement and masculinities if Syrian men felt that an established system of complementary gender roles that used to define life in Syria was subject to change in Egypt? It seems that Syrian men were aware of the changes in and around them and that they observed with worries the repercussions of their forced displacement to Egypt. The idea of how men ought to be that envisaged men to be providers and women to raise children could not be taken for granted anymore. The instability, uncertainty and unpredictability of their future played out in the concrete experiences of need for shared responsibilities that replaced the idealized system of gender roles they had taken for granted. While most men had been brought up and lived in family constellations in which their role as father and main bread winner was pre-determined and foreseeable and was also what needed to be presented to the outside, the inner family structures as well as the overall system were shaking during forced displacement and saw first fine fissures.

Building masculinity on women's ascribed weakness

In addition to a general preference to ignore women's contributions to the labour market, I observed that several young Syrian men used yet another strategy to masculinize against women: they described women as being unable to live the life they as bachelors lived on their own in Cairo. Hani, the medical student, said the following when we were discussing what it was like to live without his family in Cairo:

> If I don't want to cook, I order food from the restaurant. Food is not so important. For the guy, it's normal, but a girl might care more about what she wants to eat. It's not like a family or like a woman who has children and she is alone and she needs someone to help her. If you are a man alone, you can manage. Maybe for her, if she will marry without rights, it's better for her than to stay alone. It's better than staying alone and the people disturb her. There are really bad people. But for the guy he can do anything: he can eat, not eat, sleep, not sleep. And if he cooks and the food is bad, he can eat it without problems.

Hani presented yet another time his access to 'the good life' in Egypt as someone who had the means to order in from a restaurant. I read this as a sign of belonging to the affluent ones in Egypt. Hani takes women's 'pickiness' with regard to food and sleep and their presumed inability to defend themselves against harassment as a proof of men's strength and endurance in times of hardship. He also takes it as a reason to justify living in an unfair, unwanted marriage. The version of masculinity he creates achieves meaning and depends on the contrasting definition of weak femininity.[12]

Likewise, Majd differentiated between men and women's varying resiliences when I asked him whether life for Syrian women in Egypt had changed:

> Dealing with the girls in the Syrian families is the same as before, but they are a bit more concerned about them because of the situation in Egypt. The nature of the country here is strange. If the guy goes out, something will happen to him. If it happens to a guy, for sure it will happen to a girl.

Akram, the Arabic primary school teacher, recently got engaged. He related women and men's 'naturally' different capabilities to adapt and women's assumed weakness to men's enhanced responsibilities for women's safety:

> In Syria, she goes out and buys the things herself – here no! She can meet my family and get to know them. In Syria, the girl [he refers to his future wife] would have lived among my family, but here I don't really know the people who are around me. So, I stay with her at home. If we need food, I will go to bring it. If she wants to go out with her sisters or friends, I'll bring her out. There is the unknown fear and the absence of security here in Egypt, but it is the responsibility of a man to make her safe.

In contrast to Abu Walid who argued that men in Syria had immense duties, Akram described how the hostility of the unknown place they lived in increased women's dependence on men's support. The combination of women's weakness and the prevalent insecurity in Egypt catapults Akram in the position of the responsible, caring, protective husband-to-be. He verbally positions himself close to ideal middle-class provider masculinity.

Young Syrian men managed to gain masculine capital, by describing that they were able to live on their own, that they could eat bad food, and that they could survive on the street on their own, while they stressed that Syrian women were unable to do so, and thus needed constant support from men. In this context, notions of masculinity achieve meaning through the construction of patterns of difference (Barrett 1996: 133). Syrian men devalue women turning them into their 'others' (Kimmel 1994) against whom they can project a respected masculine identity.

Facing unemployment in Egypt

Having discussed the various approaches to Syrian working women and the difficulties Syrian men had in accepting their participation in the labour market, I turn to a theme that was of concern for most Syrian men: unemployment was perceived as the most dramatic misfortune a man could find.[13] In almost every neighbourhood, there seemed to be gossip about this one unsuccessful male figure, who used to be a well-paid manager, doctor or engineer in Syria, but had not found adequate work in Egypt, even though he tried, which made him eventually stay at home. Such stories about a man 'failing' his family in Egypt despite his professional background in Syria circulated, and while most Syrians appeared to feel sympathy for this unsuccessful man, a lack of understanding was also prevalent – especially if the consequence of not finding a job was for the man to stay at home.

Wasim, a social worker in a community centre for refugees, talked mostly empathically about unemployed men. I met him in his office together with two peers who enjoyed listening to our conversation and sometimes jumped in to correct Wasim or add a story or thought. The centre, located in an old, spacious building in a lower middle-class neighbourhood, was empty when I visited Wasim; however, it bore the signs of the different activities that were offered there, such as cooking classes, child care and computer lessons. The community centre used to receive financial support from UNHCR. However, this support was cancelled a couple of months before I met Wasim. For this reason, the amount of volunteers and employed social workers decreased sharply and most initiatives had come to an end. He described the situation for the Syrians in the neighbourhood in the following way:

> The Syrians were shocked because of the long working hours, 13/14 hours. Mostly, the work place is not close to the house. It's always far and we are not used to it. The salaries are between 700 and 1000 LE only. The people were shocked. There are some people who started to work. There are other people who stayed at home. They started to suffer socially and psychologically.

Having highlighted what was different for most Syrian men upon their forced displacement in Egypt, Wasim described the prototype of the 'failing man':

> There are several men who just stay at home although some of them were managers of companies back in Syria. The husband of Samiya [a woman in the neighbourhood] was working in programming. He is not working now and when he finds a job it is usually only a small job and the salary is not enough so until now he is staying at home. This puts a lot of pressure on him and on the family. I think that men are the neglected ones. The aid associations focus on children and women. No one looks at men. No one looks at their problems! It is correct that many men are working, however, I think that associations should focus on men that are older than thirty years. These people don't work or study, they just stay at home which puts more pressure on them, especially, when he is at home and his wife is working instead of him or if he sits down and his brother in Saudi Arabia or the Emirates sends him money.

Wasim describes the severity of the experience of unemployment and how the pain of being unemployed and not in the position of providing for the family anymore is aggravated if female relatives work instead of men or if men become the recipients of financial support from more affluent male relatives. The men Wasim is concerned with fail as the providers of their families. Being unable to comply to this role takes away their position as men that they can hold up as a protective shield. They risk being stripped off their honourable and respected position in society, in the family and in front of themselves.

In contrast to Wasim's benevolence for unemployed men's plight, Qays, the founder of an NGO, who talked to me predominantly in Modern Standard Arabic, was less compassionate, even though he acknowledged, when talking about the reasons why he founded an NGO, how exhausted Syrians in Egypt were and how they struggled with the conditions they faced. Nevertheless, when it came to unemployed Syrian men, he characterized them as idle, dishonest and wishing to live off others:

> The majority of men could find jobs and men who didn't find work are just trying to escape from work. The Syrian in general is characterised by his ability to create job opportunities and to find economic solutions. I don't recall that men ever had a problem finding work. We could find jobs for all the people who asked us. There are some Syrians, as it is the case in every society, who like to have privileges without working.

Qays did not only look down on unemployed Syrian men, but also denied them the status of proper 'Syrianness', since, for him, 'Syrianness' was defined through high work ethics, commitment and creativity. The theme of how 'Syrianness' is related to success in the labour market runs like a common thread through this chapter. Being a man, a Syrian and a (successful) participant in the labour market is inevitably interlinked. The creation of groups – like the refugee in Europe versus Syrian men in Egypt who cannot be described as refugees – is again used as a method here, when Qays makes a distinction between labouring Syrian men and those who are unemployed and do not meet the standard of 'Syrianness'. This strategy is used to establish an acceptable version of manhood for oneself.

Another issue that came up in the form of gossip was the value of work. Abu Muhammad told me disparagingly and indignantly about a Syrian man living in his neighbourhood, who decided that he would not work in Egypt if he could not earn more than 500 to 1,000 LE per month (approx. 60–110 US dollars in 2015). Because of this man's refusal to work, his children and wife had to provide for the family. Abu Muhammad assumed that the man was not altogether sane. However, at the same time, he excused such a sentiment by explaining to me that it was difficult for men, who used to be successful business owners back in Syria, to come to terms with the modest salary they would get for their labour in Egypt. Again, a man's failing to find work is judged in especially hard terms if it means that his wife and children are on the suffering end and have to replace the man in his position as the family's provider. At least, a man should try, struggle and strive – prominent markers of neoliberal, middle-class positioning.

What I have presented so far regarding the theme of unemployment are men's narratives and judgements about the 'other' unemployed man. Many Syrian men were strongly opinionated about this theme as long as it was another man's issue.

They used gossip and harsh judgement in order to distance themselves from the 'failing' unemployed Syrian man. By doing so they created proper 'Syrianness' as incompatible with unemployment. Referring to the failing, unemployed man put them automatically in a better position, whether or not they could maintain the prestige and status of their former employment in their new profession in Egypt. Syrian men established a continuum between the poles of respected and failed masculinity (see Kleist 2010: 199). They used the positioning of 'others' at the pole of failed masculinity to express their own relative success as labouring men. They restored and normalized their own practices as men through stories about these 'others'. Thus, Syrian men managed through their judgement and rejection of unemployed 'others' to create a distinction and claimed for themselves belonging to the 'real' Syrian men, who are economically successful, hard-working and striving.

Men's unemployment and women's involvement

As mentioned above, I did not meet many men who talked openly about their own experiences of unemployment. Often, it was through women that I would hear about their husbands' joblessness. This was the case with Um Basim. Um Khalid had put me in touch with Um Basim. She had to be the main provider for the family – her husband, two teenage sons and one daughter – since her husband had lost all his savings when he tried to do business in Egypt with several partners, who eventually cheated him out of his money. Um Basim told me when we met for the first time that her husband used to be a 'boss' in Syria, a successful and influential businessman and owner of an ironworks, and that she did not have to work. When the family arrived in Cairo, he tried to run several business projects with different Egyptian partners but was tricked by all of them, which caused him to lose all of his savings. Um Basim vividly recalled the day her husband found out that his last project was not viable and that he had been tricked and robbed of his investment yet another time. 'He didn't speak for three days', she remembered tearfully. Since then, Um Basim's husband had developed hearing difficulties, distractedness and bursts of rage and irritability. He barely talked but repeatedly said that he wished to die. Um Basim took her husband to the doctor but he could not diagnose anything. Having lost its main provider, the family struggled to survive and Um Basim, after having sold her gold jewellery, tried to establish a business at home as a hairdresser together with her daughter. Once, when I visited her, she showed me a huge plastic bag filled to the brim with ointments and tablets. She explained that she needed the medication to cure the various forms of pain she suffered all over her body. Sometimes, the pain in her hands, arms and neck was so strong that she could not work for days. We usually met in her unorganized flat; however, whenever I visited her, her husband was not at home – or if he was, he would not appear. Often, she would ask me if I could help her with the monthly rent or if I knew someone who I could ask for financial support on her behalf. Knowing that the current situation was unbearable for her husband, Um Basim tried to protect him in front of others:

I don't want to shame my husband by telling people that I am working. He was an important man in Syria.

Her reluctance to speak in public about the family's poverty because of her husband's former status in Syria shows the irreconcilability of their lives in Syria and in Egypt. It describes the shame of having a husband who was not only unemployed but even stopped trying to find work which meant that wife and children had to take over providing. Um Basim's attempt to protect her husband shows the importance of women's conduct and behaviour for the establishment of manhood and that women were strategic in the way they represented the efforts of their husbands.[14] Um Basim was aware of her ability to bestow on or take away recognition from her husband and tried to guard his reputation in public for as long as possible. However, it might not only be sorrow and pity for her husband that motivated Um Basim, but also that it somehow guaranteed some dignity for her and her children if she hid her own labour. According to Stolleis (2004: 30), women in Damascus were cautious with what they shared about their own contribution to the household income. If they had admitted that their labour was significant for the family's survival, they would have undermined not only their husband's reputation but also their own. Syrian men's unemployment did not only challenge men in their striving to be providers, but also undermined his family's value and reputation. Men and women alike feared being judged and misvalued by others. And thus, if women like Um Basim wanted to protect themselves, they had to be strategic and hide their husband's failure to provide for them and the family.

When I met Salim, I experienced a similar interaction in which women protected the 'failing' man in front of me. Salim came to the office of an NGO where I spent the day volunteering. His clothes were worn out and dirty, his beard and hair needed cutting. After entering the office, he immediately asked for the food that the secretaries shared behind the desk and ate it eagerly. He emphasized that he had experience working in Dubai as an engineer and that his wife was the first French teacher in their area back in Syria. In Cairo, however, Salim could not find work, despite his professional background, which was causing him a lot of distress. He could not afford the rent for his small flat in a slum in 6th of October City and did not know how to buy food and clothes for his four children. He had started to work as a street vendor next to the Husari Mosque. In our conversation, his mood changed from angry to friendly, aggressive to sad. Among other topics, he expressed his anger and disappointment in the UN staff and other aid agencies. He complained that at the UN office he was told to come back another day but never got an appointment, and the two aid agencies he had approached had also refused to help him. Eventually, he directed all his anger and disappointment at me. He asked me what I could do for him and demanded that I wrote down the identification number on his 'yellow card' in order to support his case at the UN office in Germany. When I expressed doubts about my ability to influence his case, he shouted angrily as to how could I refuse to help him, while I was obviously getting paid for my research and could live a good life by using his and other Syrians' stories. He only calmed down after I told him that I was a student and not paid by anyone. He apologized, said that he was only joking and added that the whole situation was making him stressed and nervous. After his outburst of anger he left, but not before making me promise to try to help him and his family. When he was gone, the Syrian women working as secretaries told me to be sympathetic: Salim had been a respectable engineer in Syria, had lost everything when he came to Egypt and could barely make ends meet. One of them told me that I should understand that unemployment and the consequent struggle destroyed men's psychological well-being and that I should not take his anger personally. The secretaries came to Salim's defence and appealed to me to understand the challenges he faced so as to better classify his reactions. Like Um Basim, the secretaries defended a man who was broken by the circumstances and consequently unable to fulfil his role as a provider.

Disguising need

Like Salim and Abu Basim, Abu Nabil was unable to provide for his family, although he chose a different way to hide this piece of information in public and from me. He was in his fifties and came to Cairo in 2012 with one of his wives and the two children he had with her. Abu Nabil was not unemployed but worked as a salesman. I met him several times in a shop selling orthopaedic shoes and medical supplies located in a dark side-corridor in one of the malls in 6th of October City, which belonged to an Egyptian businessman. The mall, the corridor and the shop itself had seen better days and it did not seem as if many customers found their way to it. The shop was empty and Abu Nabil was sitting alone behind the cash register every time I passed by. I also met Abu Nabil at his flat where I was offered tea and juice and was introduced to his wife and daughters. Soon after these first meetings, Abu Nabil began to ask me for money in order to give it to Syrian families he knew, who were in need of financial support. Um Khalid, who had put me in touch with Abu Nabil, was the one who explained to me that through these requests Abu Nabil was asking for financial support for himself but was too shy and embarrassed to tell me that. She begged me not to reveal that I knew he was in dire need of money and that his story of providing for other families was made up. Thus, I did not challenge, though not without discomfort, his continuous requests for help and donations for poor and needy acquaintances. Once, Abu Nabil asked me to get medication from an Egyptian pharmacist I knew, who had offered to help Syrians by selling his products at a huge discount. When I delivered the medication, Abu Nabil's wife opened the door and thanked me cheerfully for bringing the medication for Abu Nabil's mother. She obviously had no idea that Abu Nabil asked me for money and support by positioning himself as a fundraiser helping Syrian families in need, rather than admitting that he could not afford the medication for one of his closest relatives.

And finally, there was Abu Khalid who had introduced himself to me as community leader. Several times I gave him bags filled with clothes that an acquaintance of mine had collected in the school where she was working. After one clothes donation, I met him and he was wearing one of the suits from the bags of clothes that he had promised to give to Syrian families in need. It made me wonder whether he himself was disguising to be in need just like Abu Nabil. Another time, I received a phone call from Abu Khalid asking to meet me urgently. Once we had sat down in a quiet café in 6th of October City, he told me that he himself needed money, that he had helped so many families over the years and that it was his turn now. He explained that he needed the money urgently to be able to meet his family in Turkey. He said that he was embarrassed to confess in front of his family that he did not have enough money for the ticket from Cairo to Istanbul. Furthermore, his wife needed to see a doctor and the whole family needed to find the financial means to settle down in Istanbul. During this time, I often chatted with his son in Turkey. He said the following with regard to my interaction with his father:

> Don't expect of someone like my father to tell you the truth about all the small details, especially in these days. It's considered embarrassing. [...] I hope you don't misunderstand the fact that he wouldn't be able to be honest about these details. To tell you the truth, even I wouldn't like to talk about these details. We don't consider it bad lying. It's just something unnecessary to share ... You wouldn't like someone to worry about you even if you aren't totally okay.

For Abu Nabil and Abu Khalid, it seemed most important to prove in public that they were in control of the situation and that they were still able to provide for their family. There was an embarrassment related to admitting helplessness and the inability to get out of one's situation independently that men seemed to avoid and circumvent for as long as possible; in Abu Nabil's case, through hiding the truth about his desperate economic situation despite his efforts to work.[15] What was at stake for men like Abu Khalid and Abu Nabil was their ability to adhere to the ideal of 'Syrianness' defined by economic stability and success. For this reason, they adopted in front of me the position of providing men who were able to take care of themselves, their families and their communities. This was their way of masculinization.

Conclusion

In the Egyptian labour market, Syrian men faced difficulties in reclaiming their middle-class masculinity. They were confronted with the pain of starting again from scratch, of status loss and an inability to prove their skills and they experienced humiliation, dependency on others and vulnerability in the labour market. Unemployment was especially feared and considered to be the opposite of proper manhood which was defined by the ideal of provider masculinity. Hence, several Syrian men who interacted with me could not admit their inability to provide and were instead hiding this from me – if necessary, by circumventing the truth.

This chapter has presented various forms of shame: Syrian men shamed 'others', expressed their personal sentiments of embarrassment, unease and depression regarding their specific circumstances in the labour market and engaged in certain practices to deal with shame, such as disguising their need. This chapter has also discussed pride: most Syrian men spoke about a form of seemingly universal 'Syrian' moral and gendered codes and schemes. They extracted pride from belonging to a community of Syrians that was defined by their high work ethics and values. Syrian men kept referring to an idealized version of gender relations, in which men remained the main and sole breadwinner while women could stay at home. The notion of the masculine provider is thus entrenched in a particular idea of the household with complementary, gendered responsibilities. This vision of the ideal household and family was deeply classed. Syrian men's nostalgia for and indulgence in an ideal Syrian culture stood in sharp contrast to the reality they faced in Egypt on a daily basis. In Egypt, a number of Syrian men could not be the providers they aspired to be but were confronted with various obstacles, such as little payment, work in low-profile professions or precarious work conditions. Their respective challenges in the Egyptian labour market evoked shame, embarrassment, unease and depression in most Syrian men who reflected about their work conditions. Nevertheless, at the same time, several Syrian men made an effort to highlight Syrians' commitment and love for hard work, their inventiveness, knowledge and energy. Notions of shame and pride were closely related: pride in one's inventions and new ideas alternated with fear for one's existence; the feeling to be better off in Egypt than somewhere else interchanged with anger about Egypt's strict work and immigration laws. Men expressed pride in their love for and ability to do hard work that they directly related to being Syrian. They were proud of Syrians' expertise in the labour market and the knowledge Syrians brought to Egypt from previous education and work experience in Syria. At the same time, they were fearful of being unable to earn sufficient income despite their expressed love for work and expertise, and they felt ashamed and humiliated when being reduced to their role as precarious beings who had no ground and stability under their feet to complain or claim appropriate work conditions.

Some men struggled with their position in the Egyptian labour market in a specific way: young men, who had to interrupt their education due to their forced displacement, suffered from being excluded from the privileges of being young, while they were at the same time unable to properly access the sphere of grown-up men. In a similar vein, fathers were at a specific intersection that caused a certain form of suffering, namely, the inability to function as the backbone of the family and the children's guarantor of stability. An intersectional analysis proves to bring to the forefront those specificities of suffering and negotiations of masculinities.

Based on the dominance of the ideal of provider masculinity, women's participation in the labour market could only be understood as a threat that undermined men's status, power and self-worth. Consequently, several Syrian men I met ignored the fact that Syrian women were present and visible in the Egyptian labour market and had been economically active in Syria. Instead, they masculinized against women by defining them as weak and themselves as their 'natural' and 'traditional' protectors and providers. Their self-positioning and their endeavours to control women discursively prove again that several Syrian men found it difficult to put their middle-class masculinity, essentially built on providing, on stable ground in Egypt. Apart from the strategy of masculinizing against women and the unwillingness to approve and recognize women's position in the labour market, men engaged in judging others and demarcating themselves from them especially when it came to the topic of unemployment. The circulation of gossip and the judgement of unsuccessful Syrian men also involved the fear of being judged, exposed and humiliated one day. To reinstate masculinity there was again a need for the 'other' as well as a need for the 'weak woman' and a need for references to patriarchal traditions.

Chapter 4

LOSS OF STATUS AND 'GROOM-ABILITY': MAKING SENSE OF CHANGES IN MARRIAGE NEGOTIATIONS

It's too early to think about [marriage]. The situation is difficult so it will be delayed. In Syria, it was possible because there was a house and a car, but here I don't have this idea.

Bashar said this to me when we sat together with Hani and Mazin in Mazin's flat. Um Mazin had made delicious food for us and after food we sat down for lemonade and some cake in the small living room. We were talking about marriage and whether the young men were thinking about finding a spouse and getting married at that point in time in Egypt. As young men in their mid-twenties almost at the end of their studies, it would have been the 'right' time to start considering marriage – at least in pre-2011 Syria.[1] However, the three of them agreed that since they could not gather the necessary financial and material resources to get married, they did not want to think about falling in love at that moment. Bashar's description of the status quo includes several aspects that also came up in conversations I had with other single Syrian men in their late twenties or early thirties: acknowledgement of displacement as a difficult and exhausting situation, referring to the capital and status they held in Syria that would have made it possible to get married, and the inability to think about marriage in their current situation in Egypt. Overall, I sensed, when spending time with Syrian men of this age group, that the topic of marriage was a heavy burden on them. I was told that the engagement and marriage procedures that were prevalent in Syria had changed since they had come to live in Egypt and that they had to find a way to deal with these changes if they did not want to delay their marriage.

This chapter deals with the changes in marriage patterns experienced and observed by Syrian men in Egypt. In the words of Salamandra (2004: 70), 'marriage, entailing as it does the alignment of families and the melding of cultural and economic capital, is a primary locus of identity and sociability'. Marriage is

Some aspects of this chapter were published in the article 'Defining the Other to Masculinize Oneself: Syrian Men's Negotiations of Masculinity during Displacement in Egypt', in *Signs: Journal of Women in Culture and Society*, 43(3), 665–86.

still commonly understood as a necessary stepping stone that defines the life of men and women in the Middle East (Kreil 2016; Schielke 2015; Singerman 2013). Furthermore, marriage in the Middle East is a family concern (Tucker 2008) described by Schielke (2015: 95) as following 'the double logic' of rational strategizing and meticulous planning on the part of the families, combined with a step into the unknown and the inability to estimate what the future will bring for the married couple. Several Syrian men felt challenged in their ability to perform successful masculinities in the roles of groom and husband. Gendered identities, ideals and power relationships had to be renegotiated since men risked to be undermined if they failed to get engaged or married (Ghannam 2013: 72).

The importance of social class background for Syrian refugee men in Egypt appears in an urgent and highly visible form in the context of marriage. Because of forced displacement, Syrian men asking for a woman's hand in marriage frequently experienced misrecognition based on the in-laws' lack of knowledge of their former status. The development of a marital relationship was directly related to one's economic stability and future perspectives, and consequently it was not only the groom's lost symbolic capital but also his decreased economic capital that hampered the marriage process. The financial burdens of marriage for the majority of young men and women and families in the Middle East have been in the focus of discussions for a while (see, for example, Assaad et al. 2010; Singerman 2013). It is still common to demand the availability of a flat, household items, furniture and a *mahr* (dower), usually provided by the groom's side, before a couple can get married (Schielke 2015; Singerman 2013). Furthermore, a husband is supposed to provide in accordance with the wife's class background (Hasso 2010).

Emotions such as anger and fury frequently guided conversations and Syrian men's sharing of their experiences in the marriage market. Especially Mahmud was often angry when he had gone out again to present himself to a woman looking for a groom and was rejected by the family afterwards. His odyssey to find a spouse was a recurring theme we discussed during our meetings. It informs this chapter significantly. Another aspect that warrants analysis in this chapter is the marriage of Syrian women to Egyptian men. Syrian men had difficulty accepting this situation and blamed Syrian women's weakness for intermarriages. As suggested in the previous chapter, Syrian women's conduct and behaviour were of high relevance for constructions of masculinities.

Remembering marriage traditions in Syria

I begin this chapter with Um and Abu Mazin's memories of marriage traditions in Syria. They had been married for almost forty years and happily shared with me the story of how they met, became engaged and got married, which was intertwined with the experience of when their daughter got married in Syria ten years ago. Abu Mazin used to work at an electricity company owned by the Syrian state and Um Mazin took care of their, now grown-up, children. Um Mazin told me almost every time I met her about the possessions and social position they previously had in Syria. She frequently spoke about their real estate properties in the city they came from, in the countryside and at the beach. Abu Mazin often talked about his social life and his political and voluntary work at the communal level in his home town. Once he proudly showed me a business card indicating that he was member of a political party in the city he came from, which he pulled out of an otherwise empty wallet and carefully put back after I had looked at it. When I asked them about their engagement and marriage, Um Mazin recalled how sharing a house with the family was the norm for newlyweds forty years ago, whereas nowadays brides would ask for a house of their own, a car, a chalet and a lot of gold. Their wedding celebration was modest, Um Mazin said, with home-made food and a party in the house of the groom, while 'nowadays the party takes place in a hall and costs a lot more'. When I asked them how young men could pay for all these expenses, Abu Mazin explained that the family of the groom would usually step in to support him financially. Their engagement period was short, Um Mazin continued to explain, because they were related and already knew each other. Their marriage was arranged, she said, stressing that 'until now men prefer that the family chooses'. Abu Mazin added that the main criterion for choosing a suitable groom was the family's reputation: 'even if he only has little money we care the most about his family background'. He cited a Syrian proverb to illustrate expectations in a future spouse:

Don't be afraid of someone who got hungry after he had been sated. Instead, fear the one who is sated after he was hungry.

According to this proverb, the poor man is not trustworthy while the noble man remains noble and keeps his manners and morals, even if he encounters problems. Abu Mazin said that this proverb meant that the prospective spouse should not be from a poor family because he or she could turn out to be greedy once he or she had access to wealth. There is an immanent relation to class formation and frontiers that could be read into this proverb. The way Abu Mazin uses it describes a lack of trust and respect for people from a lower-class background, who are seemingly eternally marked by their poor background.

In order to find out whether the family of the potential spouse fit the criteria and was suitable for marriage, fathers would ask around among neighbours and friends, Um Mazin explained. Again, Abu Mazin made use of a proverb to explain the situation to me: 'Each person considers his colleague an idol', meaning that one's choice of friends and acquaintances speaks volumes about one's morals, interests and educational background. Abu Mazin's ascription of utmost importance to the reputation of the groom's family and the enquiry taking place in the social circle of the groom resonate with Rabo's (2005: 80) finding that, among Aleppian traders, the family name, the name of the father, the quarter where one lives and where the father grew up establish a 'frame of reference' by which the potential groom gets socially classified. The more that is known about the family of the groom or the bride, the more one is able to vouch for the character of the individual (2005:

90). Likewise, Salamandra (2004: 41) describes for the context of the capital how the place of residence in Damascus is linked to the status of the people who inhabit it. What is described here is the individual's 'symbolic capital' – assets like public acknowledgement, recognition and honour, perceived by others as 'self-evident' and permanent (Bourdieu 1985: 731). Reay (2004: 57/58), who engages in a feminist analysis of Bourdieu's work, writes, 'symbolic capital is manifested in individual prestige and personal qualities, such as authority and charisma'. A Syrian man can acquire these characteristics through his name, place of residence and his family's reputation.

Certain aspects of the engagement process in Syria were entirely female-dominated. However, women only searched for a potential bride on behalf of a marriageable bachelor, not vice versa (Stolleis 2004: 152). Young women and their mothers ought to wait for offers. If men and women found someone without the help of relatives, both families needed to be convinced of the suitability of the arrangement. Young men usually depended on the financial support of their fathers and the young woman's family needed assurance that their daughter would have a standard of living similar to what she was accustomed to at home (Rabo 2005: 89/90). Um Mazin explained that usually it would be hinted to the mother of a son that there was a girl of marriageable age suitable for her son. Thereafter, the mother of the groom would go and meet the girl and her family.

> She makes an appointment by phone and then she goes to see the girl. When she enters, the girl brings her coffee. The girl offers the coffee to her, then, she leaves. […] The mother of the groom returns to her house and tells her son that the family is good and the girl is pretty. Then, the mother makes another phone call and tells the other family: 'I liked the situation. Can I bring my son to see her?'

After the first official encounter of bride and groom-to-be, both families make a deal about the *mahr* and how the couple will live.[2] In the case of Um Mazin's daughter, the engagement period was introduced through *katb al-kitab* (signing of the marriage contract). Afterwards, the couple had the chance to get to know each other: they went to cafés together and the groom visited the home of his future parents-in-law frequently. Over the time of the engagement, Um Mazin's daughter received many gifts, such as gold jewellery, from her fiancé. Gift-giving, especially of gold, plays an important role in the context of marriage in most parts of the Arab world (see Nasser el Dine 2018; Singerman 2007; Moors 2003; Hoodfar 1997). The wedding process is then completed by the wedding party, which, according to Johnson et al. (2009: 15), is a central aspect of the performance and production of identities. The final part of the process is the consummation of the marriage.[3]

Um and Abu Mazin were not the only ones who spoke with me about marriage traditions in Syria. Firas and Yasmin, whom I met during a meeting initiated and organized by my friend Mahmud to help me with my research, eventually engaged in a lively discussion about marriage habits and customs in Syria. Yasmin was from a rural town in the east of Syria and mocked Firas, who was from Damascus, for what she perceived as snobbery and an ignorance about life back in Syria. She related his unawareness to his class status and to the fact that he was born 'with a silver spoon in his mouth'[4] meaning that he was born rich and privileged.

- Firas: My wedding was for a big amount of money: 120,000 dollars. It was for the house, the *mahr* and everything else. When I got married, I bought a house in Damascus and I furnished it and I rented a wedding hall for 8,000 dollars. For the honeymoon, we went to Turkey. So, all in all, it was for 120,000 dollars. I paid for everything. The woman in Damascus has a value, so she doesn't pay for anything. She is more respected than the Egyptian woman.
- Magdalena: How did you meet her?
- Firas: It was a family engagement. These are the old traditions. My mother went out to see girls and when she liked a girl she told me and then I went to see her. I was engaged for two years so we could get to know each other. At the beginning, she was a stranger to me so you should spend time to know her. I continued for two years with her until we agreed and confirmed and then the engagement was completed. Getting married in Damascus is very challenging.
- Yasmin: What do you mean? Are you saying that in [my hometown] they don't value a girl? Is marriage just a commercial thing? Is it marriage or trade?
- Firas: In these days, it has become a little bit like trade.
- Mahmud: Yes, it became like trade in Syria. In Egypt, it is the same.

Firas' account confirms the financial burden traditionally put on the shoulders of the groom's family and also shows his pride in having been able to fulfil these expectations. His wealth and level of consumption play an important role in the way Firas describes his wedding. After Firas and Yasmin had left, Mahmud told me that he was shocked by the amount of money his friend had spent on his wedding. Where he comes from, in the suburbs of Damascus, he said, it used to be possible to think about marriage when a man had accumulated 2,000 US dollars. Firas' and Yasmin's dialogue speak to Schielke's (2012: 136) argument that wealth and consumption translate into respect, recognition and the promise of a good life and happiness. Consumption proves to be 'the key register in which people judge various social relationships, most notably marriage and social standing' (2012: 136) Through his wedding and by enumerating what he bought for his wife, Firas is able to claim respect and recognition for himself.

Meeting a potential bride in Egypt

Challenges surrounding the issue of marriage were various. For Syrian men who were already engaged when they arrived in Egypt, the family reunion proved to be difficult, as I learned during my conversation with Wasim who was sitting together with his friends in his office at the community centre in which he worked.

> I got married here in Egypt and Ayman [he points to one of his peers sitting next to him] also got married here, but maybe our experience is different from that of others. There are people who came to Egypt and they were already engaged or in a relationship with someone in Syria. Firstly, there is no possibility to bring a woman to Egypt, there is no visa for her and it is impossible to make her enter. Maybe you can do it if you bribe. You have to pay 1500–2000 Dollar. I brought my back-then fiancée from Syria and I paid 1000 Dollar and I am lucky, very lucky, because usually you have to pay more. Another topic is the challenges Syrian men face who want to marry Syrians in Egypt, but there is no money and no house. There are some families that make it easier to marry in terms of conditions. There is no problem. We are all refugees, we are the same. However, there are some people who believe that they still live in Syria.

Wasim mentioned what appeared like a canon that I heard frequently when I talked with young Syrian men about getting married: they found it extremely challenging to meet the requirements of the potential in-laws and could not always rely on their understanding for young men's economically unstable situation as forcibly displaced newcomers to Egypt. Ayman added to Wasim's description that there were several other obstacles to getting engaged and married in the 'traditional Syrian way' in Egypt: Syrian men and women of marriageable age did not have venues to meet and in many cases their female family members were not around to take over the introduction.

> I want to add something. It happened with me last night. I met a Syrian guy who has a job and would be able to provide comfortably for his future wife. What's his problem? His family is not staying with him. Usually our habits and traditions demand that he brings his family with him so that the families get to know each other. The problem is the initial meeting between a man and a woman. This guy is 29 or 30 years old and his work is excellent. He imports products from China and he sells them here. He is able to buy four houses. However, his problem is that he lives in Kafr el-Sheikh and he doesn't know any Syrians. When he found out that I am working in a place with Syrians he told me: 'please, I beg you, I just want the names of some girls and I will tell my family to see them in Cairo.' The problem is that the people don't know each other. The Syrians don't meet each other, especially in some areas. Any Syrian man who is able to marry but doesn't know any Syrians in his surroundings won't get married. For sure and frankly, he won't marry an Egyptian. It happened the opposite way: a Syrian woman can marry an Egyptian, but the other way around is very rare.

Ayman's summary of the problems that Syrian men in Egypt experienced sparked a discussion between Wasim, Ayman and Bashir who had been silently following the conversation so far. The three friends did their best to explain all the details to me clarifying the urgency of the matter and the ways in which marriage was a burden on young displaced Syrian men.

- Bashir: The problem is that the guys cannot meet the girls and at work they only meet Egyptian girls and if they study they also only meet Egyptian girls.
- Ayman: If you meet a girl and propose to her family and then they find out that you are here alone without your family, will her family accept you? No, for sure not.
- Wasim: It's the problem that the families are conservative. If I am in one place and my family is in another place, it makes marriage really difficult. There are some families who are sympathetic. I personally was engaged to my wife before leaving Syria and for one year I was trying to bring her here. It was a difficult matter.
- Magdalena: Was it common in Syria that spouses were not from the same city?
- Bashir: It didn't happen a lot. I am from the south of Syria. I didn't know anyone from Homs or from Idlib. Even from Sueda, which is close to my home city, only 45 minutes away, I didn't know anyone. Here in Egypt, I got to know people from Aleppo, Homs, Idlib, everywhere.
- Wasim: This is a positive point. Concerning the question of marriage, if someone from Deraa marries someone from Idlib, it is something positive. However, it is the only positive point of being here.
- Bashir: As for marriage, this doesn't make it easier. The in-laws should be able to enquire about you by asking your relatives and your family. So the people here are a bit afraid. If I want to marry a girl from Idlib and I go to her family, her family will ask about me in my hometown. And if they know someone there, it will make it easier because they can ask the person and his contacts. However, if they don't know anyone in the city of the prospective groom, this might be a reason to refuse him. And in this situation, the family brings bad luck to the man and the woman.

Young Syrian men experienced that they could not rely on previous patterns of getting engaged and married. The loneliness of their displacement with families scattered over various places directly impacted on their chances vis-à-vis potential in-laws. The 'frame of reference' (Rabo 2005: 80), through which they used to be read and socially classified in Syria, could not migrate with them to Egypt and thus Syrian men were always on the edge of being misrecognized, misread and misplaced in the social hierarchy they once took for granted.

The conditions of forced displacement that Wasim and his friends experienced as challenging and draining aspects of the journey to marriage during forced displacement did not evoke the same reaction in every young man I met. Qutayba, who was introduced to me during a party at a friend's house, welcomed the changes he observed in the way Syrian men and women got to know each other in Egypt. Qutayba was not looking for a spouse but believed that in Egypt there was the possibility to meet and fall in love with a woman 'just like it happens in the movies'. In Cairo, young Syrian men and women could meet and get to know each other in the workplace, cafés or restaurants, he told me enthusiastically, while we were sitting in my friend's living room with people around us dancing and drinking. They would meet, fall in love and tell the family later, he said. This rhetoric describes a classed opportunity to get to know each other. Access to the spaces in which Qutayba dreams of meeting a spouse is due to the high prices restricted to the middle and upper class. Adeley (2016: 104), who conducted research among unmarried men and women in Jordan, argues that new ways of falling in love outside of family-organized gatherings are available because of the increased number of cafés that opened in Amman over the past decades, which are however only affordable for university-educated and employed young adults. In contrast to most young Syrian men I met, Qutayba also considered it positive that, due to forced displacement, families were scattered over various countries and could no longer uphold the tradition of choosing a spouse. While it was not uncommon in Syria to marry one's cousin or someone else from the extended family, this had become more difficult since families were spread over various countries, he explained. Qutayba appreciated a gradual distancing from 'traditional' forms of getting to know each other in favour of 'new ways' of finding courtship.[5]

Being a fish out of water

Akram, in contrast to Qutayba, wanted to get married when I got to know him and did not welcome the fact that he could not rely on his relatives' judgement and recommendation in the process of finding a potential spouse. He was a primary school teacher in his late twenties from a small city in the north of Syria and told me how he got engaged to his fiancée. The first challenge he faced was to make sure that the woman he liked had 'good' morals:

> If I want to marry a girl, I should ask about her and her family, as I told you, to find out if she is from a good family. Before I get engaged to her, I should know her morals, if she is good or not and also if her brothers are good. So, I talked with [my fiancée] frankly to find out what she was like.

Akram ascribed high relevance to finding a bride of a social and cultural background he considers appropriate and suitable. It is not just the future wife who had to pass the test but also her family should meet his standards.[6] Akram decided that, due to the absence of his female relatives and because his father with whom he had come to Egypt had passed away a few months earlier, he had to speak to the woman he liked. He wanted to be able to judge whether they could have a future together. He did this even though he felt that it was against the 'traditional' way to meet a woman back in Syria. Once Akram was convinced that she was a suitable spouse for him, he introduced himself to her father. That they were not from the same region was reason enough for her father to initially resist. However, his future father-in-law knew someone from Akram's hometown and could therefore enquire about his background. In addition, his prospective father-in-law used the opportunity that Akram was working as a teacher in the very same school he had founded in Egypt and observed his behaviour for a while before he eventually agreed to the marriage. In addition to the complicated way to being accepted by his in-laws, the negotiations about the *mahr* between Akram and his father-in-law were challenging because his father-in-law did not know the financial background of Akram's family. Akram's father-in-law initially requested 75,000 LE (in 2015 approximately 9,700 US dollars) arguing that his daughter's cousin had got married for the same amount and that he did not want his daughter to feel less worthy. However, Akram could not afford this amount and because his father-in-law knew that his daughter loved Akram and wanted her to be happy, they eventually agreed on 50,000 LE (approximately 6,500 US dollars).

In summary, what hampered and complicated the engagement process was the fact that Akram and the woman he wanted to marry were not from the same city and could not read each other's background:

> [...] She [the potential bride] should be a girl from my place. Her father would know who I am because in the village the people know each other. They would say: 'this is the son of so and so and they are good people.' So, he might agree. You can give what you have in terms of money and it will be fine. It's the issue that I told you before regarding the origin of people and the family so and so ... this is lost here in Egypt.

Away from his home town, his comfort zone, Akram could not rely on his family's reputation that might have outweighed the unavailability of the necessary financial resources. Bourdieu and Wacquant's (1992: 127) metaphor of the 'fish in water' comes to mind:

> Social reality exists, so to speak, twice, in things and in minds, in fields and in habitus, outside and inside social agents. And when habitus encounters a social world of which it is the product, it is like a 'fish in water': it does not feel the weight of the water and it takes the world about itself for granted.

As long as Akram remained in his comfort zone, where his name and background were known and his class status was valued, he did not feel the challenges of getting married to the extent he experienced it in Egypt. It only turned into a severe burden on him when he could not take his position at home for granted anymore during displacement in Egypt. And thus, Akram's situation has turned into that of a fish being out of water, in which habitus encounters an unfamiliar situation and 'the resulting disjunctures can generate not only change and transformation, but also disquiet, ambivalence, insecurity and uncertainty' (Reay et al. 2009: 1105).[7] Being a man in search for marriage during forced displacement in Egypt thus required a change in conduct and form of masculinity that relied less on one's frame of reference and more on how one presented oneself. Being a man meant being aware of one's former privileges and the lack thereof in Egypt and necessitated coping strategies.

Looking back, even though he perceived the process of getting engaged in Egypt as challenging, Akram found a positive aspect:

> All the people here are in the same situation. We all became refugees and displaced. The person who was rich has lost all his money and became poor, and the poor is still poor, so all the people are now in the same class. It was like melting and all are now in the same container. This is a positive factor that we found here in Egypt.

Describing himself as being from the 'normal class or middle class in Syria', Akram believed that if they had not been displaced but had met in Syria, his father-in-law would have rejected him because of the class differences between the two families. His father-in-law was rich and had many real estate properties that had been destroyed in the war; in Egypt, his father-in-law was, as Akram said, 'just like us'. Akram was aware of social class divisions in Syria and how they would have made his engagement impossible. In Egypt, he finds some form of solidarity and cross-class alliances due to forced displacement.[8] While Akram bemoaned, on the one hand, that his frame of reference and good reputation could not travel with him to Egypt, he was, on the other hand, convinced and appreciative of the fact that the challenges of being refugees in Egypt lead to compromises and a softening of social divisions. Interestingly, this argument stands in sharp contrast to the hierarchies which Syrian men established during forced displacement regarding 'real refugeeness' and men's employment. Syrian men were outspoken about who was a 'real' refugee and who did not define as one. Similarly, they created a continuum of successful men and failing men in the labour market. In the context of marriage, however, Akram found that several families prioritized their mutually experienced plight in Egypt as refugees abstaining from drawing lines of separation, which then made alternative marriage arrangements possible. And thus, Akram was both hampered and advantaged by the renegotiation of class and status due to forced displacement. On the one hand, he faced difficulties because his father-in-law misrecognized him and his financial situation. On the other hand, however, he saw in the possibility of their engagement a potential for change and a new form of solidarity due to the common experience of social hardship in Egypt.

The multifacetedness of social class belonging as played out during forced displacement and Syrian men's challenging endeavours of re-claiming their middle-classness are especially present in the context of marriage. With a frame of reference from Syria that could either not be relied on anymore or proved unfitting under the new social conditions, negotiations of masculinities meet a social context in which known and taken-for-granted patterns, norms and values do not hold anymore while new forms of social encounter and cohesion are not yet established.

Politics entering marriage negotiations

In contrast to the difficulties Akram had to face when he wanted to get married, Dawud experienced that the differences of opinions regarding politics that fragmented Syrian society since the uprising had entered marriage negotiations. Dawud had just got engaged and was eager to share his story with me. It was during a restaurant visit together with his sister, that he saw his fiancée for the first time. He decided to go to her table to talk to her and managed to get her father's phone number, who was absent on that evening. A few days later, he called her father and asked for her hand in marriage. The marriage negotiations were challenging and were about to fail because Dawud, even though he had lived in Damascus for a long time, was not originally from Damascus, which his potential family-in-law was. Dawud recalled that it was an advantage that he had picked up the Damascene accent. His case thus not only illustrates the importance of one's background and frame of reference, but also proves the uninterrupted significance of the Damascene/non-Damascene and the urban/rural divide (Rabo 2012: 83; Salamandra 2004: 12). Because Dawud was not born in Damascus and only moved there later in life, it was difficult for him to prove his social class background vis-à-vis his in-laws, a well-known Damascene family that he described to me as upper class. The long-lasting negotiations with his father-in law further included an enquiry about his political views. His father-in-law asked him about his opinions regarding the uprising in Syria and Dawud remembered that he tried his best to guess what his father-in-law would appreciate as an answer, wondering whether he was with or against the regime. Furthermore, he was conscious of the fact that his unstable financial situation in Egypt could make marriage problematic. In contrast to Syria, where Dawud possessed all the assets necessary to marry, such as a car, a flat and a good job, in Egypt, he rented a flat, his work was not secure and he could not afford a car. In Syria, he could have asked for any girl's hand, he assured me confidently, but in Egypt he had to hope for her and her family's sympathy and understanding about his financial situation. Despite all his worries, Dawud's father-in-law accepted him and once they had agreed about the *mahr*, Dawud's family in Syria and the in-laws in Cairo talked via Skype and then Dawud and his fiancée read the first *sura* of the Quran as a confirmation of their engagement.

As if making a plea for young men facing similar conditions, Dawud summarized their situation emphatically:

> There is a sadness and difficulty like: 'I don't have an income, I cannot find a job, I cannot pay my rent, I cannot marry, I cannot send money to my family ... '. The people are not anymore like they were in the past. Maybe the crisis made young men very old before they should have become old.

There is a form of exhaustion that was unknown to young men before the uprising relating to their struggle as grooms in the marriage market. Overall, the stories that were shared with me often reminded me of the myth of Sisyphus (see Camus

[1955] 1979), who is forced by the gods to put all his effort into pushing a stone up a mountain before it rolls back down and Sisyphus must start all over again. The torture is, according to Camus, that Sisyphus is deeply aware of the 'whole extent of his wretched condition' (Camus [1955] 1979: 109). In a similar vein, Syrian bachelors had to begin anew to accumulate the capital they needed if they wanted to get married in Egypt. Often, they had already gathered this capital back in Syria, such as a flat of their own, a stable job and a car. However, in Egypt, the stone they had struggled to push up the mountain had rolled down and they needed to gather the economic resources to get married again. Similarly, they had to find a way to reinstall their status and give weight and credibility to their reputation that was once an intrinsic part of their identity.

Marriage and economic capital

The uninterrupted importance of financial resources in order to be classified as a potential groom meant that young men who were financially unstable in Egypt had to postpone their plans for marriage indefinitely. In Fadi's case, the prospect of getting married was directly related to finding work and graduation from university as he summarized in the following way in 2016: 'I want to get married, Magdalena. If only I could complete my studies.' After Fadi had successfully passed his high school diploma, he began studying engineering in the summer of 2015. However, he had to interrupt his studies several times: firstly, because he had to help earning money for his family and, secondly, because he could not afford to pay 1,000 US dollars per year to continue studying. Hence, he was thinking about working in a second job in the evening after his eight-hour shift at his parents' shop to be able to accumulate the university fees. For Fadi, there was a direct connection between completing his education and being ready to get married. Being forcibly displaced caused that it was considerably more difficult for Fadi to finalize his studies while being at the same time one of the main breadwinners for his family.

Being stuck in one's masculine trajectory, unable to reach what one had imagined to have achieved at this time of one's life had it not been for the uprising and forced displacement, caused distress and discontent among many Syrian men. Mazin tried to confine his disappointment and presented it as a simple equation: even though he would have thought about getting married at this point of his life in Syria, under the new circumstances, marriage had to be delayed, and work and securing his future took priority. In Mazin's words:

> If I were still in Syria, I would have thought about [marriage] by now, but here it's difficult. I don't know if I am staying here and also economically it's difficult. I cannot get married until I know that I will stay in one country and that I have work and make money.

Forced displacement, unemployment and insecurity about one's future prospects meant that marriage had to be postponed indefinitely until his life was normalized.

It is important to contextualize the temporal aspect of Mazin's statement. Because of the recentness of the Syrian civil war, the consequent displacement, uncertainty about the war's outcome and the stability of the whole region, Mazin did not feel able to think about marriage. He did not know what the near future would bring and unless there was a minimal form of stability in his life he felt that he could not make a marital commitment. Loizos' (2007: 193) analysis of the experience of time in the context of forced displacement comes to mind. He argues that there is a period of 'radical cognitive and affective uncertainty' that relates to where and how one's life will continue.

Not being groom enough

In contrast to Mazin who wanted to postpone marriage until he felt some form of stability in his life, Mahmud's frantic search for a spouse had been ongoing for a year. During our meetings, he would describe in detail the strategies he had applied to find a bride: he asked his Syrian acquaintances to act as matchmakers; he posted an ad about himself in a Facebook group that was designed for Syrians of marriageable age in Egypt; and he asked his uncle, who also lived in Cairo, to find him a bride. In his search, he had already met various families and was used to the different questions he had to answer: he was asked about his political views, his religious beliefs and practices and his future plans. One family he visited wanted to know whether he was planning to flee to Europe. When he replied that he was not, 'the mother raised her eyebrow and asked me if I had no ambitions', he remembered. One time, I met Mahmud after a potential bride and her family had just rejected him. The woman was twenty-nine years old, which was far beyond what was considered the marriageable age for women, Mahmud told me angrily. However, she was educated and had a similar interest in tourism, which had convinced him to meet her. During the meeting, she and her family expressed doubts about his morals and religiosity, because Mahmud was in regular touch with foreign women due to being a tour guide. Mahmud was outraged that a woman of her age demanded that he should change his profession and shouted:

> The Syrian women who are in Egypt deserve to be treated like the girls in Zaatari Camp, where men come to pay the families to marry and exploit them.

His fury and call for women to learn to appreciate what they had in Egypt are evocative of the feeling of misrecognition and status loss he felt whenever he was rejected by a potential spouse and her family. Even though Mahmud rarely shouted and reached a level of rage comparable to that day, there was a general sense of anger that he expressed regularly when I met him. He felt that it was unfair that so many women he met in Egypt were hesitant, demanding and arrogant, even though he assured me that he ought to be considered a good match with his career, language skills, relatively assured income, savings and high education. What increased his anger was the fact that most of the women who rejected him had in his opinion nothing to offer, since he considered them neither beautiful nor young enough. He met these women, he told me, because he was desperate to get married and always hoped that they would somehow be a match for him.

According to Taylor (1994: 25) misrecognition can cause severe damage to the individual's self-esteem:

> A person or a group of people can suffer real damage, real distortion, if the people or society around them mirror back to them a confining or demeaning or contemptible picture of themselves. Nonrecognition or misrecognition can inflict harm, can be a form of oppression, imprisoning someone in a false, distorted, and reduced mode of being.

Taylor's argument can lay the foundation for contextualizing Mahmud's outburst of anger after he felt misjudged, misunderstood and misvalued by a potential bride and her family. A woman, whom Mahmud did not consider of being in his league, reflected through her rejection a picture of him that did not approve the social status he tried to claim for himself. This caused Mahmud's condemnation of all women in Egypt who he considered undeserving of men with honest and good intentions like himself. Mahmud's anger is an acceptable, manly emotion, in contrast to the expression of sadness which is expected to be controlled (Ghannam 2013: 140).

Likewise, Abd al-Rahman, who had got married to Israa in Egypt a year ago, observed a change in perceptions of marriage among Syrian families and in their expectations of a groom albeit for his benefit. He compared what men had to pay in Syria before the outbreak of the civil war and how they got married in exile in Egypt.

> [The bride] was always dreaming about her soulmate, who will come to her on his white horse and she doesn't agree to get married unless [the groom] is a doctor or an engineer. When the revolution started, many young men were killed and many others took up arms so the number of men decreased. Before the revolution, people were giving around 200,000 or 300,000 Syrian Lira[9] in gold to the bride. However, since the beginning of the revolution only the ring is enough even without the white dress that the girl has always dreamed about. [..] The important thing is that you take good care of the bride.

Indeed, the photographs that Abd al-Rahman and Israa shared with me that were taken on their wedding day showed them in a living room with about ten guests. The pictures were taken in the moment in which Abd al-Rahman gave Israa the *shabka*. Another picture showed Israa's father giving gold to his daughter. Israa told me later that the impressive wedding dress she wore was only rented for that day. Abd al-Rahman's account suggests that the expectations that Syrian women and their families had of potential grooms used to be considerably more ambitious and had come to be reined in through the experience of the uprising and consequent forced displacement. He even mocked women for their unrealistic expectations and appeared to feel satisfaction and a sense of justice knowing that women could not ask for as much as they used to in Syria. Again, women are condemned for not appreciating honest intentions, but rather sticking to unrealistic dreams and expectations in a man. Being judged and rejected by these women would mean that Abd al-Rahman could not pass as the good match he considers himself to be. These women's misrecognition is a threat to him in his standing as a valuable man and husband and thus he cannot hide his satisfaction regarding the new developments since the uprising.

Abd al-Rahman was not the only one who argued that Syrian men's absence, due to their death or because they were fighting, would change the meaning of marriage and engagement with a Syrian man. After I shared with Rafi during one of our trips to 6th of October City, who was usually calm, introverted and polite and had got married more than ten years ago in Syria, that a Syrian friend of mine had been left by his fiancée, he told me fiercely that a woman who would break up with a Syrian man was stupid for letting him go, since there were no Syrian men left. His eyes pinned on the road, he said firmly that she was to be blamed if the relationship did not work out and that she ought to be aware that she would not find another Syrian man easily because their number had decreased. The topic seemed to bug him and even after we had stopped talking about it and several minutes had passed, he opened the conversation again saying that he was convinced that not only in Egypt but also back in Syria the number of women ready to get married was bigger than the number of men and thus women should demand less from a Syrian groom.

That several Syrian men I met blamed women for being picky or too demanding suggests that these men had felt 'not good enough' and humiliated at some point of their search for a spouse. Being in Egypt without their family, without the reputation they used to have in their hometown, and having lost what would have made them a favoured match in Syria explain the rigour and anger expressed by Mahmud and Abd al-Rahman. The loss of social context and the consequent misrecognition equal loss of their masculine identity as grooms in which they had invested extensively through accumulation of various resources. These men could not rely on being read in the ways they wanted, their being and accumulated resources were nullified in Cairo and thus they responded with anger when getting mirrored from their surroundings that they were 'not good enough'. Eventually, both men's odyssey came to a positive end: Abd al-Rahman had got married to Israa and Mahmud married the daughter of his uncle whom he had asked for help in his search for a suitable spouse in 2016.

Syrian women marrying Egyptian men

Many Syrian men I talked to shared with me their concern about marriages between Syrian women and Egyptian men, which were commonly assumed to take place even though not many men knew Syrian-Egyptian couples in person. During my fieldwork, I met and talked to only one Syrian woman who had married an Egyptian, but, according to gossip, there was in fact a small number of women who had recently married Egyptian men. Being strongly opinionated about intermarriages seemed to be connected, on the one hand, with Syrian men's stress related to being forced to compete with Egyptian men to win Syrian women's favour. Their once-solid position appeared to be in question by the presence of more men among whom Syrian women could choose. On the other hand, Syrian men expressed a sense of possession over Syrian women.

Qutayba experienced that several Egyptian men, such as taxi drivers and even his former professor, asked him about a Syrian woman they could marry. Such a question was usually phrased as offering 'help' to Syrian women and their families. Qutayba did not appreciate such offers and he answered along the lines of: 'You don't want to help us, you only try to find a cheap opportunity to marry.' He heard of families who had to accept 'cheap' marriage proposals by Egyptian men because of their devastating financial situations. Qutayba, when referring to 'us', suggested that when Syrian women married Egyptian men, it was not about individual cases, but rather about the 'us/them' binary and that women belonged to the Syrian community. This reminds of an argument put forward by Yuval-Davis and Stoetzler (2002: 340), who state that women are commonly constructed as 'symbolic boundary guards of the collectivity and as representing the collectivity's honour'. The critique Qutayba and Syrian men voiced towards marriages between Syrian women and Egyptian men was similarly related to these women's disruption of the 'us/them' binary and to being 'lost' to the Syrian community.

According to Nur, 2012 was the year in which Syrian women were 'sold' to Egyptian husbands for 2,000 LE (approximately 200 US dollars in 2015). She recalled that there were offices in 6th of October City that functioned as agencies, in which women were 'advertised' for marriage to Egyptian men. However, she remembered that Syrian men had put an end to this by destroying those places in rage, forcing the marriage brokers to stop selling Syrian women. Anger and rage were the dominant emotions, directed against Egyptians who seemingly did not value Syrian women as their brides and against Syrians who supported these practices.

Miss Fatma, a middle-aged, strictly religious woman of Syrian/Egyptian descent who had opened a nursery for Syrian children knew the Syrian community, especially the women, in her neighbourhood well. She knew who needed donations, a job, a new flat and tried her best to answer to these needs through the channelling of donations. She said the following when I asked her about Syrian-Egyptian marriages:

-   Magdalena: Are there many Syrian women who marry Egyptians?
-   Miss Fatma: It's very rare. I don't think they are smart, the men …. I don't think they are serious. I know some ladies who did get married. But they are not from the cities. They are from the villages. The divorced ones. Her husband died there and then she has no one to take care of her and her daughter. I know two in Dar al-Salam, one in Maadi. Just three.

- Magdalena: Do you see that many Egyptian men are interested to marry Syrian women?
- Miss Fatma: Egyptian men are always after Syrian women. They feel that in this crisis Syrian women are ready to get married for nothing. But it's not right. They discover after time that it is not right. Most Syrian families don't want to have an Egyptian man among them. Maybe in the Facebook groups you noticed that they write: 'Syrian women are only for Syrian men!' If you are one of the members, you will read a lot about this. At the beginning there was somebody, I don't want to mention her name, who used to help those women who were raped in Syria to get married here. [...] she helps those girls to get married to Syrians, Egyptians, to whomever ....

Miss Fatma welcomed marriage to Egyptian men only if Syrian women, due to rape, divorce or being widowed, did not have high chances on the marriage market anymore. Following her reasoning, Egyptian men were in that case a second-class choice and better than no marriage at all. She foregrounded the context of war and forced displacement to explain intermarriages as better than nothing on the part of Syrian women and as Egyptian men's primitive motivation to circumvent traditional payments, habits and customs.

Furthermore, it was often assumed that Syrian women married Egyptian men only because they needed protection and financial aid. The emphasis was on single women's economic conditions that forced them to marry Egyptian men. Hani had an ambivalent opinion about Syrian/Egyptian intermarriages:

It's both positive and negative. If there is a woman and she really needs help and you as a man can help her and if you like her and you want to marry her, it's positive because you decide to stay with her all your life and to take care of her. But the negative thing is if someone wants to marry her only because he wants to give her a certain amount of money. This would be more like buying her, especially if he treats her like a slave and feels that he can leave her any time he wants. I can say that there is a phenomenon of taking advantage of Syrians.

For Hani the marriage of a Syrian woman with an Egyptian man was acceptable if the man proved to have good morals and the best intentions. Again, Syrian women are fixed in a static version of femininity – they are considered helpless without the support of a man, which makes getting married to an Egyptian man acceptable.

If men tried to explain to me why Syrian women and Egyptian men got married, it was commonly argued that Egyptian men were attracted to Syrian women because they were neater, cleaner, better cooks and more beautiful than Egyptian women – the notion of *sitt al-bayt* (queen of the house) came up frequently in these conversations. Syrian women were described as the best housewives in the region. For this reason, many Syrian men claimed that a marriage to Egyptian women was for them unthinkable. They perceived Egyptian women as loud, aggressive and even violent against their husbands. Rafi's younger brother Malik, who worked as a driver albeit with a more comfortable car, would every now and then take over the trips for Rafi if he was unavailable. In contrast to his brother who was very polite, silent and reserved, Malik enjoyed a good chat with his customers. On one of our trips to 6th of October City, he told me half-serious, half-joking that his neighbours were an Egyptian couple and at night he would hear the woman shouting and screaming. Her husband in the meantime would never say a word. He wondered whether his neighbour was a real man after all and whether he could stand up and defend himself against his clamouring wife. Malik was convinced that his poor neighbour would not only be screamed at but also be beaten by his wife.

Despite being not very common, marriages of Syrian women with Egyptian men received a surprising amount of attention. It was a way of communicating the boundaries of the Syrian community in Egypt. On the one hand, Syrian women took centre stage being elevated to the most attractive spouses and on the other cemented in a position of need and protection in which only honourable husbands could save them. The Egyptian man becomes the 'other', the competitor, the one with unruly intentions who abuses his chances to get married in a context of crisis.

Conclusion

This chapter has looked at Syrian men's position in the marriage market during forced displacement. Several conversations brought to the forefront the significance of family reputation and background for a man's 'groom-ability' and chances in the marriage market. Young men who wanted to find a suitable bride could not rely on family members and their networks anymore. They had to think about unusual and uncommon ways to get in touch with potential brides. This was met with both appreciation and rejection among those young men I met who were in the middle of their search for a spouse. The ability to spend used to be of utmost importance if men aspired to prove their middle-class belonging and proper manhood in the marriage market in Syria, which had not changed if Syrian men tried get married to Syrian women in Egypt. Consequently, if men encountered economic instability in Egypt, it could threaten their position in the marriage market. There was a direct connection between one's new economic status during displacement and one's chances of getting married. Most young men had to realize what they had lost and responded with fury to the misrecognition they experienced when they introduced themselves to potential in-laws. Young men's former status did not travel in its entirety with them to Egypt. Hence, it was extremely difficult to convince potential spouses and their families of their middle-class background and respected masculinity.

I have illustrated in this chapter that forced displacement opens the potential not only for new class formations and renegotiations of class and status but also for misrecognition. Most young men willing to get married had to reinvent themselves anew as grooms, the work of Sisyphus, since it usually meant that they needed to find a way to prove that they should be perceived as dignified, proper middle-class grooms. In the struggle for (re-)claiming one's economic and social groomability, several Syrian men blamed women's extreme expectations as a way to gloss over the fact that they could not fulfil them. Ideas of manhood and constructions of masculinities needed to be elastic and tensile to adapt to the new context. For some young men, the breaking away of known patterns, habits and norms translated into more freedom. For others, it created new forms of stress and struggle to be outside of one's comfort zone and without one's framework of reference. Negotiating, finding and claiming one's position as grooms in the marriage market prove the elasticity of constructions of masculinities. This chapter has illustrated that the aspiration to come over as a respectable, honourable groom was intimately related to notions of middle-classness. Constructions of masculinities were deeply classed.

Another challenge Syrian men felt confronted with was Egyptian men's interest in 'their' Syrian women and the potential 'loss' of Syrian women to the Egyptian 'other' men. In this case, Syrian men doubted Egyptian men's intentions, love and feelings. The discussion of the 'boundaries' of the Syrian community, in this case, Syrian women who married non-Syrian men, functions as a door opener to an in-depth analysis of who was defined as 'Syrian' and if there was a Syrian community in Egypt – themes I will engage with in the next chapter.

Chapter 5

ESTABLISHING A LIVING AMONG SEVERAL 'OTHERS' IN EGYPT

This chapter focuses on the construction of 'self' and 'others' in the context of Syrian men's encounters with fellow Syrians staying in Egypt and with the Egyptian receiving society. I begin with a discussion of sectarianism, a pressing theme and one of several aspects of life in Syria that migrated with Syrian men to Egypt and impacted on their lives there in various ways. Many Syrian men shared with me their perception of sectarian conflict and its remembered absence in Syrian society before the uprising. Furthermore, they reflected on how sectarianism interfered with their present situation in Egypt and their future. On the one hand, I approach sectarianism in this chapter by dealing with Syrian men's memories of peaceful coexistence among Sunna, Christians, Druze, Shia, Ismailis and Yazidis and how this coexistence appears irretrievable in Syrians' imagination of their present and future both in Syria and in Egypt.[1] On the other hand, I discuss how Syrian men remembered a specific form of sectarianism, namely, the oppressive encounters with the Alawi sect. Syrian men applied a form of 'selective sectarianism' against the Alawi sect by recollecting how there was unity among all the Syrian people excluding the Alawites. They applied the 'us' versus 'them' dichotomy to complain about the visible markers of the Alawites' power, to mock them and to depict strategies of dealing with them. As far as the Syrian civil war was concerned, some Syrian men considered sectarianism to be a strategy applied by the regime and felt that the civil war had been sectarianized. Others had experienced that Syrians from another sect had turned into violent perpetrators during the civil war. In the context of regime-induced sectarianism and after having experienced violence caused by Syrians belonging to other sects, several Syrian men expressed hate and uncertainty. While it is obvious that sectarianism is an important theme in understanding the situation of recently displaced people fleeing from a war-torn, fractured country, I argue that living with sectarianism should also be understood as a crucial aspect influencing constructions of masculinities. Having been confronted for one's whole life with injustice based on a system of sectarian preferences that advantages foremost the Alawi sect affects men (just as it affects women). In everyday life, it means experiencing multiple pressures, constraints and the confrontation with unfair yet unchangeable power structures if one is not part of the powerful sect. In some situations, it means silently accepting unjust treatment; in others, it means adapting to be able to make one's life easier.

In the second part of the chapter, the focus shifts to the relation between Syrians and Egyptians. This chapter includes both a focus on sectarianism as it was remembered and how it defined Syrian men's present and future and contains engagement with Syrian men's contact to and perceptions of the Egyptian host population, because studying the two themes interrelatedly can reveal practices of othering and attempts to define who is 'us'. In order to describe Syria's ties with the Egyptian receiving society, Syrian men often referred to the historical period of the United Arabic Republic (UAR). Referencing the UAR had various reasons: it was taken as a proof for good relationships with the Egyptians and as a signifier of Syria's powerful position in the region in the past. Another defining incident described to mark the relations with the Egyptian population was the Rabaa Square massacre in 2013 and its aftermath. Through narratives focusing on the UAR and Rabaa Square, I analyse Syrian men's perceptions of and demarcation from the Egyptian host society as well as their practices of inclusion and exclusion of fellow Syrians in the community of Syrians in Egypt. Moreover, I scrutinize the specific strategies Syrians used to distance themselves from the Egyptians. Emphasizing Syria's former wealth, work ethic and the quality of Syrian products was a tactic many Syrian men used to stigmatize the Egyptian 'others'. This resembles processes of constructing 'self' and 'other' via role distancing in the context of 'real refugeeness' or the issue of successful participation in the Egyptian labour market, as previously presented. Hence, I reiterate that processes of hierarchization and demarcation were among the most prominent strategies to create an integer, masculine self. The construction of an ideal image of Syrian manhood vis-à-vis the Egyptians stands in sharp contrast to the often-expressed feeling of victimhood – a sentiment many Syrian men encountered during forced displacement evoking in them a feeling of inability to hold up the ideals of Syrian middle-class masculinity.

Conceptualizing sectarianism

Sect can be defined as sharing of historical narratives, religious beliefs, political aspirations and fears. There is no essence to sect; it is not a preordained category. Rather, it is an experience depending on the individual's personal status, encounters with the state, one's practice of religion and political affiliation (Mikdashi 2014: 282/285; Peteet 2011: 16). Sectarianism needs to be read and understood in the historical context in which it developed (see, for example, Makdissi 2000). Furthermore, it is fruitful to understand sect and sectarianism as intertwined with class (see, for example, Joseph 1983: 17).

Chatty (2018: 3/4) writes that 'Syria and the Fertile Crescent have been at the heart of migrations of people, ideas, and goods for millennia'. For the past 200 years, Syria has been a destination for a plethora of different ethno-religious and minority groups creating tolerance and local conviviality. It was under French rule at the beginning of the twentieth century that sectarian tensions were aggravated. French policies created a hierarchy of citizens based on location, class and religion (Thompson 2000: 82/83). After the coup and under the rule of Hafez al-Asad, sectarianism was inextricably linked with and used to extend the regime's power (Hinnebusch 2001: 59), in which the Alawi minority held key positions. Along with Syrians from rural backgrounds, Alawites had joined the Ba'th Party in large numbers in the 1950s and 1960s because of its radical socioeconomic policies. Already before Hafez al-Asad came to power, the Ba'th Party fostered a new political elite drawn from the country's minority populations, especially from the Alawi sect, and from rural and lower- and middle-class backgrounds (Wedeen 1999: 8). By 1955, around 65 per cent of the non-commissioned officers in the Syrian military were Alawites and there was a disproportionate representation of Alawites among ordinary soldiers (Sluglett 2016: 41). Once Hafez al-Asad, himself an Alawi, was in power in 1970, he further promoted Alawi officers, employed predominantly Alawites in the coercive apparatuses and gave the whole Alawi community a reason to back his rule (Hokayem 2013: 31/32; Ismail 2011: 541).[2] Regarding the Alawites' economic position in Syria, scholars have different opinions: Hokayem (2013: 32/33) stresses that the Alawi community did have better access to jobs in the security sector and that the overall conditions of the community improved over time. Creating dependence on the regime and alienation from mainstream society, the regime was interested in keeping the Alawi community under its control, ready to be mobilized if needed. In contrast, several scholars express doubts about the Alawites' overall advantageous situation and argue that it is over-simplistic to assume that the entire Alawi community was in a privileged position (Harling and Birke 2013; Ismail 2009; Salamandra 2013). Ismail (2011: 540/541) detects in Syrian society prior to the outbreak of the uprising 'hidden' or 'dormant' sectarianism combined with political sectarianism induced by the regime. Furthermore, there was a fundamental fear that the regime could instrumentalize sectarian affiliations followed by a breakdown of society. This fear was nourished and manipulated by the regime with the purpose to preserve people's support (2018: 120). The Syrian regime had always promoted sectarianism as a lens to read and understand violent events in Syria (2018: 199). Yet, Ismail (2018: 192) opposes the view that the current conflict had its base in sectarian hatred. Rather, sectarianism had been superimposed on other divisions and processes of sectarianization had affected and coloured apparatuses of coercion, the political landscape, neighbourhoods and areas (2018: 179/191).

Remembering sectarianism in Syria

Even though I did not specifically ask about their experiences with sectarianism, Syrian men brought up the topic in one way or another in various conversations. Many Syrians highlighted their sense of an absence of sectarianism during their lives in Syria before the uprising.[3] Firas, for instance, used the absence of sectarianism as the opening statement of our conversation. When asked about his life back in Syria, he responded:

> Life in Syria was wonderful. We lived happily. The poor were able to live and the rich were able to live. The whole people lived. Everyone was happy. Women could walk in the street in the middle of the night. There was no problem. The shops were open 24/7. The people were happy. The people were together. They lived in peace. There was no racism. We didn't have a problem with sectarianism – no one was talking about Sunna or Shia. Our neighbours were Shia and under us were Alawites and we were living.

Combining his memories of the absence of sectarianism in Syria prior to the uprising with a story about his childhood, Hani shared how he used to play with children of different religious backgrounds:

> In all my life, I hadn't heard about [sectarianism]. Only during the revolution, I realised that there was a sect called Shia. [...] I remember that I was playing with all my friends, also Christian friends, and we never felt that we were different.

Furthermore, many Syrians stressed that it had not been common to ask people about their religious affiliation. However, I was told that this had changed since the beginning of the uprising in 2011.

Apart from Syrian men's memories of the absence of societal sectarianism before the uprising, there was an awareness of the existence of a political form of destructive and outwardly induced sectarianism. Majd, the student of economics with high career aspirations, explained his interpretation of Syrian politics to me once, when we were sitting in a café belonging to an international chain. He repeatedly assured me that I could use his explanations in my research as he was neither afraid of consequences, nor uncertain regarding his political opinion. Bitterly and with much agitation, he described sectarianism in Syria as a political strategy:

> The regime tried to play the sectarian game. The regime played with that issue. Before in Syria, we didn't have such a thing called sectarianism. My neighbours, for instance, were Christians and we were always visiting them and spent time with each other. The regime focused on the issue of sectarianism and started to tell the people: 'If I, the regime, leave, your sect will be erased. They will kill you!' They started to force this idea into their brains. Unfortunately, there are some classes that are very ignorant so the regime put weapons in front of them and told them: 'Defend yourselves!' At some point, the people started to be convinced that this idea is not right. Then, the regime started to request support from foreign powers. However, it will not be able to oppress the people. We are the whole people. We took up arms to defend ourselves. Even after many years, the regime won't be able to oppress us!

According to Majd, sectarianism was a strategy used by the Asad regime to arouse fear of other religious communities within Syrian society. He also made use of a classed narrative expressing that it was a matter of socioeconomic background whether the regime was successful in applying its tactics. Nevertheless, he insisted on the argument that Syrian people were one and united against the regime – a discourse that was prominent during the first years after the uprising (see Ismail 2011; Proudfoot 2016).

The Alawi sect and its dialect

Apart from acknowledging the lack of interest in sectarianism before the uprising and awareness of the regime's gambling with it as a political strategy, there was a strong anti-Alawi sentiment among most Syrian men. This was based on their belief that Alawites benefitted from an unfair and illegitimate link with power that granted them privileges in various aspects of their life in Syria. Mahmud was among the men who openly expressed how much he disliked the Alawites: when discussing the issue of sectarianism, he had initially emphasized the absence of differentiation or discrimination based on sectarian affiliation before the uprising. However, he eventually corrected himself throughout our conversation with growing anger in his voice:

> Actually, we had a problem. Now that I am here in Egypt, I realise it. There was an Alawi dialect. It was strong and if it was spoken it meant: be careful. It wasn't the language of a partner, who lived in the same country.

Mahmud further illustrated his argument by vividly recalling the story of a taxi driver, who brought his client to the desired address and asked for more money than was initially agreed upon. When the client started to use the Alawi dialect and refused to give him the extra money, the taxi driver left, intimidated by the assumption that his client was an influential, powerful person. Throughout the conversation, Mahmud departed further and further from the discourse of the absence of sectarianism before the uprising and kept insisting on sectarianism being present in the form of dominance of the Alawi sect and consequent mistrust on the part of other Syrians:

> No one trusts an Alawi in the family, even if the Alawi is part of the family for a while. We never talk in front of an Alawi. We share information and criticism only with Christians or Druze.

Here, Mahmud makes a clear distinction between relations with Alawites, on the one hand, and with other sects, on the other. He describes a form of unity shared across of all the religious groups in Syria in contrast to suspicion vis-à-vis the Alawites. Eventually, he came to speak again about the Alawi dialect:

> If you hear someone talking Alawi dialect, it means that someone threatens another person. If he wants to get privileges, then he will use Alawi dialect. People start to use Alawi dialect if they need it. […] When they speak Alawi dialect, people get afraid.

Mahmud draws a line between the Alawi sect and other Syrians unfolding the Alawi dialect as an instrument of action and power, a symbolic capital, which is bound to the speaker's position in the social structure (Bourdieu 1977: 646). Through language, the speaker does not only aim to be understood, but also wants 'to be believed, obeyed, respected, distinguished' (Bourdieu 1977: 648). This means that the speaker is in a position of authority and can control how the language is received. Mahmud experienced the use of the Alawi dialect as a signifier to communicate the Alawi sect's dominance in Syria that is accepted through enforcement on the receiver, the other sects. Thus, the Alawi dialect gives visibility to a system of power and inequality. It evokes associations with danger, coercion and undeserved privileges and causes suspicion, mistrust and fear as well as the building of barriers. Moreover, the dialect signals that certain privileges are inaccessible for Mahmud as a non-member of the Alawi sect. It reminds him, when spoken, of undeserved but unchangeable inferiority.

In a similar vein to Mahmud, who distinguished between Alawites and all the other sects in Syria, Bashar described his experiences with the Alawi sect in administrative contexts, albeit more controlled and with less emotion in his voice than Mahmud. To my surprise, he came to talk about the dominance of Alawi employees in governmental offices after I had asked him whether he was disappointed in the older generations:

> If you enter any governmental place, you feel that it represents one sect only and sometimes it makes you think that it represents only one village. You feel the injustice when they all speak in the same accent. You can feel the injustice in the country. That was a big mistake.

Bashar refers to the power of the Alawites, their dominance in governmental positions, and alludes to their origin from a similar place – Syria's coastal region. When Bashar depicts the injustice in the country with anyone but the Alawites on the receiving end, Bourdieu's (1977: 652) notion of the power of language is useful again. He stresses that language is worth what the speakers are worth, which relates to the economic and cultural power relations of the holders. He contends that when one language dominates the market, it becomes the norm against which the prices of the other modes of expression are valued. Even though the Alawi dialect does not dominate the Syrian 'linguistic market' but is only spoken by a minority, it nevertheless has the authority and power to enforce action. The dialect manifests the day-to-day sectarian injustice in Syria and provokes emotions of powerlessness vis-à-vis the established system that entails the Alawites' dominance. The dialect can be portrayed as a medium that makes the dominance of the Alawi sect visible, defines social relationships in everyday life and shows the omnipresence of the regime. The dialect references the Alawites' power, their access to privileges and their ability to threaten those who were not included in the community of speakers of the dialect.

The Alawites and the Syrians

The sense of unity across sects against the Alawites that Mahmud expressed when he mentioned how critique and information were only exchanged among non-Alawites was also clearly pronounced by Bashar. I had probed his stand vis-à-vis the older generations by asking if he agreed with their position to which he answered that he disagreed with his father but not with his grandfather. Then, he went back to talking about the Alawites' position in the Syrian regime.

> If you have a minority and a majority, the minority should not govern. This is the problem of Syria. The Alawites held the highest positions in the army and in the police. The minority governs and they rule without considering all the other minorities. So, the Syrian people is made of two types: Syrians and Alawites. Do you watch Faisal al-Qassem?[4] This person says: 'there are Syrians and there are Alawites', however, he is dealing with them from a political perspective, not from a religious point of view. This fighting now is after more than twenty years of such politics. We have had these problems since more than twenty years and they exploded now. This is what they call now a sectarian war, but actually it isn't a sectarian war, because we never cared about which religion you have or which sect you are from.

Like Majd, Bashar suggests that the conflict became sectarianized and opposes the idea that sectarianism was an inherent feature of Syrian society. At the same time, he insists on the division of the Syrian people into 'Alawites' and 'Syrians' as a result of political strategies and structures of governing the country. Dividing the people into Alawites and Syrians is evocative of the unbridgeable gap and distance that existed between the regime and its people. Nevertheless, it also shows hardened fronts and a black-and-white thinking that did not represent the reality: neither were all the Alawites in powerful positions nor were Syrians from other sects unable to benefit from the Alawites' dominance, for instance, through strategic positioning relative to the regime and through expressed loyalty (see, for example, Hinnebusch 2001).

The theme of 'us' versus 'them' applied to the Alawites and all the other Syrians was implicit in many conversations. Often, there were references to the privileged position of Alawites in Syrian society. According to Abd al-Rahman, students belonging to the Alawi sect attended better schools, received better education and had a better standard of living. When I sat down with him to conduct a recorded interview and asked him about his childhood in Syria as an introductory question, the privileges of the Alawites were part of his response:

> There were classes in Syria: the poor class, the middle class and the rich class. And there was a huge class of beneficiaries of the regime. The Alawite sect. I am not going to compare myself as a child with the beneficiaries of the regime. The

beneficiaries from al-Asad's regime could go to private schools and were able to get better education and a better standard of living.

He further described that, when he was young, his parents forbade him to speak about the inequalities existing between the Alawites and the rest of Syrians:

> We couldn't talk about the fact that we were ruled by the Alawite sect, and we were beaten up or humiliated by our parents in order not to talk about it, because they were worried about us.

Likewise, Mazin, who studied dentistry at private universities in Syria and Egypt after he had found an Egyptian sponsor, complained that, compared to the Alawites, he did not have many job opportunities back in Syria. Then, he mocked the Alawites' rural background and how their life had changed from a 'life with cows, sheep, animals and houses made of clay to palaces in Damascus and Europe'. Mazin's mockery can be understood as a way of challenging the Alawites' dominance in society – at least indirectly in the absence of any Alawites and in front of an outsider like myself. Through the use of rhetorical practices, such as jokes, people can offer alternative visions of politics, challenge the official regime rhetoric and show their awareness of the political system they live in (Wedeen 1999: 130). In addition, the narratives of both men reveal envy, jealousy and a sense of inferiority, even though both of them had been in positions of relative privilege, given that Abd al-Rahman had been able to study abroad and Mazin could afford to study at a private university in Egypt.

When I met Mu'ayad for backgammon and *arkile* in the summer of 2015 and had realized that my fieldnotes contained numerous references to the Alawi sect, I asked him if he could share with me his memories. We were sitting in the streets in front of a simple coffee shop in his neighbourhood enjoying that the heat of the day had decreased a bit. He asked me what I had heard about the Alawites so far and after having listened carefully called these talks 'a bit extreme'. He asked for fresh coal for his shisha, leaned back and informed me that he wanted to try to give me a balanced account of the relations with the Alawites:

> Look, there were those Alawites who benefitted from the regime. You find them in Damascus and in the other big cities. And then, there were the Alawites who lived in the villages close to Latakiyya. We used to go there as a family when I was young, once almost every year. No one asked: 'are you Alawi or are you someone else?' The people there were poor, simple and nice.

Mu'ayad managed to complicate the picture and re-drew the 'us' versus 'them' dichotomy. Instead of condemning the Alawi sect as a whole, he isolated and critiqued the Alawites who were affiliated with the regime pushing the focus further away from a discussion about sectarianism in Syria and closer to a critique of the regime.

All in all, the presented accounts suggest that conflicts among Sunnis, Christians, Druze, Shia and Yazidis were remembered as being absent before the uprising. Sectarianism was predominantly seen as a political strategy but not as an inherent feature of Syrian society. However, this did not apply to Syrian men's perception of the Alawites. They defined the relation of Alawites with all the other Syrians in the first place in terms of a dominant sect deeply entangled with the regime and an oppressed people. The line between discussing sectarianism and criticizing the regime thus proved to be thin. Disapproval of the regime was expressed in sectarian terms as rejection of the Alawi sect. I argue that Syrian men answered to the dominance of the Alawi sect within the Syrian regime by applying 'selective sectarianism' against them. The presented clear-cut division between oppressive relations with the Alawites, on the one hand, and peaceful coexistence with all the other sects, on the other, may be idealizing, essentializing and interwoven with nostalgia. Nevertheless, the existence of this dichotomy reveals a sense of agency and reclaiming of a dignified position on the part of the Syrian men I met. Through the creation of distance from the Alawites, condemnation of their association with the regime and the expression of unity among all the other sects, Syrian men managed to present themselves as active, informed and responsive to the situation in Syria.

Constructions of masculinities in a sectarian context

Even though sectarianism and living under a regime with a sectarian base were described without an explicit reference to notions of manhood, I argue that the structures described influenced Syrian men, depending on their social standing, in their self-perception and practices. Given the Alawites' powerful positions in society, I suggest that men belonging to other religious groups felt positioned at the lower end of a hierarchy, for instance, when being confronted with the Alawi accent. This evoked a feeling of being less worthy, less acknowledged and less privileged – sentiments that may be the catalyst of Mahmud's anger when talking about the Alawites or Mazin's bitter joke about the Alawites' initial poverty. In addition to these emotions, Syrian men expressed fear related to the Alawites' powerful position, resentment and envy. Sectarianism and one's individual positioning in the sectarian context are thus part of how Syrian men feel and imagine themselves as men.

There is a remarkable absence of scholarly engagement with masculinities in sectarian contexts. Material from which to draw a comparison can be found in the study of men and masculinities among Palestinian citizens in Israel. According to Sa'ar and Yahia-Younis (2008: 313), in a context in which direct routes to hegemonic masculinity, for instance via military service, are not available, the development of alternative versions of hegemonic masculinities takes place. This article, despite being quite static in its methodology and conclusion, gives a hint to possible consequences of living in a society, in which most paths towards masculine accomplishments are blocked by structural injustice. Monterescu (2006) analyses masculinities among Palestinian men in Yafa and traces a process of fragmentation into local, religious and regional-fractional sub-identities due to the blurred boundaries between 'self' and 'other'. For the context of the Coptic minority in Egypt, Kårtveit (2018: 20) argues that young men

> are not unaffected by their relations with Egyptian Muslims, but their masculine identities are primarily defined by ideals and practices that gain validation within their own community.

Young Coptic men subscribe to masculine norms and practices that, in their own eyes, set them apart from (working-class) Muslim men. Thus, Kårtveit (2018) contends that these men inhabit parallel masculinities that emerge under the formative impact of a masculine 'other'.

Based on Syrian men's memories of both peaceful coexistence and the unjust rule of the Alawi sect in Syria, I suggest that masculine performances in a heterogeneous place, where various power structures and structural inequalities are in place, are dependent on the different daily encounters and enforce manoeuvring the continuum of acceptable versions of masculinities. Non-Alawi Syrian men are affected by the relations with Alawites who benefit from contact to the Syrian regime. This might mean compliance vis-à-vis a speaker of the Alawi dialect in offices and in public, while mocking and joking about the regime and the Alawites in their absence. It might mean practising the exclusion of Alawites from one's circle of confidantes, while coping with Alawites in one's daily life chores. Constructions of masculinities under a regime with a sectarian base, if the individual holds the position of the less powerful, need to be elastic and dynamic, able to absorb damage since they emerge, at least partially, out of humiliating experiences with the dominant groups. This is obvious when Syrian men remember the dominance and control of the Alawi sect to which they did not have access, since they did not possess their markers such as the Alawi dialect, their network and socioeconomic advantages.

Sectarianism in present and future

Having discussed Syrian men's memories of sectarianism and relations with the Alawi sect in Syria, I turn to how sectarianism played a role in Syrian men's everyday life in Egypt and in the future they envisioned for themselves and their home country. In order to illustrate how he grew up and experienced the uprising and civil war, Akram spoke about his dreams when he still lived in Syria.

> Let's talk frankly: on the political side, there are people who don't want a certain group of people to become more important. They said that this type of people should only work for a low income in order to be unable to think

about anything. We built our dreams on this reality. My ambition was, like that of any respectable Syrian, to have a car. It is a dream that is really difficult to achieve. If a car is a far-fetched dream, what do you think getting married and having a house will be like? All these details show that life was difficult. When did we feel the value of that time? It was when I graduated, started to decide for myself and begin my life. It was 2011 and it was the period of big dreams. But then, at the time of the Syrian revolution and civil war, people started to be killed for their ideas and the society became shaped as: this is a Sunni, this is an Alawi, this is a Shiite.

Akram's experiences of growing up, dreaming, experiencing the weight of responsibility and realizing that these dreams are unlikely to materialize fall into a time in which Syria's society underwent extreme changes. His account of being identified and classified by one' sectarian belonging stands in sharp contrast to earlier mentioned memories of a Syria, in which religion and ethnicity did not play a role in the everyday life.

Abu Walid, who shared with me his experiences of being involved in weapon transfer for the opposition during the uprising, illustrated the heightened focus on sectarian belonging and spoke of his complete loss of trust in certain sects:

For the person, no matter if he is educated or illiterate, it is now generally impossible to live with other minorities. I am not talking about Christians, but about Alawi and Shia. We [he refers to Sunnites] are the ones who were massacred. The ones who massacred the country were Alawi and Shia. Their ideology is: 'kill a Sunni and you will go to paradise!' You are surprised to find him ready with his weapons after all these years. And you used to feel safe in his presence for all these years. Now, how will you ever be able to feel safe around him again? In Homs, the most famous video maker, the one who took videos for the revolution and sent them to the channels, came from America. He was Christian. He left his studies and he came to Homs. They killed him in Homs. Who killed him? The Alawites. They didn't distinguish whether he was Christian or Sunni. With these people, there is no safety. I am not talking from a sectarian perspective. I explain to you what happens if you meet anyone who lost someone, was imprisoned or came to grief, and you ask him: 'who do you hate?'. He will answer: Alawi and Shia, but he won't give you names. Bashar [al-Asad] is an individual, but he doesn't make any decisions. The decisions are made for him in Iran by the Shia. This is what happens in our country. There are many people who would oppose my opinion. They would consider my words sectarian. No, we don't want to cover the truth. Our killer is one side. I don't know if you are informed, but the percentage of Alawites in Syria increased. They killed people from all the different groups of the Syrian people. They killed Sunni, Christians, Armenians, they killed them all. In my opinion, the living together will not come back to Syria.

Abu Walid drew the picture of a society fractured by sectarianism and hate that will never be able to live together again. His bitterness, anger and insuppressible hatred of Shia and Alawites emanate from Abu Walid's situation in Syria: he and his family used to live in an area that was dominated by Shia inhabitants. With the outbreak of the uprising, his former contacts, acquaintances and neighbours turned into his enemies. Shia militias tried to kill his father, who was a Sunni sheikh and then they kidnapped Abu Walid at a street checkpoint, when he was on his way home. His family had to pay a high ransom to set him free. Having been shaken in his core beliefs about his society and previous life, leaves Abu Walid with the feeling of being unable to make proper judgement; enforces horror and insecurity that ultimately lead to hate; and creates fear, mistrust and suspicion.

In a similarly emotional mind set, Mahmud once expressed his bitterness to me about Syrians belonging to other sects. He said that he could not understand how Syrian Christians denied what was happening in Syria and continued to sympathize with and support the Asad regime. Agitated, he told me: 'I don't have any respect for the other minorities anymore!' He assured me that he had tried for a long time to remain neutral and objective, but he could not retain this attitude when witnessing the injustice and condemnations the Sunnis in Syria experienced in contrast to the other minorities. He said that he was shocked and fearful when hearing slogans like: 'Either al-Asad stays or we will burn the country' and 'Your God may step down but not al-Asad'. Mahmud, just like Abu Walid, drew the picture of a completely broken, deeply fissured Syrian society that held no hope for present and future. Another time, when we talked about a conversation I had had with an acquaintance of mine, who had a pacifist attitude regarding the ongoing civil war, Mahmud told me:

> If we have people talking like this, we will not succeed. If there is an Alawi on the street, you have to kill him immediately. No one can convince me that Shiites and Alawites are good people!

His account reinforces the sharp shift from a past remembered as defined by peaceful coexistence and a present and future that are created as inherently violent and full of hatred, mistrust and ultimately loss of humanity. Hate as an emotion features strongly in these perceptions of present and future.

I also sensed hate and outrage during my encounter with Abu Muhannad at his office in his drugstore when the conversation turned to the Syrian community in Egypt. Muhannad had invited me to meet his father so that I could ask him questions about Syria. I was welcomed politely by Abu Muhannad, got a tour through the store and was asked to follow him to his office. There, I was seated on a small chair in a corner while he sat down behind his huge, dark-wooden desk, which provided him with a sense of authority. There were several other men in the office, one of who was Abu Muhannad's brother-in-law. The others did not introduce themselves to me. They listened carefully to our conversation. Abu Muhannad asked me several questions about German foreign politics. Afterwards, he seemed more comfortable and began talking about his biography and life in

Syria. Abu Muhannad's voice was filled with rage and anger when he urged me to believe him that sectarian affiliations could not be overlooked anymore after all that had happened since 2011. He asked me furiously from behind his desk:

> How can you ignore if members of another sect are responsible for the death of your relatives and friends? Before the uprising, no one asked about your religious background, however, now, you cannot be casual about religious affiliation anymore.

He used his momentary authority in the room to try to sternly convince me of the sectarian character of the conflict giving a reason as to why hate of other sects had become an essential part of the present. The past that was defined by Syrian men's ability to differentiate between sectarianism used as a political strategy, the oppressive relationships with the dominant Alawi sect and everyday peaceful encounters among Sunnis, Druze, Christians, Shia and Yazidis is superseded by a present coloured and shaped by violence and hate. Nevertheless, it was not only hate that I sensed but also deep despair, sorrow and a feeling of being overtaken by the recent events that left Syrians in the position of refugees. There was nothing left of Abu Muhannad's momentary fury when he started to speak about his life in Syria, where he had everything to support himself and his family, when he was apolitical and simply strived for the continuation of his comfortable life.

I got a similar sense of utter confusion and sadness about how one could possible end up as refugees in Egypt, when I met Um Mazin and her family for dinner after my visit to Abu Muhannad's drugstore. She served soup, salad and kibbeh. When I helped her clear the table after food, she said:

> After all, we had everything in Syria. We had property. We had a flat for each child. We had everything and only wanted the war to stop. We don't want to go anywhere. We just want to go back to how it was before.

Making sense of hate and uncertainty

The issue of sectarianism as it was experienced in Syrian men's past and present proves crucial for the discussion of manhood, since the various aspects of sectarianism, and especially sectarianized violence, turned them into fearful, insecure, suspicious, human beings full of hate, whose former understandings of the order of the world were shaken if not completely lost. Syrian men's experience of violence caused a renegotiation of their relationships with other sects involving essentialism, totalization and homogenization of the other sects' characteristics. The violence in Syria was perceived as continuous without an actual end in sight causing various and ongoing repercussions in Syrian men's lives, even when they were physically detached from the conflict. Syrian men's experiences of the conflict reverberate with Appadurai's (1998: 229) conceptualization of ethnic violence which he brings in contact with the sentiment of uncertainty. He argues that uncertainty relates to the anxiety as to whether a person really is what they claim or appear to be. An answer to this kind of uncertainty can be violence in order to confirm with certainty who is 'them' and consequently who is 'us'. Ethnic violence is thus intimately related to a sense of betrayal, treachery and deception, which is the result of no longer being able to identify social contacts. They have transformed into monsters wearing masks behind which they hide their true, horrible nature leading the individual to sense that they have felt false solidarity and were utterly betrayed (1998: 238). Syrian men I met felt horror and uncertainty towards members of a society they once knew but became alien to them during the conflict. They answered with hate to the experience of violence in Syria and the consequent sentiment of uncertainty they felt. The hate they expressed had the effect of shaping a clear image of who was the 'other', namely, the Alawites and Shia, who were the enemies and perpetrators. They survived the encounter with sectarianized violence during the uprising and the emotional repercussions it continuously evoked, by establishing walls of hate that they cultivated and kept intact through their outrage, anger and bitterness. Othering is here not only used to establish proper manhood as seen in previous chapters, but also as a strategy to make sense of fleeing from a civil war and living as refugees.

The importance of one's origin and political opinion

I now turn to the analysis of the consistency, manifestation and everyday experience of community life in Egypt. This topic is closely related to and thoroughly impacted by the experience of sectarianized violence. The reason I began to focus on the issue of 'community' during my fieldwork was its absence among Syrians in Egypt. I sensed an extreme suspicion and scepticism in my acquaintances' dealings with each other and was often told that one would not befriend other Syrians but preferred to be in contact with immediate family only. The recentness of Syrian forced displacement seemed to play a major role in this widespread perception.

An event during the 'international day' at the American University that I spent with members of *Fursa* is evocative of how social cohesion was defined by scepticism, uncertainty and fear. Muhannad's NGO had been invited to represent Syria by setting up a booth on campus where traditional sweets were offered. Members of *Fursa* also performed traditional songs and *dabkeh* on stage. There were approximately fifteen volunteers who helped setting up the booth, took pictures, sang and danced, mingled and enjoyed the atmosphere on the AUC campus. As usual, the male volunteers showed up in white shirts and black pants. Fadi was there in his position as a volunteer. He sang a song on stage and was visibly proud of his performance and belonging to the group. However, at some point I noticed that his mood changed. When we left the campus together, he told me agitated that one of the women who performed with him wore a necklace with a pendant in the shape of the geographic borders of Syria. The pendant showed the Syrian flag with two green stars. I had noticed the necklace but was unaware of its meaning. Fadi explained that it alluded to her position as pro-Asad. He had tried to confront her but did not manage to involve her in a discussion. A couple of weeks later, I met Muhannad and I asked him about his perception of what had happened on that day at AUC. He answered:

Someone asked her [the girl with the necklace]: 'why are you wearing this?' I went to them and interrupted the discussion immediately. I said: 'we are here to represent Syria. She has your opinion and you have yours.'

Speaking about his mission for *Fursa*, he explained:

We have volunteers who are pro and against Bashar al-Asad. I respect this. However, it's prohibited to discuss politics. If political discussions were allowed, our members would fight immediately.

The conflict and its consequent focus on the political affiliation of one's counterpart were transferred to Egypt and had a direct influence on the everyday life and sense of community of Syrians there.

In order to illustrate to me how Syrians in Egypt dealt with each other, Qutayba recounted that the relationships among Syrians when they first arrived in Egypt were shaped by the overriding question of who was pro and who was against Bashar al-Asad. Qutayba remembered that the situation was explosive and that many Syrians refused to work together in case they had different political opinions. He described that political discussions were not rational between people who had lost loved ones at the hands of either the opposition or the regime forces. Furthermore, Qutayba shared with me an incident illustrating how political opinion permeated and defined encounters with other Syrians in Egypt: once, he met a girl at a kiosk in the streets of Cairo. She spoke with a Syrian accent the Egyptian kiosk seller did not understand, so Qutayba translated her words into Egyptian Arabic. Afterwards, the girl and Qutayba had a quick chat. The girl said to him: 'Please don't tell me that you are with Bashar al-Asad so I don't have to hate you!' Qutayba avoided meeting her again because he was disappointed by her judgement and general condemnation of anyone who did not share her political views. He was neither with nor against Bashar al-Asad and the revolution, he said, and wanted to be respected as such. Qutayba's illustrations imply that certain personal characteristics and political opinions have begun to outweigh other aspects of the self. He was directly judged based on his political opinions and reduced to them. Moreover, Qutayba explained how he was rejected by other Syrians when he first arrived in Egypt because his home city had only been recently under attack. Other Syrians in Egypt calculated whether to help each other and this calculation was based on whether they came from the same region or city, and if not, whether the home city of the one in need was included in the revolution and to what extent it was destroyed. The treatment he experienced stands in sharp contrast to Ismail's (2011: 544) observation of the early days of the Syrian revolution, in which the residents of one town held protests in support and solidarity with people demonstrating in other regions of Syria showing their willingness to fight and sacrifice for each other. In 2011, there was a sense of belonging to a single political community among Syrians (Khaddour and Mazur 2013) that seemed completely lost in the context of Syrian displacement in Egypt.

The heightened focus on one's origin was also obvious in my encounter with Faris, the businessman and manager of a branch of a Syrian retail chain, when he was a relatively new acquaintance of mine. He asked me to meet him in the shop he supervised. After I had a chance to look at the products he sold, we went to a café nearby. He was a far relative of Um Khalid and said that he was eager to participate in my research project when she told him about it. We spoke about life in Egypt, his life back in Syria and the uprising. When I mentioned how a contact of mine who was from Deraa had experienced the first days of the revolution, Faris reacted:

> Your friend must hate Syrians from the coast and Latakiyya. I wouldn't want to be friends with this guy and he wouldn't like me either!

I asked him why he expected this mutual rejection and he responded that all the people from Deraa would hate the regime and its supporters who lived at the coast and in Latakiyya. He disclosed that he and his family were supporters of the regime.[5]

The encounters with Qutayba and Faris reinforce the importance of one's region in Syria and how it permeates various aspects of Syrian identity. Their accounts allude to the politicization of the individual's origin, in which trust and support came to be linked to one's home city's involvement in the uprising. It also shows the ongoing repercussions of having experienced secterianized violence, the establishment of homogenized groups of 'us' and 'them' and the loss of trust in others. Why is it useful to delve into these aspects of societal cohesion and combine them with Syrian men's experiences of sectarianism in the past? I suggest that encounters with other Syrians, whether real, remembered or imagined ones, set the scene in which masculinities are negotiated. Syrian men's masculine performances are deeply affected by having been forced to flee from a sectarianized civil war. Horror, deep despair, anger and hate emerge from their exposure to sectarianized violence and impact how they imagine their life in the present and future and position themselves in it. Taken-for-granted structures and perceptions of the world have proven useless which means that men needed to reinvent themselves, needed to regain trust in their senses and needed to learn anew how to navigate their lifeworlds.

The Syrian 'non-community' in Egypt

In many more accounts that were shared with me, the absence of communal structures became obvious. Qays, the founder of an NGO planning activities for Syrians, drew a clear connection between the crisis and the communal life of Syrians in Egypt:

The crisis is big. It caused a psychological problem. This problem made the Syrians decrease their circle of friends. At the beginning, I was careful to say or show my political or rebellious opinions in order not to be hurt, and the fear reached high levels because of the injustice of the regime. The social relations are not good, so at this point our team enters.

The goal of the NGO Qays founded was to improve the relations of Syrians in Egypt and to help 'in rebuilding the Syrian society newly from scratch', as Qays liked to describe it. For this reason, his team was planning and organizing communal events, such as an activity for Syrian women on Mother's Day. Qays' narrative suggests that the uprising and the experience of sectarianized violence evoked fear, self-control, uncertainty and suspicion that defined Syrians' everyday interactions and encounters.

Once I overheard Mu'ayad when he was on the phone with his brother who was still in Syria. He urged him with a voice that did not allow objection that he was not supposed to tell anyone where he was and what he was doing. He repeated several times that no one was supposed to know anything about him and his whereabouts. He had similar reactions vis-à-vis other Syrians in Egypt. He explained his behaviour by saying:

How do I know that he is not *mukhabarat*? How can I trust his intentions? Call me paranoid and crazy, but I don't want to risk it. No one needs to know what I am doing.

Mu'ayad's suspicion and mistrust towards other Syrians were nurtured by the fear of the regime's security apparatus showing that there was not only the issue of sectarianized violence, but in fact various reasons why one ought to keep contact to others to a minimum.

In order to emphasize the lack of communal cohesion, Abu Walid described his experiences of trying to establish joint projects in Egypt:

We wanted to open a Syrian kitchen to help families. We were about twenty Syrians. There is such a kitchen in Istanbul. There are twenty or thirty families who help each other. Such a project doesn't have any success in Egypt, because you have two classes of Syrians and the two classes are very far away from each other. The ones who are down cannot help, if the ones who are up don't do the same thing. [...] The Syrians are from many areas in Syria: Damascus, Aleppo, Homs and they don't agree with each other. Maybe the women sit together in the morning and they greet each other, but regarding financial issues, they don't agree. Maybe this is because we are outside of our homeland so everyone is afraid, but I don't know the exact reason. As Syrians helping each other, we weren't successful. Usually, Syrians are famous for making groups when they live outside of their homeland and they help each other, but here we are lost. On a level of twenty people, men and women, we couldn't agree on a deal. We look like we are together, but actually we are not. When you create groups, there should be common things or affairs, but here it didn't work out.

Abu Walid describes the lack of community cohesion as a personal failure and points to feelings of isolation and of being lost because a common ground and mutual understanding had vanished and fear and suspicion prevailed. Even though he could not put his finger on the exact cause of this condition, he bemoaned Syrians' inability to overcome distance and boundaries based on social class and place of origin in order to stand together. Not only Abu Walid but several Syrian contacts of mine complained about the inability to establish support networks. Dima, a lawyer who attended one of my English classes, recalled that it was impossible to organize a group of Syrians with the aim of establishing *jama'iyyat* (associations) in Egypt.[6] Despite everyone's initial motivation, at the end, no one would pay their share and the whole project would fail. The failing of *jama'iyyat* in Egypt is another proof of the lack of trust Syrians had in each other.

The difficulty of building a community described by Syrians in Egypt shows the extent of damage Syrian society experienced and the severe influence the civil war and the witnessing of sectarianized violence continued to have on Syrians who fled the conflict. The failure of creating a community can thus be understood as the ongoing repercussions of experiences of sectarianized violence in Syria and the consequent development of fronts of hate. Furthermore, the different accounts show that living in a 'non-community' evokes a deep sense of insecurity, fragility and incomprehension. Masculine identity must be built anew during forced displacement and can only be formed on the unstable ground of living without visible communal structures – a state in which mistrust and suspicion in others are the norm.

Upholding the memory of the United Arab Republic

Having discussed the fractures, fissures and fragmentations among Syrians and the ongoing impact of sectarianized violence on Syrian men's lives, I turn in the following paragraphs to a discussion of Syrian men's encounters with the Egyptian host population which were ripe with processes of othering and forms of masculinization against the 'other'. Over the course of my fieldwork, I noticed that Syrians often defined the relations with the Egyptians by referring to the common historical period of the UAR[7] and to the Rabaa Square Massacre in 2013.

Once, when I was invited by Um Mazin for lunch, I sat down with Um Mazin and her son after food in the small living room. Um Mazin had a bad day. In tears, she told me about a relative of hers who had experienced torture. In great detail, she described the horror he had gone through. Um Mazin also shared with me that UNHCR had cut the financial support for refugees from 300 LE to 100 LE.[8] She kept repeating that she only wanted to go home to Syria. She was tired of being a drain on other people's pocket. If only Bashar al-Asad could be brought down and the family could go home to Syria, she lamented. Given the worsening situation for refugees in Egypt, I asked Mazin how he remembered his first days in Egypt back in 2012. He responded:

Egypt was different for the Syrians at that time [in 2012]. The Syrians were more respected. They [the Egyptians] used to love them more and sympathised with them more. They always remembered the union between Egypt and Syria from 1956 to 1958 [*sic*]. So, there was respect at the beginning but when the number of Syrians in Egypt rose, the situation changed. Some underlying tensions occurred between the people.

Hani reminded me of the existence of the UAR and the consequent privileges that Egyptians and Syrians enjoyed, when I asked him whether he felt that the Egyptians welcomed the Syrians:

If you remember, there was a Union between Syria and Egypt. Since that time, the relations between both countries were relaxed. There were no visas.

Moreover, Hani understood the Union as a historical proof that Syrians and Egyptian could live together. He described how the UAR brought about close relationships. Interestingly, while most Syrian men were critical of marriages between Syrian women and Egyptian men in the present, as described in the previous chapter, in the context of the UAR, marriages between Syrians and Egyptians dating back to the past were taken as a proof for harmonious coexistence.

I wonder whether they [Syrians and Egyptians] will get used to each other. But in this situation, I say that the people lost everything so … and we should remember that at the time of the Union between Syria and Egypt there were many marriages between Syrians and Egyptians. For example, I know a woman who is Syrian and she is married to an Egyptian for twenty years and they still live happily together. This woman is one of my relatives. He takes good care of her.

According to his account, the UAR gives hope for a present and a future in Egypt, in which Syrians and Egyptians live together in acceptance and appreciation. In addition, I got the sense when talking to Abd al-Rahman that the memory of the UAR was nostalgically related to Syria's past position in the region:

We hope that we go back to our homeland and don't need to stay in Egypt or Jordan or anywhere else. The Syrian people are generous. They hosted the Iraqis and the Lebanese people and didn't make any tents for them, even though the territory was small and there was not enough potential. The Syrian people had three rooms and emptied one of them to host the refugees […] I wish that the Lebanese people who treat the Syrians badly remember July War when their houses were destroyed. Where did they go? They were living in Syria for a year or a year and a half. […] Just remember how we treated the Iraqis in Syria. Markets, markets, markets were open for the Iraqis all over Syria. […] we didn't close their shops and we didn't stop them from making a living. […] I just wish that these countries remember the Syrians and the many nice things they did for them. We wish that Syria becomes a state again and we build it and we return to have strong relations with Egypt. We had strategic relations with Egypt. In 1958, there was a unity between Syria and Egypt. We wish for more care for the Syrians and that we return to build the economy and to have again treaties with Egypt or Jordan. We just wish.

Abd al-Rahman speaks about Syria's response to refugee influxes from both Iraq and Lebanon in previous decades during times of war highlighting Syria's welcoming attitude. In fact, Syria offered safety to various groups of forced migrants over the course of the twentieth century (see Hoffmann 2016). Abd al-Rahman's narrative shows his pride in Syria when it was a generous state with important international relations and his longing for Syria to be this strong, generous state again. It thus reinforces the analysis of men and their bond with the nation state. Abd al-Rahman's longing for a strong state implies suffering related to being a citizen of a weak state. Without a strong nation state in his back, Abd al-Rahman felt valueless, worthless and deprived of the ability to be generous. A strong state with economic and political ties to other states appears to confer a sense of stability, self-worth and pride. There is clearly a level of nostalgia and idealization in his reflection of the Syrian state. Furthermore, his narrative stands in sharp contrast to memories of the Syrian security service and the state's violence applied against its people. I expand on the theme of men's ambivalent relation to the nation state and the various ways in which the Syrian state granted and deprived men of their manhood in the coming chapter. All in all, Syrian men's reference to the UAR, when speaking about their relationship with the Egyptians, shows the overall yearning to be accepted as newcomers whose country of origin once held important historical ties with Egypt. Syrian men wanted to be seen as worthy and valuable citizens from a formerly generous state.

The Rabaa Square massacre

Having referred back to the times of the UAR and the sense of an initial positive welcome in Egypt, most Syrians continued talking about their experiences in Egypt by mentioning another landmark, namely, the Rabaa Square massacre in 2013 and how it destroyed their initial positive relationship with the Egyptians. Had the beginning of their stay in Egypt been defined by then-President Morsi's political support and an overall welcoming attitude, they felt that they had to accept that these days were gone. Dawud, for instance, described the period after his arrival to Egypt by referencing the UAR and a culture of welcome before turning to the challenges Syrians faced since Morsi's ouster.

It wasn't so complicated unlike now. It was normal. My stay here was more touristic back then. I went to Alexandria. I knew the monuments and drawings of Egypt, the habits of Egyptians. I talked with many people. It's the opposite of what you may think: the Syrians were welcomed by the Egyptians. The Syrians and Egyptians have the same history because there was the union in the 1950s, the days of unity. Those days, when Syrians were welcomed, were beautiful. It was during Morsi's presidency. There was a lot of support for the Syrians. There were visas, projects, support. They allowed you to work and didn't stop you for details, but after Morsi's ousting everything turned upside down. I noticed that there are not a lot of Egyptians who understand politics. The Egyptians started from the point that Morsi was supporting the Syrian revolution. And for this reason, everyone is against the Syrians nowadays. There are disadvantages: you have to renew your visa, if you leave Egypt you cannot enter again, and it is very difficult to bring someone from abroad to Egypt. The documents for the application to bring someone are very complicated and they will finish with 'rejected'.

Indeed, the ousting of former president Muhammad Morsi and the Rabaa Square massacre had a lasting effect on Syrians living in Egypt. Hostility towards Syrians was on the rise even before 2013, when Morsi extended protection and public services for them in 2012. By presidential decree, Syrians were allowed to access public education and the healthcare system – privileges denied to most other refugee groups in Egypt (Fritzsche 2013; Davis et al. 2017: 30). A speech by Morsi in June 2013, in which he expressed his full support for the Free Syrian Army, ordered the closure of the Syrian embassy in Egypt and demanded the Egyptian people's participation in the fight against the Asad regime, further triggered anti-Syrian sentiments (Ayoub and Khallaf 2014: 20). After this speech, Syrians began to be accused of interfering in Egypt's internal politics by supporting the Muslim Brotherhood (Ayoub and Khallaf 2014). Hostility towards Syrians was exacerbated when Syrian refugees were publicly denounced for participating in the sit-ins on Rabaa Square organized by Morsi supporters after his ousting (Fritzsche 2013). The media fuelled the anti-Syrian sentiments with TV presenter Tawfiq Okasha warning Syrians to stop supporting the Muslim Brotherhood within the next forty-eight hours, if they did not want Egyptians to destroy their homes (HRW 2013). According to Fritzsche (2013), Syrians in Egypt were utilized to polarize the country and delegitimize the Muslim Brotherhood. While the Brotherhood was portrayed as a foreign-led entity, Syrian refugees were demonized and depicted as a threat to Egypt's national security. Indeed, several of my Egyptian acquaintances voiced a strong sense of rejection of Syrians' assumed interference in Egypt's national politics and a lot of anger that Syrians who were tolerated as foreigners and guests would intrude in Egypt's internal issues.

Mahmud remembered that the summer of 2013 was defined by fear and insecurity. He avoided speaking Syrian dialect in public in order not to be identified as Syrian. He was called names and was treated badly by Egyptians. Fadi recalled that Egyptians said 'bad stuff' in front of him about Syrians and that he felt forced to speak in Egyptian accent in order not to identified as Syrian. Mu'ayad remembered how he ran into a policeman in the summer of 2013 who said to him, after looking at his Syrian passport, that he should not be in the streets but rather at home. After this incident, he continuously reduced his presence on the streets of

Cairo until he spent almost all his time at home unable to earn money and provide for himself. When I asked Rafi, who regularly gave me a ride to 6th of October City, why he did not want to live there but instead chose to settle in another area of Cairo, where the Syrian presence was less visible, he answered that the Egyptians treated him better in areas with less Syrian presence. Rafi clearly enjoyed spending time in 6th of October City. He said that the smell, the names, the shops and the chitchat on the streets reminded him of his life in Syria; however, he experienced rejection there. Once, when he entered a shop in 6th of October City, the Egyptian vendor immediately insulted him, saying 'you are not good people!' He assumed that the shop owner had had a bad experience with a Syrian and felt that all Syrians were the same. In order to avoid this sweeping rejection, Rafi decided to live in an area of Cairo where fewer Syrians were living.

Bashar, the student of medicine, compared the Egyptians' hostile attitude after the Rabaa Square massacre with the perception of Syrians before Morsi's ousting in 2013:

> When they heard the word 'Syrian', it was a very positive term and they used to say welcome.

This stood in sharp contrast to the situation after the summer of 2013, in which, Bashar remembered, 'if you say "Syrian", you feel that it's nothing'. Furthermore, he explained that the changing attitude towards Syrians was most obvious in the immigration department:

> In the past, they dealt with me like a Syrian – a guest. Now, you have a window and it's written on top of it 'Syrian'. Next to it, there is a window for Palestinians and another window is for all the remaining Arab countries.

Bashar refers to the introduction of visa requirements for Syrians in 2013, bemoaning how Syrians became a special case in need of their own window, comparable to the situation of Palestinians. After having been part of the bigger group of 'Arab countries', Syrians are now excluded from it and reduced to the level of a people who are without a nation state. The underlying theme is again the loss of a strong nation state that is on an equal footing with other Arab states. Referring to the pro-Morsi demonstrations on Rabaa Square and the assumed Syrian presence there, Bashar proclaimed that Syrians in Egypt were accused of 'things they didn't do'. In fact, only a few Syrians I met assumed that there was an actual presence of Syrians on Rabaa Square as had been propagated by the Egyptian media. If they believed that there had been Syrian participation in the demonstration, they either strongly condemned it arguing that these protesting Syrians did not know that they had no right to interfere in domestic politics, or they assumed that these Syrians had been 'bought' by the Muslim Brotherhood. They related this assumption to the initial widespread support for Syrians by Egyptian aid organizations affiliated with the Muslim Brotherhood and presumed that this drew Syrians into supporting the Muslim Brothers in demonstrations. Abu Mazin, for instance, told me that those Syrians who attended the Rabaa Square protests were extremely poor and had been forced to participate by an Egyptian sheikh of a specific mosque in 6th of October City, where he had provided Syrian refugees with material support, was in possession of people's passport and was thus in the position to force them. He called the strong reaction on the part of the Egyptians to the participation of a small number of Syrians in the protests their search for a scapegoat.

In contrast, Faris, the manager of a clothes shop, did not try to find excuses for the assumed presence of Syrians in the demonstrations, but argued that the attitude of Egyptians towards Syrians understandably changed for the worse because of 'bad Syrians' partaking in the pro-Morsi demonstrations. He assumed that the Muslim Brotherhood had paid them for their participation. These Syrians, he stressed, did not understand their position as 'guests' in a host country. While Bashar used the term 'guest' as a status of respect that Syrians had lost because of the ongoing civil war, for Faris, being a guest translated into the need for neutrality and staying out of the political issues of the host country. Both definitions are congruent with common concepts of hospitality in the Arab world (see Mason 2011: 354). Being an appreciated and respected guest holds the risk to transform into silencing of the individual, enforcing complicity, docility, submissiveness and humiliation and ultimately making the individual agentless. In fact, I found self-restraint and political apathy derived from the 'guest' status to be present in several political debates, during which Syrian acquaintances preferred to remain silent. There was an awareness that activism and engagement in Egyptian domestic politics could endanger the collectivity of Syrians in Egypt and several Syrians reiterated the discourse present in the Egyptian host population. Another theme occurring in Faris' rejection of Syrians on Rabaa Square is the stigmatization of those who presumably participated in the demonstrations in support of the Muslim Brotherhood as 'bad'. He engaged in an internal selection as to who defined as 'good' Syrian, and those presumably participated in the demonstrations on Rabaa Square were downgraded because of their behaviour.[9] I mentioned this strategy of internal selection and condemnation of behaviour that was not considered to be appropriate and 'Syrian' in previous chapters, for instance, in the context of employment. The reiteration of the Egyptian discourse against the Syrians thus offered men like Faris the opportunity to purify themselves through the creation of distance from the 'bad' Syrians and to render themselves acceptable in the face of the regime and the biased Egyptians. Consequently, the aftermath of Rabaa Square is not only an important signifier for Syrian-Egyptian relations, but also defines negotiations among Syrians. Syrians in Egypt had to make sense of being scapegoated by the Egyptians and had to negotiate their new position as merely tolerated 'guests'. This led in some cases to the creation of a new 'bad other' from their midst, against which they could construct a purer and 'better' version of Syrianness.

Making sense of 'self' and 'other' through stereotypes

In addition to accusing 'bad Syrians', several Syrians I met blamed the influence of the media and the Egyptians' ignorance for the rise in xenophobia, intolerance and suspicion against Syrians after the Rabaa Squar massacre, as expressed by Abu Walid:

> Now here, who is controlling Egypt is al-Sisi. I can tell you in one word that he is with Bashar [al-Asad]. So he always disturbs the Syrians. Every day he makes a new decision which makes life hard for the Syrians. The same Egyptians who used to say yesterday that we are their beloved ones; now they are saying that we are terrorists. The Egyptian people changed completely. There are two Egyptian channels on TV and what they say in these channels is what the Egyptians believe. If the TV tells the Egyptians that we are terrorists, then we are terrorists. If we are good, then they believe that we are good. Last year you put me on your head and now you believe that I am a terrorist? We started to see this in their eyes.

Apart from Abu Walid's sense that Syrians were in contrast to the Egyptians politically more aware, he described a feeling of insecurity in a country in which the population was 'moody' and could easily change its opinion. Abu Walid was not the only one who shared with me the belief that Egyptians lacked political acumen, which was obvious when they blindly followed the media's definition of the Syrians as scapegoats after the Rabaa Square massacre. A similar sense of ascribed ignorance and lack of understanding is present in Abd al-Rahman's account, when he recalled his stay in Egypt since he came as a student in 2006:

> From 2006 until 2011, I was a *basha* (respected man) in Egypt. Any Egyptian would call me *basha* and I was loved because there were not many Syrians in Egypt. When the incidents started in Syria, they thought that we were fleeing from the war and that we needed them. However, the money that any Syrian paid for the flight ticket for him and his family can provide living for one year for an Egyptian family. The costs of the trip from Syria to Cairo can cover the living for any Egyptian family! We see a lot of Syrians living in 6th of October City in nice houses and they opened very fancy restaurants. We see how the Egyptians left the Egyptian restaurants and came to eat in the Syrian restaurants.

Abd al-Rahman's use of the term *basha*[10] is evocative. During my stays in Egypt, I recognized how Egyptians friends and acquaintances used the term *basha* in everyday conversations in an informal manner. According to Yussif, an Egyptian student and contact of mine, *basha* these days defines someone with money, property and influence, someone with high social status and a good life. In Abd al-Rahman's account, being *basha* also relates to economic capital and success. Losing this status, which he recognized and bemoaned, can thus be understood as a feeling of degradation in terms of class, status and respect. While being Syrian used to be an influential, valued status, the Syrian crisis and civil war diminished Syria's standing and consequently the position of a Syrian man in Egypt. Abd al-Rahman clearly exaggerates the overall wealth he ascribes to Syrians in order to give more strength to his argument. He was one of many Syrians who made use of stereotypes and exaggeration to describe themselves and stigmatize the Egyptian 'others'.[11]

Masculinization through stereotyping

In addition to discussions of Syria's presumed wealth and Egypt's poverty, many Syrians I met displayed the exceptional work ethics of Syrian employees and entrepreneurs and the high-quality products produced by Syrian factories and companies as a strategy of setting themselves apart from the Egyptians. I often heard that Syrian houses and restaurants were cleaner, that Syrian doctors were more educated and trustworthy, that Syria's streets were in a better shape or that Syrian employers were preferred even by Egyptian workers. Qutayba, for instance, complained about the inadequate way his office was cleaned by the Egyptian staff. He said that he usually had to tell the Egyptian cleaner to come back and redo their job three times before his desk reached a satisfactory level of cleanliness. He added that he kept his own rag in his closet so that he could clean his desk and workplace if he remained unsatisfied. Qutayba believed it was Syrians' high standards, their level of expectations in themselves and in others, which differentiated them from the Egyptians. He was convinced that the Egyptians forgot the incidents that occurred in the summer of 2013 as soon as the Syrians had established themselves in Egypt, were in possession of many factories and shops and were appreciated for their work and the quality they produced. Syrian men could assert themselves and regain their reputation as valuable men through hard work.

Mahmud had set up his own office in his flat and had created his own material for tours he offered to tourists. He remembered a conversation with his Egyptian landlord, in which the landlord told him that Egyptians could learn how to be creative from Syrians. He admired the fact that even though Syrians were facing a war in their home country, they could come up with original, innovative ideas in Egypt to make a living. In another conversation, Mahmud spoke at great length about jealousy he saw in Egyptians, which was, in his eyes, an understandable outcome of their encounter with the more meticulous and diligent Syrians:

and sometimes there is envy on the part of the Egyptians. Why? Because, as I noticed, many Egyptians told me: 'you are excellent in everything! You are the best in restaurants, you are the best in clothes. You open a dentist clinic here and you are the best. You open bla bla bla ... !' I hear it from many people. I feel happy but at the same time I feel that the Egyptians who work in the same field are not happy because of the Syrians. And they are right sometimes. I am in my country and someone comes to my country and he starts to make any food and the people go to his place. Some Egyptians ate *hawawshi* [an Egyptian meat dish] in a Syrian restaurant with me and they said that it was the best *hawawshi* they ever had. But *hawawshi* is Egyptian! Imagine if another restaurant here that is very famous hears that *hawawshi* is the best at the Syrians! And the one who said it is Egyptian. They will say: Fuck Syrians!

Mahmud's talk of the danger of being too successful in the host country echoes the discussion of being a tolerated guest who has to keep his head down and should not stand out in any way. It also reverberates with the discussion of being successful entrepreneurs and reminds of the main theme of several Egyptian TV shows in which Syrian men were described as hardworking, diligent and innovative in contrast to the idleness of the Egyptians. Islam, an Egyptian friend of mine, told me that the Syrians in Egypt had become 'stronger, smarter and more active' than the Egyptians, that they loved to work and had money and businesses. At the same time, Mahmud's account reiterates the image of the ideal Syrian middle-class man who is characterized by creativity, ingenuity, diligence and productivity. The ideal of the self-made man who sets up his own business features strongly. Furthermore, his narrative is ripe with generalization, exaggeration and stigmatization – tactics of masculinization through othering.

Focusing on the food industry, in which many Syrians in Egypt managed to make a living, he continued:

So, this is the difficulty: if you want to work, you might face problems because you may not be good. However, Syrians have a different problem: they are famous for being good. And maybe they are not good. I met someone in *Midan Lubnan* and I asked him where he used to sell shawarma in Syria and I discovered that he was smith back in Syria. He wasn't doing anything with shawarma before. But he opened a shawarma shop in Egypt and wrote 'Syrian Shawarma' on the signboard and all the people trusted him immediately. I found the shawarma okay, not very special.

There is a strong sense of stigmatization in Mahmud's narratives. Through the comparison with the Egyptians, he reclaims Syrian middle-class identity and successful Syrian masculinity. At the same time, he manages to lower the standing of the Egyptians who cannot keep up with Syrians' inventiveness and hard work. Having been publicly scapegoated and blamed for interference in Egyptian politics and support of demonized Islamism, Syrian men engaged in stigmatization of the Egyptian host population by emphasizing definitions of successful masculine identity.

Like Mahmud, Firas talked at length about the difference between Egyptians' and Syrians' approaches to work. When I met him, he was unemployed and was preparing to travel to Europe via the Mediterranean. He had initially tried to open a factory in Egypt but for many reasons could not do so. At the point of our meeting, he was unable to provide for his wife and two children. Nevertheless, he described extensively the success of his factory back in Syria, where they 'worked with big contracts [and] used to work for France and Italy'. He ascribed the failure of his project in Egypt to a lack of work ethic among Egyptian employees, who, in contrast to the Syrian workers, were in his opinion 'not productive'.

> The difference is that Syrians are very hard workers. They love to work. The Syrian likes to eat from the sweat of his forehead, while the Egyptian likes to abuse and likes to steal. This is the thing. There is a big difference between Syrians and Egyptians, isn't it? In their personality, there is a difference. They are cheating and they are not honest. The Egyptians are very lazy people. He thinks about the day only. The worker in the factory takes the salary at the end of the month. The next day he doesn't come to work because he has money. He will come back when the money is gone.

Throughout the conversation Firas frequently described the Egyptians as 'cheats' and bemoaned that everyone just wanted his money. He drew a clear picture of a certain type of man and his antagonist. There is the meticulous, diligent, enthusiastic Syrian worker, who appreciates the fruits of honest work and its opposite is the lazy cheat, the liar, the thief, personified by the Egyptian. Firas defines the Syrian masculine self by referring to honourable traits and creates the Egyptian other by stripping it off these valuable characteristics. Knowing that he did not fit into this idealized picture of a Syrian man, being unemployed and preparing to leave for Europe in order to apply for asylum, Firas seemed to be even harsher in defending his perception of Syrian characteristics. Firas made use of a strategy that I identified already in previous chapters: he defines Syrian masculinity in the first place by what it is not, namely, cheating, lying or stealing. He uses the value of hard and honest work to degrade the Egyptians and give praise to the Syrians. The 'lazy' Egyptian embodied the opposite and abject notion of ideal respectable Syrian masculinity and allowed him to reinstall a sense of success, dignity and manhood in a situation of displacement that disrupted his pre-flight goals and lifestyle. Stereotyping, exaggeration and stigmatization were part of his strategy to masculinize against the other.

Not all stereotypes only implicitly referred to images of ideal masculinities, some prejudices explicitly referred to characteristics of ideal manhood with the purpose of distinguishing Syrian men from their Egyptian counterparts. Mahmud told me that after the fourth anniversary of the Egyptian revolution there was a public outcry in Egypt following the killing of Sheimaa al-Sabbagh[12] that Egyptian men had no *rujula* (masculinity). Mahmud told me that on the pictures and videos of her dying moments that went viral, he saw several men passing by without stopping to help the dying woman and the man who was holding her. To strengthen his argument, he added that Egyptian men on a bus ride would commonly not offer their seat to women and would rather watch them being harassed and stared at by other men. He said that in Syria, men always interfered if a woman was harassed, while in Egypt, men had not understood that masculinity would not only include words but also actions.

Likewise, Mustafa, a student busy with his final exams, who participated in a variety of trainings and courses in his free time and came over as very self-confident, made use of stereotypes that related to work ethic in addition to emphasizing on Syrian men's appeal. He had joined Fadi and me to the café, where we used to spend some time after the end of each English class we prepared together. Mustafa was eager to talk about his experiences in Egypt.

> Nowadays, I get accepted. The beginning was hard. You have to enforce that you get respected. At first, Egyptian men treated me badly, but when you enforce respect by showing that you are a respectable man, then everyone treats you well. At the beginning in Egypt, you have to learn how to find your place. Egyptian men treat Syrian men badly because all the Egyptian girls are now attracted to Syrian boys more than to Egyptian boys. Also, Egyptian employers prefer Syrian workers, because they work very hard and much better than the Egyptians. [...] The Egyptians are now used to us and they love to deal with Syrians.

Mustafa describes women's preferences in and choices among men as having an impact on men's standing, in this case, a superior position vis-à-vis the less attractive Egyptians.

Various narratives about Egyptians and Syrians were entangled with strategies of masculinization – through othering. Ascribing honourable manly qualities to Syrians and denying them to Egyptians allowed Syrian men to present themselves as the valuable middle-class men they aspired to be.

The victim aspect and compromises

Apart from the glorification of Syria's former wealth, Syrians' hard work and high qualifications and the consequent creation of ideal Syrian masculinity, another quite different discourse occurred in several conversations. It was the recognition of loss and the inability to maintain this value system. Abu Muhammad said:

> We are making ourselves victims because sometimes we go to the Egyptians and we tell them: 'please can you bring me this product?' In this situation, we don't ask for the price but we just give him what we have because we need it. Hence, we make ourselves and others victims because the Egyptians can dominate and control the price and the Egyptian also knows from where to get the product. The same holds true for Syrians: when they bring something that the Egyptians don't have they make the prices higher. For example, a product that costs 100 LE can be sold for 120 LE if many people want it. Many Syrians do this because after three years of not working, you can imagine everything. This is a small example, but there are some people who sell something worth 1,000 LE for 2,000 LE. In this case, they are controlling each other and dominate each other. This creates hate but it's inside. You hear them say that they love each other but inside of them, there is hate. This is the same among Syrians and Egyptians.

There are many layers in Abu Muhammad's description: he acknowledges that Syrians in Egypt are often in a situation of need, in which they cannot bargain and negotiate on an equal footing but must accept the conditions set by the Egyptians. At the same time, he recognizes a change in the Syrians, who depart from the above described idealized notion of middle-class masculinity defined by honest and hard work, making business in a similar way to the Egyptians, fuelled by their role as 'victims' who 'can imagine everything'. Abu Muhammad connects the transformation he finds in fellow Syrians with the consequences of Syria's civil war and consequent displacement and the contact to Egyptians. Syrian men's poverty in Egypt demands new measures and economic strategies in order to survive. Hence, people adapt their ways of bargaining and of doing business. Compared with the idealized narratives of Syrian men's outstanding qualities, Abu Muhammad's account has the aim to emphasize the difficulties Syrians face during forced displacement rather than their success. It appears like a less sugar-coded depiction of the situation of Syrians in Egypt and can add to the idealized descriptions of how Syrian men managed to remain providers for their families and hard-working entrepreneurs. Nevertheless, Abu Muhammad does not miss to engage in the stigmatization of the Egyptians as frauds, while he describes Syrians as merely reactive to the circumstances and poverty they face in Egypt.

In a similar vein to Abu Muhammad, Abu Walid recognized in his surrounding that many Syrians 'became Egyptianized'. We were sitting together in a small café next to the accessories shop in which he worked, where he often spent his daily break. I asked him whether he felt that Syrians had changed in Egypt.

There are people who kept the good habits and there are people who don't care. Some of the Syrians' children became Egyptian. The kids become Egyptian in the Egyptian schools. They become baltagy (thug). Some people kept their habits. There are some Syrian children who don't have a private school or kindergarten, so they are always in touch with the Egyptians and they become like them. I also saw adults who took over the personality of the Egyptians. They start to be dishonest as well. Egyptians are famous for abusing others and Syrians take over these habits. Maybe some of the Syrians already had these habits in them in Syria, but in Egypt it shows. They begin to consider it smartness.

Again, a rather negative image is created: Abu Walid draws the picture of a community that is forced to adapt, assimilate and copy the immoral behaviour of the Egyptians. Being in constant contact with Egyptians 'rubs off' on Syrians. Morals and values upheld in Syria are now exchanged for a better strategy of survival. Highlighting the core differences between Syrians and Egyptians, he clarifies that is was due to the dire circumstances of forced displacement that Syrians habits, attitudes and morals changed. Nevertheless, he maintains the picture of Syrians' intrinsic dignity and morality.

And then, there was Jaafar who used to work as a caseworker providing psycho-social services to his community before he decided to switch positions. I met him in a huge building exhibiting bathrooms where he worked as a retailer. The exhibition was still under construction and not open to the public. While he was employed by an Egyptian at his current workplace, he used to own a similar company back in Syria, he told me proudly. He welcomed me to give me an idea about the Syrian community in Egypt, based on his previous experiences as a caseworker. In order to help me with my research, he introduced me to his former colleagues and to Rafi, his Syrian driver, and invited me to his office several times to discuss the situation of Syrians in Egypt. Jaafar sensed that Syrians who experienced the civil war aged: boys became men and men became old men because of the sadness, despair and fear they went through. He was convinced that most Syrians in Egypt would lie in their daily lives because of feeling ashamed to be vulnerable, impoverished and in need. He was upset and angry whenever he heard about someone lying or behaving in an immoral way, since he felt that it bestowed on the Syrian community a negative reputation. Frequently, he stressed that the Syrian people had always been educated and full of culture and that it broke his heart to see the dignified Syrian people suffering, queuing for food vouchers and begging. Jaafar repeatedly questioned my position and the results of my research assuming that people would make up stories out of hope that I could do something for them. He as a Syrian could comprehend someone's intentions; however, I as a foreigner just like Egyptian staff in NGOs, would not be able to distinguish lie from truth and good from bad.

According to Dawud, the transformation of many Syrians was not only due to their inherent, but hitherto, hidden characteristics and the consequences of forced displacement, but also to their treatment by the outside world:

> When the people see a Syrian family, they will only welcome them, if they have an interest of their own in them. Maybe they think that one of them can marry the daughter. Actually, all the relations became relations with interest. There is nothing human. This is the reality. [...] Syrians always had dignity, but now the majority of people who want to help you want to take advantage of you. However, we always expect the good intentions. This is how we grew up. And then, we meet people who say that they want to help but inside they have bad intentions. We are not used to that.

Dawud refers to a poisoning of Syrians who used to have a strong and naïve belief in the other one's good intentions. Only when being confronted with the bad intentions of the outside world, did Syrians understand the cruelty of others and eventually adapted and transformed their otherwise 'pure' character. Forced displacement is described here as a force that has changed Syrians to the extent that they cannot uphold their ideals anymore and recognize how the others' behaviour infiltrates Syrian values and morals.[13]

The narratives show a sense of victimization that Syrians ascribed to the circumstances of their forced displacement and create the idea that Syrians were no longer in the position to make decisions solely based on their background and ideals, but the crisis enforces a re-evaluation of approaches to life. At the same time, these narratives do not fail to highlight Syrian men's inherent values, morals and dignity.

Conclusion

This chapter began by discussing the various connotations that were associated with sectarianism. Conflict with most sects was remembered to be absent before the uprising; however, there was an awareness of the regime's strategic use of sectarianism. Syrian men remembered that there was a form of sectarian injustice present in their daily lives, namely, living as a non-Alawite in a country that was ruled by a regime with a sectarian base. Furthermore, this chapter has shed light on the emotions of anxiety, anger, betrayal, uncertainty and hate related to having had to flee from a sectarianized civil war and to the horror, loss of context and inability to understand what Syrian society had become. The sectarian violence that had become part of the Syrian civil war made Syrian men feel that they learned the truth about fellow Syrians who used to be their neighbours, acquaintances and friends but ultimately betrayed them and showed their 'true' faces. Syrian men responded with a new awareness of who was 'us' and who was 'them' and reported to have become hostile, suspicious and hateful vis-à-vis other Syrians. Sectarianism and accompanying emotions and memories carried on from Syria could not but influence Syrian men's encounter with other Syrians in Egypt and thus impacted on their experiences of community and social contact. Viewed from an intersectional perspective, living in a sectarian context is but one of the axes that define Syrian men's understanding, construction and practice of masculinities. Consequently, sectarianism can be conceptualized as a form of 'baggage' that followed Syrians to Egypt and impacted on their social relations and lives there. During forced displacement, Syrians experienced an absence of community cohesion and the form of living together in Egypt Syrian men described could only be conceptualized as a 'non-community'.

Moreover, this chapter has dealt with Syrians' encounters with the Egyptian host society that were often narrated by referring to the UAR and the incidents on Rabaa Square. Both discourses do not only describe the contact of Egyptians and Syrians, but also illustrate processes of ascription and denial of an ideal version of Syrianness to other Syrians. They also hint to how Syrian men felt challenged in their positions as citizens of a strong nation state. The stereotypes that were used to describe how Syrian men managed to outdo Egyptians in the contexts of work, innovation and stamina speak to the image of the ideal Syrian middle-class man described in the previous chapters. These processes show how Syrian men reconfirmed their masculinities, namely, through othering and the use of essentialism and homogenization.

Chapter 6

MASCULINITIES, INTERACTION WITH THE STATE AND THE MIGRATION OF FEAR

Shortly before Abu Muhammad and his family travelled to Germany, I met him for a last time in a café close to his shop. Abu Muhammad told me delighted that he and his family were packing and preparing for their trip and suggested that I should meet his cousin Layla and her daughter, who would remain in Cairo after his departure. He gave me strict instructions regarding my behaviour during the visit. He informed me that his widowed cousin and her teenage daughter were in a precarious situation, because Layla's son had gone to Sweden and there was no man in the flat. Abu Muhammad advised me to meet his cousin in her flat wearing appropriate and decent clothes in order to avoid any gossip from the neighbours. Moreover, he suggested that if I wanted to interview her, or in fact any other Syrian contacts of mine, I should record in secret, keeping the device hidden in my pocket (an advice I did not follow). He also encouraged me to ask questions relating only to societal and economic issues and strongly advised against asking any kind of political questions, especially those referring to political affiliations and preferences. He said that the Syrians in Egypt were exhausted and anxious and that most of them would assume that I was a spy if I decided to ask political questions. Abu Muhammad further anticipated that it was difficult for Syrians to assess me as a person, my intentions and the reasons behind my research. In order to clarify the relevance of his instructions, Abu Muhammad mentioned an Egyptian American volunteer, who taught English for *Fursa* volunteers like me, and had just posted pictures from a trip to Israel on Facebook. Abu Muhammad announced that people, and especially our students – his son was one of them, were 'scared of both of [us]', since they did not know our motivations and political positions.

In this chapter, I analyse Abu Muhammad's sense of fear, distrust and suspicion that motivated his clear instructions and explanations. I argue that Syrian people's past encounters and experiences with the Syrian state created a ubiquitous fear in their lives. This fear was induced by the immense power of the *mukhabarat*, the infiltration of surveillance in the private sphere and its influence on the family and on growing up in Syria. This fear did not stop at the borders of Syria, but travelled with most Syrians I met to Egypt, where it turned into a pervasive anxiety and suspicion of the Syrian embassy, the Egyptian state and its authorities, as well as individuals believed to be allied with either the Egyptian or Syrian state.

Furthermore, this chapter deals with the encounters between Syrian men and the Syrian and Egyptian state administration. I investigate how Syrian men in Egypt remembered their interactions with the state apparatus in Syria – especially in terms of bureaucratic procedures and the need to make use of bribes and *wasta* (connections) to manage them. In this context, this chapter asks: What does it mean to leave behind a life under an authoritarian regime only to arrive in a country with comparable features, such as a corrupt bureaucratic system and a powerful security service? I analyse how Syrian men navigated their encounters with the Egyptian state and how the 'taste of *wasta* and corruption', similarly to the fear of the *mukhabarat*, stayed with many of my interviewees and affected their lives in Egypt. Syrian men approached the Egyptian state in the same manner as they used to encounter the Syrian state, albeit with less security and grounding because of their loss of networks and social status as refugees in Egypt.

Ultimately, this chapter identifies both the fear of state authorities and the problematic strategies Syrians had to adopt when approaching the Syrian state as aspects that influenced Syrian men. Regarding the influence of fear on constructions of gender, Green (1994: 230) who conducted research among women in Guatemala argues that an understanding of their lives necessitated an analysis of their state of fear. She found that getting used to a life in terror and crisis, which ultimately destroys the social fabric of society, 'allows people to live in a chronic state of fear with a face of normalcy' (1994: 231). In a similar vein, an understanding of Syrian men's lives requires an analysis of fear, 'a pillar of the state's coercive authority' (Pearlman 2016: 21), as a form of normalcy in everyday life that defined various parts of their lives in both Syria and Egypt.

With its focus on state-induced fear, this chapter sheds light on how living under an authoritarian regime destabilizes notions of manhood, evokes shame and threatens the contours of any form of viable masculinity. Fear, shame and discomfort accompanied the transition from citizen under an authoritarian regime to refugee in an authoritarian host state. Syrian men's notion of fear was active, 'sticky' (Ahmed 2004: 16) and in motion, docking to new objects and persons in Egypt. The focus on uncomfortable practices, such as making use of *wasta* and bribes, shows that men both back in Syria and in Egypt were in the first place reactive and responsive to the authoritarian system and had to juggle their morals, values and beliefs with their economic survival. This juggling made most men uncomfortable evoking in them self-loathing.

State Surveillance in Syria

Because of the omnipresence of the *mukhabarat*, Syrians lived in a climate of fear and encountered other Syrians with scepticism and suspicion. By the 1990s, Hafez al-Asad had expanded the military and security apparatus of the country so that 15 per cent of the country's total workforce was employed in these sectors (Chatty 2010: 43). The Syrian security apparatus had considerable social, political and economic power (Perthes 1995: 146). Having established an 'Orwellian system of surveillance' (Ziadeh 2013: 24), the Syrian regime could maintain an atmosphere of uncertainty, fear and compliance infiltrating deeply into Syrian society. Citizens could not be sure whether one's counterpart was somehow involved in the structures of the *mukhabarat* and would reveal information about them (Schneiders 2013: 233). The knowledge that anyone could work for the *mukhabarat* and could pass on information, even family members, created a general sense of distrust, suspicion and self-censorship amongst many Syrians (Van Eijk 2016: 13). And thus, dealing with the security service had to be part of people's strategies for survival (Perthes 1995: 148).

Meeting Syrians in Egypt, I was eager to discuss with them their experiences with the *mukhabarat* because I still remembered vividly the constant gaze of the regime I used to feel when I was in Syria in 2009 and 2010 as a language student. Various experiences still coloured my memories of Syria: once, I asked a friend of mine from Hama on a car ride from Damascus to his hometown, what had happened in the 1980s to the Syrian Muslim Brotherhood and what he knew about the massacres that had taken place in his home town.[1] To my surprise, he simply stopped talking to me for a while and we sat in awkward silence before he introduced another topic, completely ignoring my question. I was also surprised to find that whenever my language partner wanted to say something critical about Syria, he would close the curtains of the windows in the living room and start to whisper. And eventually, I got to experience the arbitrariness of the Syrian security apparatus: when I left the country in February 2010, hoping to come back for a longer stay after graduation, the border police at the airport stopped me and left with my passport and my ticket only to come back to tell me that I was not allowed to enter Syria again. When I said, utterly confused and in a panic, that I was just a language student and that I was not doing anything wrong (thinking of all the things I learned not to do while being in Syria, such as travelling to Israel or publishing journalistic pieces about Syria), he coldly and stoically repeated that it was written on his computer that I would never be allowed to access Syria again. Scared and shocked, I boarded the plane.

'Walls have ears'

Once I asked Mazin when he started to be against the regime. Responding in great detail to my question, Mazin explained how the Alawites used to be preferred, while the rest of the country suffered under Hafez al-Asad's rule. Eventually, he turned to the omnipresence of the security apparatus and suspicion of being overheard in Syria using two idioms I should hear frequently during conversations with other Syrian acquaintances.

> For a long time this happened [the mistreatment by the Asad family], but we couldn't say anything. We used to say that the walls have ears. It was difficult to talk about this. If you talk, they will take you behind the sun. Since the revolution started up until now, you still find people who are afraid to speak.

Mazin's described his disappointment in the Syrian regime paired with an inability to express critique because of a constant paranoia of being spied on and controlled by the regime's informants. His account reveals how in repressive political systems 'citizens were trained to view each other suspiciously in a world of mutual surveillance' (Betts 2010: 49). It shows the extent to which Syrians had internalized the system's rules and how the fear of consequences, if they critiqued the regime, endured.

A couple of days after I had this conversation with Mazin, I asked Mahmud how he understood the idiom of taking someone behind the sun. He interpreted it in the following way: 'they will take you and no one will know where you are'. His interpretations suggest the cruel consequences people can expect if they speak critically about politics in public. The anticipation of unknown but real punishment when citizens express their political opinion in authoritarian regimes was an effective way for the regime to consolidate its power and enforce citizens' obedience (Wedeen 1999: 147). Ismail (2018: 166) points out that the Syrian regime made use of horror as a modality of rule through specific performances of violence. This way of governing created citizens who were knowledgeable of what the regime was able to do, constantly awaiting acts of violence that never missed to reinstate a sense of horror. Furthermore, Ismail (2018: 114) argues that the regime installed a sense of abjection in citizens making them feel unworthy, humiliated and degraded.

In a similar vein to Mazin, Abd al-Rahman came to speak with me about the high level of surveillance to which Syrians were subjected. When we were talking about his studies in Egypt between 2006 and 2011, Abd al-Rahman remembered that every time he came back to Syria from Egypt, 'someone from the Syrian security' came to him:

> Sometimes, I would arrive very late at night, even without telling any of my friends; still, in the morning, the security would knock on my door to tell me: 'Good to have you back!' It is a police state. They were asking me: 'What did you do in Egypt?' [...] I always told them that I was a student, that I just studied in Egypt and that I came back for the holidays, nothing else. This is what they call a political investigation.

Abd al-Rahman's narrative exposes the authorities' focus on and disruption of the citizen's private sphere.[2] The penetration of the home had the effect of contaminating the individual's body, psyche and life (Feldman 2000: 47). And indeed, Abd al-Rahman's memory shows his inability to ever feel completely safe and not subjected to someone else's will. Comparing the situation in Syria with his experiences in Egypt when he had first come to study in Cairo during then-President Mubarak's rule, Abd al-Rahman remembered his surprise on finding Egyptians cursing and mocking Mubarak in public:

> When I arrived in Cairo, I saw freedom. It is true that Hosni Mubarak was a dictator and that he was trying to starve the people in order to prevent them from

actively engaging in politics, but nonetheless, I saw a kind of freedom that you might not find in Syria even after fifty years. Freedom did exist in Mubarak's era. The president was cursed while he was still in power and no one said anything. I remember a meeting of the Arab league, for which the Arab presidents came together. I was watching the meeting in a coffee shop. I heard one of the guys, who were watching with me, saying: 'Where is our dog?' If these words had been said in Syria, not only the guy who said it, but also his whole family would have disappeared.

Abd al-Rahman portrayed a situation of relative freedom of speech under Mubarak's rule in Egypt which he could not imagine experiencing in Syria. He also sheds light on how the Syrian regime managed to attack and threaten what was closest and most important to its people, namely, the family. It is thus not only the fear for one's own life, but also the fear of losing loved ones that controls people and makes them compliant.

The picture that emerges is that Syrian men experienced and remembered living under constant surveillance in Syria as a form of omnipresent danger that had a concrete impact on their everyday life in the form of expected threats as consequences to critique, unwanted encounters with representatives of the surveillance state and the raising of worries about family and loved ones.

Memories of being imprisoned

Using the example of his father's imprisonment, Khalid, the teenage son of the two community leaders in 6th of October with whom I used to meet several times before he left for Turkey with his mother and sister, described what could happen to someone who was not afraid to speak about politics in public and had 'knowledge about what's going on in the world'. Because 'he talk[ed] about what is in his heart' and said what he thought about the government, his father's name was mentioned to the government by an informer – an old school friend of his, a couple of years before the outbreak of the uprising. Soon after, the whole family was woken up one night by someone knocking on their door. When Abu Khalid asked who was outside, the answer was: 'We're the police!' 'They didn't say "we're the *mukhabarat!*"', Khalid recalled. Then, ten heavily armed men entered their flat and searched it. They took Abu Khalid with them, saying he would only undergo interrogation and would be back after two hours. Eventually, he returned after forty-five days of imprisonment. Fifteen days after Abu Khalid's disappearance, the family received information about his whereabouts. In prison, Abu Khalid was interrogated repeatedly, described by Khalid in the following way:

They made him repeat his life story lots of times. They did this to find out whether he was lying. If he did not tell the truth on one occasion, then he would forget and would make a mistake the next time he told his life story. He just wanted to get out and do nothing but obey. However, once my father didn't want to answer

and the officer said: 'if you don't answer we'll get your wife here!' My father tried
to kick him but couldn't reach him because he was handcuffed and blindfolded.

Khalid's description of his father's imprisonment sheds light on various issues: the
danger of being politically aware and speaking about it in public; the possibility
of being betrayed by one's acquaintances; the immense power of the regime; the
illegitimate and inhumane measures of the authorities including the authorities'
strategy to threaten the family, and compliance as the only way out. The presented
memories and experiences alert to the 'pedagogy of fear' that the Syrian regime
developed through its monitoring and disciplining of citizens with prisons,
massacres and forced disappearances as part of its infrastructure (Ismail 2018: 74).
This 'pedagogy of fear' had a constant and draining effect on Syrian men's lives. They
experienced disregard for their homes and privacy, arbitrary imprisonment and the
consequent inability to ever feel completely safe, as well as the authorities' threats
of their family members. Beyond this, we can also read from Khalid's description
that he was proud of his father's knowledge which caused the imprisonment, his
smartness vis-à-vis the interrogators and his readiness to defend his wife's honour
and safety. It can be retrieved from this account that respectable masculine traits
in an authoritarian regime relate to being aware, to manoeuvring the encounters
with the regime's powerful security service and to surviving them.

Consequences of state surveillance

While Khalid explained the most severe control mechanisms of the Syrian
authorities and what it meant to him and his father, Bashar highlighted subtler
outcomes of Syrian state control. He assumed that the ubiquitous suspicion that
one's words might be overheard and one's actions might be controlled led to a
misrepresentation of politics and an inability to imagine a variety of opinions. He
was one of the interlocutors who asked several questions about the intention of
my research and gave clear instructions about the way a recorded interview could
take place:

Maybe in Syria we have a different mentality from people in other countries.
Our thinking was focused on how to work. There was only one party and no
other political parties, which made us hear one opinion only. There was no
opposition. You only hear one opinion. There were no discussions at all except in
closed rooms. When they wanted to speak in closed rooms, they even kicked out
the children so they could not share what has been discussed at home in front of
others. If these kids had said anything, you would have got many problems. We
used to hear about the events and about what happened in the 1980s. We heard
that many people were killed, but no one would speak clearly about it.

Bashar portrayed the anxiety of the older generation to express their opinions, to
mention the regime-induced massacre of the Muslim Brotherhood in Hama in the
1980s, their fear of spies and lack of trust even in their children. He links this state

of mind in society to the absence of political opposition, the sole availability of vague and opaque knowledge and lack of diversity of opinions. The self-censorship that resulted from the feeling of a constant gaze on oneself heavily impacted on information that was shared and accessible even within families. A consequence of this lifestyle is a focus on 'how to work' – that is, establishment of a sense normalcy despite the omnipresent fear (see Green 1994).

In a similar vein to Bashar, Abd al-Rahman stated how surveillance affected the family and the way children grew up in Syria. When we met, he usually ended up lamenting about the conditions back in Syria under Asad's rule. Since the first time I met him he clarified his political position and never seemed concerned about expressing his critique of the Syrian regime in front of me. This is way his voice features strongly in this chapter.

> In general, each Syrian child was aware of the care of his parents. The parents looked after him, but nonetheless, there were external factors impacting on him. He was not allowed to talk, was always ruled, always suppressed, couldn't express his freedom, couldn't write a story or a poem, couldn't talk about any subject related to the state until the beginning of the Syrian revolution. The Syrian revolution came to set the country free of the dictatorship, the rule of Bashar al-Asad.

After a while, he continued:

> The era of Hafez al-Asad was very tough. It was the era of Al Ba'th party. Any person who belonged to Al Ba'th party was more powerful than a general in the army. We were always afraid to talk. In school, we were controlled. Tyranny was practiced on us in a very tough way. [...] After we had finished the preparatory and the secondary school, we realised that we couldn't talk about anything. Not about freedom. Not about improving our lives. [...] The Arab rulers and dictatorships led us to accept this life as normal without any hope or ambitions. All what a child thinks about is to finish his university education and become a teacher or a doctor, nothing more just to practice his job. They destroy the ambition. They destroy the willing. They destroy childhood. They destroy the feeling of willing.

The child in Abd al-Rahman's account is in a paradoxical state of feeling at the same time taken care of and protected within his family, and left alone, unprotected and controlled by his surroundings. There is, on the one hand, care, warmth and protection, and on the other, an external threat that invades the private sphere and denies the child his agency, freedom of expression and artistic development. Regime politics were in fact deeply ingrained in family relations in Syria. This caused that the family was remembered to be both: 'constraining and protecting' (Ismail 2018: 110/113).

Laith, Mu'ayad's friend who used to invite us every now and then for shisha, described that dealing with the presence of the *mukhabarat* in his life was a slow process of learning and adapting to its omnipresent threat. Said Laith:

In school, we were taught that al-Asad was the right and only president. We didn't hear any other opinion. There was one TV only and it showed only state channels. This was the same in the whole street – so how could we build another opinion? At some point in our lives, we learned about the existence of the secret service and we learned to include this knowledge in our everyday lives. You realise at some point that there is something fishy, but no one would tell you anything until you are a bit older.

Both Abd al-Rahman's and Laith's statements regarding the external control that the child experiences show how surveillance gradually conquers the individual's body, mind and learning. From a very young age, the child feels an external power that controls his life and reduces his freedom of expression, agency and space for critical thinking. This shows how Syrian men's masculine trajectory has always been strongly forged by adaptation to an authoritarian regime and its secret service. Becoming a man in Syria cannot be disentangled from what it means to grow up under an authoritarian regime. It requires a conceptualization of masculinity as elastic and tensile, able to incorporate these conditions. Again, the sense of upholding normalcy despite fear features strongly in this narrative. The effects of living under state surveillance were self-censorship, political apathy and ignorance, suspicion, feeling dominated and enforced compliance. Syrian men's frequent references to the private sphere, namely, the family or the home, and how this sphere was under attack by state surveillance prove the regime's efforts and success in challenging the family through observation and denunciation.

'How do you think men feel under such oppression?'

Once, when I was sitting in a shisha café with Mu'ayad, we got involved into a discussion about life back in Syria. I wanted him to go beyond the usual chitchat and asked him if he could put into words what it meant to be a man in Syria. He said that growing up and living under a repressive regime meant that certain aspects such as the fear of speaking about politics were still ingrained in him and haunted him, even though he had left Syria four years ago. Then, he raised a question without raising his voice or looking at me, a stern look on his face:

Aren't men supposed to provide for and protect their family? So how do you think men feel under such oppression? They feel useless.

I detected shame in Mu'ayad's rhetorical question and the answer he gave to himself in a sarcastic tone. Mu'ayad was the only one of all my interlocutors who drew an explicit connection between his sense of manhood and living under an authoritarian state. His account alerts to the shame of being unable to uphold provider masculinity and being the protector of the family because of the state's interference through oppressing state surveillance. He hints to a sense of impotence to be in full control of the situation and fulfil gendered expectations for the family.

Even though Mu'ayad made the only explicit reference to his sentiments as a man, I see similar indications in the previously presented accounts: Abd al-Rahman describes deprivation of agency and individuality and the pain of being forced to comply; Khalid speaks of humiliation, threats to life and family and simultaneously displays his pride in showing backbone to protect loved ones; and Mazin mentions that there was a painful discrepancy between the knowledge of injustice and the wrongdoing of the regime and the inability to stand up and oppose it. Syrian men were aware that the state had major control over their lives and that they were congealed and stuck in a form of being that they could not outgrow, did not perceive as honourable and that was inherently defined by paralysis and anxiety. I conclude that constructions of masculinities under authoritarian state control are defined by being forced to react and succumb rather than being in the position to act freely and show individuality. This means that masculinities can be merely lived as pragmatic, responsive and reactive and the ideal of provider and protector masculinity seems out of reach. Moreover, masculinity was inherently intertwined with sentiments of anxiety, shame and paralysis.

Remembering corruption in Syria

Syrians I met in Cairo did not only discuss frequently the influence of state surveillance on their lives, but also engaged in debates about the practices they used to apply when they approached the Syrian state. On the evening I met Firas and Yasmin, for instance, the topic of corruption became the subject of a heated debate.

- Firas: We didn't talk about politics because we were living our lives. We were happy. No one cared about politics. No one thought about it. We lived, we were happy and there was money.
- Yasmin: I feel that the interview takes place in Syria and not here! Were you happy with the regime and the police?
- Firas: There were mistakes, but we were used to them and we were happy. Corruption was in our blood! Whenever you [he points at Mahmud] enter a public office, the first thing you do is to try to put 500 SL on the employee's desk. It is your nature. It is our nature.
- Yasmin: The poverty led to corruption.
- Firas: No, the poor and the rich were getting on with their lives, we were living!
- Yasmin: Give the message in a correct way! What do you mean with living? The poor were living eating falafel and the rich were living eating kebab. You should make this message clear.
- [...]
- Yasmin: The corruption was spread all over Syria because of poverty. The dictatorial regime ruled with an iron fist. Any policeman or soldier can stop and check any Syrian citizen at will. The corruption comes from

above, not from below. The soldier takes money in order to feed his children, because the salary is low. The regime follows a strategy of making people hungry. The regime just gives you a little bit, so that you can only think about how to feed your children and not about politics. [...] There were people who lived in rubbish to find food and there were people who lived in palaces. You can find men who die of a heart attack when they are forty years old because they cannot feed their children. [...] Corruption comes from poverty. It doesn't come by itself. The state employees take money because of poverty and so do the police. Even the ordinary citizen gives bribes because he is implicit in corruption. Why? Because he needs to obtain certain documents and the salaries are not high enough in order to make us not think about politics. We were living like cattle!

In this dialogue, several important issues are addressed: Firas, who presented himself as privileged, is teased for talking as if the interview took place in Syria implying that there exist certain ways of speaking either inside and outside Syria; there is a sharp class distinctions and difference in experiences and opinions based on one's class background; there was an absence of political debate back in Syria; there was extreme poverty among some parts of the Syrian population and indifference by the regime about how the poverty impacts on the people, so that men die, as described by Yasmin, because of the pain of failing as protectors and providers of the family. Yasmin defined corruption, poverty, the regime's indifference and the malaise of the system as an environment in which the individual lives and feels inhumane. Living conditions that are hardly acceptable for animals are defining features of the life in Syria which Yasmin remembered. The inability to be the provider of the family is addressed again and considered the reason for men's untimely death. Whether the inability to provide is described by Mu'ayad to cause a feeling of uselessness or, by Yasmin, as the reason for a man's absolute exhaustion, it reiterates, on the one hand, the importance of the ideal of provider masculinity, and, on the other hand, the authoritarian state being the obstacle keeping men from becoming proper, respectable providers and protectors.

Citizens' contact with the state that gave the opportunity to engage in corruption, bribery or *wasta* was institutionalized and used as a tool of control. Under the rule of Hafez al-Asad, the number of state employees in Syria increased dramatically between the 1970s and the 1990s. The expansion of bureaucratic procedures facilitated access to the state, while, at the same time, the regime made its presence visible all over Syria. Perthes (1995: 142) argues that public employment was a means of political and social control. Through voting cards, identity cards, passports and various permits required by citizens wanting to travel, build, marry or work, people were bound to the state's bureaucratic apparatus (Rabo 2014a: 220) and corruption was widespread within this system. Consequently, there was a need for the people to keep in with authorities and civil servants. Connection to state employees was often essential to gain what one was legally entitled to (Perthes

1995: 142). The explanation Yasmin gave for the existence of corruption closely resembles the justification Rabo (2014a: 219) regularly heard while conducting research in Syria among Aleppian traders and merchants, which is that bribery and corruption persisted because of general poverty and the low salaries of Syrian public employees. Furthermore, Yasmin excused ordinary citizens' engagement in corruption: they had been left with no other choice, she argued, because without the use of bribes they would have not received their legal entitlements. Corruption was, in her opinion, a tool in the hands of the regime, thus coming 'from above' rather than being an inherent characteristic of the Syrian's nature, as Firas described it. Similarly, Rabo found that her interlocutors excused their own use of bribes by arguing that the state would not grant its citizens rights without a bribe. Moreover, Yasmin bitterly assumed that the existing poverty and consequent corruption were a conscious strategy of the regime to keep citizens under control and too busy to develop an interest in politics. In contrast to Yasmin, Firas perceived corruption as a natural trait of the Syrian people and as a useful technique and strategy to ease one's life. Both Yasmin and Firas explained the contradictions of being part of a corrupt system and negotiate in albeit different ways the paradoxes they used to experience every day.

Developing strategies to approach the state

While Yasmin tried to explain why corruption and bribery existed in Syria and Firas defined paying bribes as a 'natural' and an entirely acceptable and useful habit during our evening-filling discussion, Abu Muhammad, the father of four who was about to move to Germany, insisted that he was against bribery, even though he was clearly aware of its existence and power in Syria:

> In Syria, life was beautiful and things were going well. Regarding our jobs, we faced limitations. You could get a governmental job through *wasta*, nepotism, and corruption. We didn't object to this. If there was a problem at the border at the customs office, we were only able to resolve it with money. Money had the power to resolve problems and also nepotism was really important. So, life in Syria was nice, the only problem was the existing injustice and domination.

Throughout our conversation, Abu Muhammad repeatedly mentioned that he had felt helpless and unable to escape the corrupt system in Syria: 'They ask for impossible things and you won't be able to do them', he explained referring to state officials who could stop people randomly at the Syrian border or in the streets. These state officials then arbitrarily created a problem and pinned it on the person in front of them, he explained. If the accused person wanted to get out of the state officials' grip and leave, then 'you had to pay a bribe', said Abu Muhammad. He compared the situation citizens faced in Syria to enforced adaptation and creation of normalcy in dire conditions:

It was impossible to object. When the price of bread increased, we didn't say anything. We didn't have any objection. I simply started to buy less bread. There was nothing called resistance, you just had to manage yourself. [...] The government didn't feel the suffering of the people. You should pay for everything. You had to pay for any service or item you wanted, no matter if you should have had the right to get this item and service for free in the first place.

His descriptions illustrate an arbitrary, inescapable control that citizens encountered and had to respond to individually by adaptation – in Abu Muhammad's case, through changes in his lifestyle. Even though he perceived opposition and objection as a reasonable reaction to the injustice, he experienced that resistance simply did not happen. Instead, money was the tool to encounter and survive in every part of the system. Through the right amount of money, he could clear any bureaucratic hurdle and get out of encounters with the authorities.

Since Abu Muhammad was opposed to the payment of bribes and tried to avoid it whenever possible, he employed a middleman if he needed something, such as documents or other state services, that could require the payment of bribes:

I didn't like paying bribes. What did I do? I phoned someone whom we call middleman. I paid him and I didn't care whether he paid bribes or not. I just gave him the money he requested because I didn't like to deal with this. [...] I said: 'I don't want anything to do with bribes, you do everything.' We can consider him an ordinary person, who has relations with the employees in the state administration. He is not a lawyer. Whether he pays bribes or not, it's not my problem. Generally, the problem with bribes in Syria was big.

Even though Abu Muhammad distanced himself from the payment of bribes whenever it was possible, this did not mean that he subverted the system, but rather that he found a way of reconciling his moral values with necessary survival under a corrupt regime. He knew that he was part of the unjust system that he rejected. In order to live in an authoritarian, corrupt system, Abu Muhammad's strategy of surviving was the creation of a double valence to acknowledge both the immorality of corruption and the personal involvement in it (Das 2015: 323). Using this double valence, Abu Muhammad was both vocal about the bad impact of corruption on his life and simultaneously described his own way to navigate the corrupt system by balancing morals and values with the need to survive socially and economically through the use of an external agent, who may or may not use bribes while working for Abu Muhammad.

In addition to employing a middleman, there were other practices of engaging in corruption. Mu'ayad explained to me that a person in an influential position (*mas'ul*) could be described as a lock. If one needed something from the *mas'ul*, the first step one had to do was to find the key. The key was a person whom the *mas'ul* trusted and who took over the position of the mediator. As a mediator, the key could tell the one in need of a favour from the *mas'ul* what kind of bribes were accepted. Bribes could be anything from personal favours to money or jewellery for the *mas'ul's* wife. Mu'ayad's account shows that bribery was not simply an economic transaction but a cultural practice that required a high level of knowledge and performative competence (Gupta 1995: 380). However, according to Mu'ayad's description, knowledge and competence were not enough, but needed to be furthered with risk-taking, financial and material resources, and network.

Anderson (2013: 468/469), who conducted research among Aleppian merchants, found that his interlocutors were acutely aware of their incapacity to distance themselves from a political system they opposed in thought and belief. In a climate in which it is dangerous to identify power holders and in which a clear-cut distinction between the oppressors and the oppressed could not be drawn easily, narratives of scorn were a form of political agency. Since relations with the local regime and bureaucratic officials were an essential part of everyday life in order to secure one's social and economic survival, the practices and ideas of power and resistance became blurred and diffused. The daily involvement with unjust structures and the constant practice of immoral actions led to a feeling of guilt or complicity. And thus, Anderson maintains that the subject is not simply oppressed by the circumstances, but is actually tainted, transformed and influenced by them. Making a similar argument, anthropologist Alexei Yurchak (2005: 9), analysing late socialism in the Soviet Union, stresses that in order to capture the paradoxical mix of 'alienations and attachments' that existed among the people, there is a need for language that avoids dichotomies, such as 'state and people', 'official and unofficial' or 'oppressor and oppressed'. I contend that an analysis of life under the Syrian authoritarian regime requires nuanced language that accounts for what lies in between binary categories of 'moral and immoral' or 'involved and external to state practices'. Syrian men I met described to have been neither oppressor nor entirely oppressed; they were neither completely clueless nor the manipulator behind the scene. Their engagement in corruption was conscious and intended to further their needs; however, it was not with pride that most Syrian men reported to have been involved in these practices but rather by expressing a sense of shame and pain.

The urgency to engage in bribing

Beyond the practice of bribery, Mu'ayad explained that it was in many cases the desperate situation in Syria that made people accomplices of the authoritarian regime and made them accept corruption and bribery, often against their will and with no other solution in sight. He said:

> If your family is in danger and you know that the only way to protect them is through bribes, you would engage in bribery, even if you had said in times of peace that you would not get involved in such practices!

Mu'ayad was convinced that people had to navigate their principles and that with more pressure applied from the Syrian regime, the less focus people could give to their morals, values and convictions. The severity of a situation enforced the use of certain measures that one would avoid in less stressful and dangerous times. As suggested by Anderson and Yurchack, there is no clear-cut distinction between involvement and rejection.

The urgency behind the use of certain measures is also obvious in the way Fadi described his father's use of *wasta* after he took part in a demonstration in 2011.

> The son of an officer of the *mukhabarat* saw me in a demonstration. He threatened me by saying that he would tell his father, but we managed to solve the problem. My best friend talked to him and convinced him not to tell his father that he had seen me in the demonstration. But then, a member of the *mukhabarat* called my father to tell him that he wanted to interrogate him and me. My father needed to make use of his *wasta* to solve the problem.

In both Mu'ayad's and Fadi's accounts, it is the family's well-being that is under threat and in order to protect it, the use of connections and bribes is not only accepted, but even required and little attention can be given to whether this ought to be considered an 'immoral' practice in less threatening situations.

The omnipresence of bribery, *wasta* and corruption urged each individual to make sense of their actions, failures and inabilities to live up to moral standards. Whether one accepted bribery and corruption as part of the system and used them as a tool to extend one's power, like Firas, or whether one tried to reconcile the necessary payment of bribes with one's moral outlook, like Abu Muhammad, accepting that payment guaranteed survival – a negotiation of one's stance towards bribery, corruption and *wasta* was necessary and inevitable. This process of making sense of one's 'immoral practices' could prove in a painful way a man's inability to live up to personal standards and values showing with clarity that he yields to the external pressure of the regime and caves in. The daily need to make use of *wasta*, bribes and corruption in order to survive under an authoritarian regime could create feelings of fault, loathing and pressure and needed to be incorporated in any image that is created of constructions of masculinities among Syrian men.

Navigating encounters with the Egyptian state

Having described the colouring of everyday life and survival in Syria by the regime's practices, the following paragraphs engage in Syrian men's daily live in Egypt and how it was tainted and influenced by their past experiences and encounters with the Syrian state. In Egypt, the prerequisites of Syrian men's contact with the state had changed: they were not citizens anymore, but had to deal with the Egyptian state from the position of a foreigner, 'guest' or refugee. Syrian men did not only need to navigate encounters with the Syrian state in their past, but also in Egypt they had to find ways to deal with the Egyptian bureaucracy and state authorities. Abu Walid, for instance, shared with me his experiences with the Syrian and

Egyptian state authorities. Abu Walid was involved in pro-opposition activism in both Syria and Egypt, had been imprisoned in both countries and had not only similar experiences, but also used the same strategy of paying bribes to get out of prison. In Syria, his imprisonment by a Shia militia after the outbreak of the revolution ended because his parents paid the ransom to free him. Abu Walid spoke with me about the immense danger in which he had put his mother and about the great risk she took when she met his kidnappers to hand over the requested sum. After his imprisonment, Abu Walid had to leave Syria. He was told 'you are wanted!', so he and his family arranged to flee immediately. His flight to Egypt was only possible because his father paid bribes to obtain the travel documents for his son, and again at the airport, so that Abu Walid could leave without difficulty.

When Abu Walid was imprisoned in Egypt, he was again dependent on the financial help of his parents to be able to get out of prison. He had vivid memories of the horror of his imprisonment and of how his psychological state deteriorated afterwards.

> I used to go to Libya illegally at that time, as did several Muslim Brotherhood supporters. There, they arrested all of us and delivered us to the Egyptians. The Egyptian police were surprised to find Syrians in the group. They said to the Syrians: 'You are with the Muslim Brotherhood'. And this gave them an opportunity to blackmailing. If we, the Syrians, wanted to be free, we had to pay. I paid a lot of money in order to call my family. I had to pay 1,500 LE. My family transferred money to me. I paid the colonel 5,000 LE to let me go. [...] Another time, I was arrested in Cairo Downtown. The Muslim Brotherhood supporters were demonstrating, that's why they were arrested, but I was not with them. I had the yellow card and the passports of my family with me. It was obvious that I had nothing to do with the demonstrations, but was on my way to the UNHCR office. They beat me because I was Syrian and they considered me to be pro-Muslim Brotherhood. My charge was defined before they even interrogated me. I paid again. The existence of corruption in Egypt helped me a lot. It's good that you can pay in such a situation. I paid and left. After the imprisonment, my psychological state was really bad.

Bribery is here described as a solution in a situation of despair and danger, in which human treatment and a fair handling of the imprisoned cannot be relied on. Furthermore, the opportunity for bribery was described as a lucky, positive occasion that guaranteed Abu Walid's survival and temporary safety. In another situation, Abu Walid contacted people working in the Syrian embassy to find out whether he was truly wanted by the Syrian regime. He bribed them to get this piece of information. Again, bribery was used to receive a crucial piece of information that had life-changing significance. Knowing that he was wanted in Syria and assuming that this piece of information had been shared by the Syrian government with the Egyptian government made him reduce his presence on the streets of Cairo and his contact with Egyptians to an absolute minimum.

Mahmud, as a tour guide for foreigners receiving many bank transfers from abroad, also had an encounter with the Egyptian authorities. He was contacted by the security service responsible for the economics section and was asked to appear at their office. Scared and stressed, he did not know what to do and asked an Egyptian friend for advice. His friend suggested bringing a lawyer to the meeting and also recommended someone whom he trusted. During the meeting, Mahmud was asked why he received so many bank transfers from abroad. Through a contract with a hotel and by showing his website and Facebook page, Mahmud was able to prove to the secret service that he was a tour guide and thus received income from abroad. The secret service was specifically interested in the money transfers he received from individuals who had names of Arabic origin. Mahmud explained that several tourists he guided had grown up abroad and wanted to see the country of their ancestors. The secret service officer told him that they wanted to make sure that he did not receive this money for terrorist purposes. Mahmud told me that he was allowed to leave after this interrogation. The Egyptian lawyer sat silently next to him throughout. When Mahmud asked the security state office whether he should expect more trouble, he was told that he would have not been allowed to leave unless everything was considered fine. Looking back at this incident, Mahmud was convinced that the lawyer's presence had been one of the main factors that helped him in his encounter with the Egyptian authorities.

Mu'ayad also had to come into contact with the Egyptian state. When he tried to apply for a residency permit for his cousin, who was in Syria at that time, he spent hours and hours in the *Mugamma*, waiting for the papers to be processed. Eventually, he was told that there was a problem and that he could not finalize his cousin's papers without a letter of authorization. His cousin made some phone calls and eventually Mu'ayad was phoned by an Egyptian friend of his cousin who told him to go to the office of a general in the *Mugamma*. The next day, Mu'ayad visited the employee's office and the bureaucratic procedures were completed within minutes. Mu'ayad did not describe this way of solving the problem as a heroic act of performing power. Instead, he spoke of the fear and anxiety that haunted him during the process and the even bigger dread of causing problems for his cousin that made him accept his request to make use of *wasta*.

Abu Walid, Mahmud and Mu'ayad were neither surprised nor entirely helpless when confronted by the Egyptian authorities. They had all experienced interrogation before, and in Abu Walid's case, even imprisonment. They seemed to have expected that they would have to deal with the Egyptian security service at some point and that they would have to make use of certain methods and coping strategies, such as bribery or *wasta*, when dealing with the Egyptian authorities. All of them reacted pragmatically, thinking of solutions that could ease their situation and using techniques that were common in Syria. This did not mean that they felt proud, empowered, 'smart' or in control of the situation. Instead, according to Mu'ayad, paying bribes could rather be perceived as a necessary and familiar tool to be used in Egypt, whose system resembled many aspects of that in Syria. Corruption was perceived as a means to circumvent greater problems, as a measure applied in times of despair and as a tool to save oneself.

Connecting what the three Syrian men experienced to an analysis of the plight of forced displacement could prompt the conclusion that the experience of loss of social networks and lack of in-depth knowledge about the context they lived in were, in their cases, partially retrieved. Based on their previous experiences in Syria, the three men handled their encounters with the Egyptian state by applying measures, such as bribery or making use of *wasta,* to resolve their everyday problems with the state's bureaucracy and authorities. Despite the high level of stress and anxiety all of them reported to have felt during their encounters with the Egyptian authorities, it could be argued that they retrieved a sense of agency and control over the situation, thus countering the loss that defined their experience of displacement. This could even be analysed as a way of regaining masculinity constituted through 'mastery, activity and power' (Treacher 2007: 292). However, while it is tempting to define the described narratives as a reclaiming of power and control over one's situation and a consequent boost for one's position as a man, the humble and reluctant way in which the four men described their encounters with the Egyptian state and the changes in Abu Walid's life which was induced by his contact with the state authorities made me analyse them in a less positive way. Fear and despair were the driving forces behind their engagement in bribery, *wasta* and corruption. They were vulnerable with regard to their status in Egypt, could not assess the uncertain economic and political future of the country, had just experienced a rise in xenophobia among the Egyptians and had great deal to lose. Nevertheless, in one way or another they were forced to deal with the Egyptian state – an actor considered an opponent, whose corrupt system and disrespect for human rights were well known to them.

Consequently, instead of understanding their experiences with bribery and use of connections in Egypt as winning back agency and control over their lives, I argue that the engagement in bribery, *wasta* and corruption in the new country of residency was an even more dangerous endeavour born out of the necessity to avert worse things from happening. Even though coping strategies were known from their life in Syria, in the new context in Egypt, Syrian men lacked contacts, networks and practical experiences, and were thus in an even more precarious situation when being forced to engage in bribing or making use of *wasta.* Rather than celebrating a regaining of power among Syrian men in Cairo, I argue by using Hannah Arendt's (1973: 293) voice that the loss of the 'entire social texture into which they were born and in which they established for themselves a distinct place in the world' is aggravated. As far as constructions of masculinities were concerned, Syrian men were again merely responsive and reactive rather than agents in control of their lives. They were in the hands of an authoritarian regime and had to comply with its rules.

The migration of fear

Not only *wasta,* corruption and bribery had a lasting impact on Syrian men's lives, likewise, the fear vis-à-vis the state authorities and security services continued to affect them. Majd, the student of economics, emphasized that the fear of sharing one's opinion was lasting and kept some Syrians from expressing their opinions in Egypt, even though they were no longer under the direct threat of punishment at the hands of the regime:

> Magdalena: Can you talk about politics here in Egypt?
> Majd: Yes, you are outside of Syria so it's no problem. Nevertheless, some people are still worried about their relatives in Syria and that's why they are not talking about politics here in Egypt. If the regime finds this out, those people in Syria will be in danger. In Syria, you cannot oppose anything. You are deprived of your own opinion. This is how the regime works. As for my friends and myself, we are talking about politics, but some of them are also afraid of doing so because of their relatives. Furthermore, their name could be put on the list of wanted people by the regime.

Despite being a long distance from Syria, many Syrians in Egypt did not voice their opinions out of fear for their loved ones. As described by Arendt (1973: 433/434), the totalitarian regime does not only threaten the individual's well-being, but also knows about the individual's connection to loved ones. This adds another layer of stress and enforces compliance in a perfidious way, even if the individual is no longer within the immediate scope or reach of the regime. Moreover, the fear of the *mukhabarat*, their omnipresence and survival techniques impacted on Syrian men's encounter with other Syrians in Egypt. In the words of Hani:

> At the beginning [in Egypt], I faced problems. For example, if I meet you and I know that you are Syrian, it is difficult for me to tell you immediately that I am with the revolution. I will think that it is possible that you were sent by the regime. This happened to me.

Hani's account shows that Syrian men lived with a constant suspicion, wondering whether the all-pervading gaze of the Syrian regime made it all the way to Egypt. This reduced opportunities to get in touch with other Syrians and paved the way for the existence of a 'non-community' as described in the previous chapter.

The Syrian embassy in Cairo

Syrian men's fear and anxiety were also noticeable when they spoke about the Syrian embassy in Cairo. Mu'ayad described the embassy in the district of Dokki as having the exact shape and appearance of a *mukhabarat* branch back in Syria. He thus made a revealing comparison especially when framing his statement with literature revolving around how different forms of material culture, such as uniforms, documents or buildings are central to 'how the state comes to be imagined, encountered, and reimagined by the population' (Sharma and Gupta 2006: 12 cited in Hull 2012: 260). The Syrian embassy, following Mu'ayad, with its architectural shape induces resentment and seems to remind the visitor of the power and presence of the Syrian regime. Generally, the Syrian embassy had a very bad reputation and most Syrians I met tried to avoid setting foot in it whenever they could. It was perceived as the long arm of the regime and many horrible stories grew around it. Abu Walid, for instance, shared with me the devastating story of an acquaintance of his: the Egyptian secret service had arrested his friend, and had handed him over to the Syrian embassy in Cairo, from where he was taken to Syria, where he was murdered. Similarly, Samir, who worked in an NGO providing aid to refugees, told me about the case of a Syrian contact of his, who had relatives in Syria who supported the opposition. This man went to the Syrian embassy in Cairo to renew his passport. When the employees at the embassy saw his name, they connected it to his brother in Syria, who was with the FSA. His passport was immediately destroyed and he was asked to enter the embassy. However, he ignored their request and ran away. Rumours and stories about the embassy circulated among Syrians. They are, following Feldman (2000: 48), the necessary complement to the diffuse, capillary system of state surveillance. Through these rumours the state apparatus achieves visibility and physical presence. And indeed, the undefined but present power of the Syrian state had become localized in the form of the Syrian embassy and Syrian men's migrated fear had connected itself to it.

Abu Walid compared the Syrian embassy in Egypt to 'the ministry of the interior', since it had the 'power to arrest anyone'. Based on what happened to his acquaintance, Abu Walid was tremendously afraid of any interaction with the Syrian embassy and with the Egyptian security service:

> I am wanted by the government. They will arrest me. And if I have any problem with the Egyptians, I will end up in the embassy and the embassy will send me to Syria, just as happened to my friend. The Syrian embassy has power. These days, I only go from my flat to the shop, and back. I try to avoid any contact with the Egyptians because I am afraid that the embassy has already shared my name with the Egyptian *mukhabarat*. I always try to avoid the embassy. Even if they ask for documents, I don't go.

Abu Walid's fear of the Syrian security apparatus had extended to include not only the Syrian embassy, but also the Egyptian authorities as collaborators with the Syrian regime. This fear defined and controlled various parts of his life and caused the negotiation of various constraints: if Abu Walid risked not going to the embassy to get the documents he needed to work, drive or enrol his children in school in Egypt, he would face numerous problems in his daily life. However, if he yielded to the pressure that he was exposed to by not having the documents and went to the embassy, his life could be in danger because of his past in Syria and the cruelty of the Syrian regime. He had to weigh up and negotiate the two evils. Abu Walid's situation powerfully illustrates how the power of the citizenship-giving state does not stop at the border, but follows refugees into exile, where it still has the strength to influence, affect and control their lives. The state is not defined by its geographical boundaries, but expands well beyond them.

Likewise, for Akram, who desperately needed to go to the embassy in order to get married legally in Egypt, the embassy represented the ubiquitous power and absolute sway of the Syrian regime.

> The Egyptians do not have any idea about what we face at our embassy here. The embassy presses on us if we want to renew or apply for documents, because they relate our situation here to our military situation back in Syria. There are documents that you cannot apply for unless you have finished your military service in Syria. This is the pressure coming from the Syrian government, which follows us everywhere and always, always, always ....

Sarcastically he continued:

> The beautiful thing is that if I have a problem and I want to resolve it, my embassy tells me to bring a document from Syria which confirms that I completed my military service. However, I escaped from Syria in order not to do the military service!

Akram described bitterly how the Syrian regime haunted him wherever he was, and that he, even though he had physically escaped the country, could not escape the regime's procedures, control, gaze and regulations. He was in a vulnerable situation since the Syrian state could even control and impair his life abroad – because he had not completed what the state defined as his male responsibilities.

Conclusion

This chapter has shown the importance of paying attention to men's position vis-à-vis the state of origin and the state of asylum when conceptualizing masculinities in the context of forced displacement. The state's security apparatus had left a mark on Syrian men, fixing in them suspicion, self-surveillance and anxiety they could not get rid of. Growing up in Syria meant learning to live with an omnipresent and controlling state and this knowledge instilled in Syrian men self-control when it came to the expression of their political opinion, their interests and ideas. Furthermore, this chapter has discussed how most Syrian men struggled to come to terms with the criminality of the Syrian regime: it was known to them that the regime and its authorities engaged in illegal activities, such as accepting bribes, and Syrian men were aware that the state's criminality dragged them into the same illegal structures. They had to comply with a system, that was immoral in most men's eyes, and they blamed the state for the immorality enforced on them. They were aware that the state had major control over their lives, potential, development and aspirations. Having grown up under a dictatorial regime and having fled to a country with a similar regime impacted on Syrian men's everyday lives and caused self-censorship, suspicion, fear, depression, isolation and self-loathing. Green (1994: 227) analysed fear in Guatemala as 'a way of life', 'a chronic condition' and a 'collective imagination'. She argues that fear is a reality 'that is factored into the choices women and men make'. In this chapter, I have expanded her argument by pointing out that the omnipresent fear and suspicion Syrians experienced in their home country did not stop at the Syrian border. In fact, it was mobile and not geographically fixed and located, but travelled with many of my interlocutors to Egypt where it connected itself with the embassy, other Syrians and foreigners. I suggest that the palpable presence of the Egyptian and Syrian states in men's everyday lives affected their sense of manhood: it bent and twisted them to an extent that they were unable to develop and show agency, subjectivity and selfhood. There was a constant threat to their ability to protect their loved ones from suffering the same fate. Syrian men reported to experience that they were left with no other option but enforced obedience and adaptation to the authoritarian systems they lived under, no way to break free from the ubiquitous states, no opportunity to convey the knowledge they had to their children and loved ones to give them access to a better, more informed, self-determined life. Ultimately, this chapter has illustrated how Syrian men move on from a form of paradoxical, insecure citizenship to a similarly insecure status as refugees in Egypt. Both legal statuses require interactions with the state that do not conform with Syrian men's morals and values. The overriding theme defining interactions with both states is the anticipation of severe consequences for oneself and one's family, if one does not accept the states' practices and thus men endure constant anxiety and engage in self-censorship.

CONCLUSION: ON MASCULINITIES, FORCED DISPLACEMENT, MIDDLE-CLASSNESS AND RELATIONS WITH THE NATION STATE

Fadi's reaction to a begging woman on the streets of Cairo made me question my assumed knowledge at the beginning of my fieldwork in 2014. This ethnographic vignette has helped me to introduce this book with its obvious and underlying themes and topics. With a description of his actions I started this work and with a reference to his situation I will end it. Despite all his efforts, ideas and trials, Fadi did not manage to remain on the path he aspired to follow. His dream is to become an engineer; however, he had to interrupt his studies at the university after he had successfully finished his first year. He could not afford the university fees and his family needed his support in the little corner shop they had bought. For a while, Fadi thought about leaving Egypt for Europe, he wondered whether there were scholarships for which he could apply and he calculated that if he took on a second shop in the evenings after he finished his shift in his parents' shop, he might be able to go back to university to continue with his studies. He hoped that after graduation from university he would be able to get married and live a more settled life. In 2018, when we chatted he did not talk about his return to university anymore. He wanted to attend a couple of English courses, he said, and thought about volunteering again. His dreams and ideas about the future seemed to align with the life that was in reach in Egypt. The work on this book has finished after several years, but Fadi's as well as other Syrians' struggles in Egypt, other parts of the Middle East and Europe are far from over: their daily challenges in finding work, dealing with the refugee label, coping with uncertainty, liminality and the loss of their home, status and capital, the coming to terms with their memories and experiences of Syria, the uprising and the civil war, as well as the challenges to find a secure future and liveable present, are an ongoing condition.

Having travelled to Egypt for three short visits after the official end of my fieldwork at the end of September 2015, I went to Cairo for a last time in the spring of 2016. Um Mazin and her family had left Egypt for Germany, just like Firas and Abu Muhammad with their families; Mu'ayad and Laith had settled and found work in Sweden; Abd al-Rahman, Israa and Israa's family had moved to the Netherlands; Nur had recently arrived in Sweden; Um Khalid's family was still in Turkey, and Abu Walid's family had been resettled to Scotland. Over the past two years, I heard that Mazin, Laith and Mu'ayad had got married and became fathers just like Abd al-Rahman. Similarly, Mahmud, Akram and Dawud, who were still in Egypt, had become fathers in the past years and also Rafi's wife gave birth to their fourth child; Layla's daughter managed to graduate from university; Majd had got engaged; Abu Nabil and Abu Khalid still contacted me every now and then to ask whether I had access to donations for Syrians in need; Muhannad worked on a second project aside from *Fursa* and travelled the world to participate in workshops and conferences to talk about his experiences as a young, Syrian CEO of an NGO. Life went on and my fieldwork that took place between August 2014 and September 2015 appeared like a fleeting visit that had allowed me to gain a brief idea about my interlocutors' lives at a specific point in time. It had given me a glimpse of their masculine trajectories that were deeply defined by the uncertainty, liminality and insecurity that marked the first years of their forced displacement. Not only my interlocutors' individual lives had moved on, the scene in which my fieldwork had taken place had changed as well: Europe had experienced the so-called 'refugee crisis' in 2015 and 2016 turning the spotlight to refugees from the Middle East and especially to refugees from Syria. Frequently, the specific situation of refugee men was publicly discussed, for instance after the image of Aylan Kurdi and his grieving father went viral. The plight of refugee men and its representation during the so-called refugee crisis have also gained scholarly attention (Allsopp 2017; Pruitt et al. 2018). The Middle East has seen further uproar with protests and demonstrations in Sudan, Iraq and Lebanon. Yemen's war is still ongoing and similarly there is no end to the Syrian civil war in sight.

On (constructions of) masculinities

My aim in this book was to focus on Syrian men's experiences during forced displacement in Egypt. Committed to an intersectional analysis, I attempted to show the various forms of social differentiation that played a role in the lives of Syrian refugee men I met in Egypt. My main focus was set on formations of masculinities during forced displacement. Firstly, I used masculinity as a lens to get a sense of the different challenges that defined Syrian men's lives during displacement, such as their memories of sectarianism, growing up with militarization or their relationship with the Syrian and Egyptian states. Secondly, I paid attention to men's active formations of masculinities. I found othering, the creation of hierarchies, masculinization against women and a combination of various registers of manhood according to their availability in the specific social context to be especially prominent among Syrian refugee men in Egypt. Thirdly, I found that constructions of masculinities proved to be elastic and tensile in contexts of forced displacement.

When using the study of masculinities as a perspective to understand difficulties that Syrian men face, it is possible to analyse 'the flexible as well as not-so-flexible and the durable as well as not-so-durable aspects of construction of gendered identifications and how their interplay shapes masculine trajectories' (Ghannam 2013: 168). I found that in direct and indirect ways growing up under a repressive regime and being exposed to militarization by the hands of the regime impacted on ideas of manhood. It meant both enforced adaptation to the normalization of violence in the everyday and active strategizing and manoeuvring. In a similar vein, memories of injustice based on a system of sectarian preferences that advantaged foremost the Alawi sect proved to have a significant impact, despite rarely accounted for, on formations of manhood. If certain groups are more directly associated with authority and social power, then men who do not have access to this authority can only exist at its periphery. Again, on the one hand, men need to adjust and comply with pressures, constraints and the confrontation with unfair yet unchangeable power structures and accept its influence on them, and, on the other hand, men prove their awareness and active coping with it in everyday life. And finally, the everyday encounters with the nation states, the constant surveilling gaze of the regime and the fear thereof become defining features of men's lifeworlds during forced displacement if analysed from a gendered lens. The palpable presence of the Syrian state in Syrian men's lives causes both active negotiations and self-surveillance, suspicion and self-loathing proving its direct and indirect influence on constructions of masculinities.

Syrian men engaged in various processes with the aim to clarify their position as respectable men. Most prominently, there was othering as a tactic in Syrian men's constructions of masculinities. Through othering – that is, 'to compete in a situation in which they will always win' (Kimmel 1994: 134), men could establish themselves as respectable men at the opposite end of the continuum. Essentializing, homogenization and stereotyping were the concrete strategies Syrian men applied in their narratives to create the other and consequently a more successful version of themselves. To mention but some of the 'types' that Syrian men created as their other, there was the refugee in Europe who preferred being fed over hard work, there was the unemployed Syrian man who accepted his female kin's labour and there was the lazy Egyptian who engaged in all kinds of practices to avoid hard work. Stereotypes that had expediency related to low work ethics and lack of morals and to those character traits that could not be aligned with respectable forms of manhood. Then, there was the tactic to highlight different registers of manhood when it was helpful in a specific context, featuring the idea of compositeness. Composite masculinities are

> contingent and fluid constellations of acts, attitudes, relationships and physicalities that men weave into coherent masculine selfhoods through a variety of social and bodily practices. (Wentzell 2015: 179)

I value in Wentzell's concept the focus on coherence, since I found that most men tried to turn ambiguities and uncertainties into logical, consistent masculine identities which often required considerable effort.

As far as the elasticity of masculinities was concerned, I do not aim to essentialize constructions of masculinities and ascribe to them an inherent quality. Rather, I recognize 'the layering, the potential internal contradiction, within all practices that construct masculinities' (Connell and Messerschmidt 2005: 852). Yet, I found that Syrian men I met in Egypt performed their manhood so that I could only think of them as tensile and elastic able to incorporate blows, 'unmanly' emotions and strategies that the circumstances of forced displacement enforced on them. Among these challenges and blows to masculinities were threats to Syrian men's roles as providers, questions on their 'groom-ability', as well as Syrian men's remembered encounters and experiences with authoritarian, sectarian states. Several scholars have described men's confrontation with, and responses to, similar challenges by making use of the notion of 'masculinity in crisis'. Even though I recognize the severity of the various issues Syrian men were confronted with, I abstain from using the term 'crisis' and suggest instead to conceive of masculinities as responsive, elastic and tensile. Syrian men found ways to reconfirm themselves despite sentiments of self-loathing, humiliation and shame. Being broken as a man by the circumstances was not an option. Rather, Syrian men engaged in various narratives, discourses and practices to present an acceptable version of manhood in front of others. These narratives, discourses and practices had to incorporate emotions and other aspects that could not be associated with ideal images of masculinity.

This work has shown that masculinities are relational and that they are dependent on and connected with others. Formations of manhood are a 'collective project' dependent on views, instructions and conduct of the people around them (Ghannam 2013: 166). An important 'other' for Syrian men is women. Women symbolized the weaker, less able and resilient counterpart, who were defined as in need of support and help from the hands of men. Women's devaluation and the creation of a static image of femininity helped men to form a complementary valued form of masculinity. Masculinities and femininities were interrelated and interdependent (Connell and Messerschmidt 2005). The existence of femininity, defined as weak, dependent and less resilient, guaranteed that men were never positioned in the lowest part of their social lifeworld. Nevertheless, this does not mean that women were merely 'an oppositional mirror against which men define themselves' (Ghannam. 2013: 166). In fact, women had enormous power to protect or destroy men's reputation, bestow or deny men recognition and legitimacy and were aware of this power. Women even had the ability to severely challenge men's standing, for example, as unreachable and demanding brides or as 'lost' women, who married Egyptian men. In addition, women defined the contours of the community. Their value equated the standing of Syrians as a whole, and thus men had various reasons to aim to control 'their' women. If Syrian women were perceived as 'cheap' or 'easy to get', it automatically caused a diminishment of 'Syrianness' and Syrian men's position and ability to 'save' their women, as laid out in the fourth chapter. Conversely, women's position could also become a 'proof' of men's success as providers for the family, as grooms and as caring fathers. Consequently, I suggest conceiving of masculinities as not able to exist without a form of femininity, which is as much as possible discursively created by men themselves. Men construct femininities with an intention and a purpose – in this work I presented that femininities were formed to be the 'other', the controlled and the 'boundary guards' of the community.

Engaging in an intersectional analysis brought to the fore the specific challenges that young men encountered. Similarly, men who were fathers faced explicit difficulties. Young men were in the ambiguous position of being at the scope of the militant parties involved in the civil war; at the same time, they could not decide freely about whether they wanted to participate in the war or not. They were 'protected' by their families and did not have to actively take a stance pro or against military masculinity. Thus, it was not clear whether the family's interference was blessing or curse. Young men also struggled as not-yet-grown-up-sons who could not enjoy the perks of their position but had to shelve their own plans and personal growth to prioritize support of the family in Egypt. They had to defer studying, getting married and roaming the streets with their friends in their everyday lives. In the first place, these young men were sons and were treated as such with all its advantages and disadvantages. Being a not-yet-grown-up-son during forced displacement meant control of emotions and functioning in the way that was best for the family. In a similar vein, fathering men were in a specific position. On the one hand, they were burdened with responsibility for their children. Several Syrian men felt strained by the fact that they could not live up to the ideal father they aspired to be. It is for the sake of their children that they try to be stringent, in control and ready to meet their parental obligations even if challenged by their current circumstances. Implicit in the position of fathers is being part of a generation that tolerated and adapted to a repressive regime for too long and allowed for this situation to happen. However, this is not the complete picture: several Syrian men I met seemed to benefit from their position as fathers. It was one of the available roles when other acceptable and respectable notions of manhood were temporarily or permanently inaccessible.

Being a middle-class man

Belonging to the middle class was a dominant and defining marker of identity among Syrian men in Egypt. They associated middle-classness with success, education, hard work, creativity, smartness, resilience and stamina. Their continuous struggle to confirm their class position shows that for Syrian men losing their middle-class status was not an option. Being middle class was seen and used as a proof of their intellect, behaviour and access to the world. Furthermore, being middle class guaranteed respect, aspirations and self-esteem. A major aspect of concern that related to their middle-classness was Syrian men's access to paid labour. Paid labour in an accepted and respected profession was a way to prove their inherent values, such as creativity, diligence, hard work, stamina, inventiveness and their education. In Egypt, however, Syrians were confronted with vulnerability, instability and precarity in the labour market, and what peeked around the corner, seemingly waiting for them at any minute, was unemployment, to which shame, idleness and dependency were ascribed. When looking at the importance of work in an honourable profession and the fear of unemployment, as described in the third chapter, it can be argued that being middle class was directly related to a constant fear of being unable to prove it (see Heiman et al. 2012).

Moreover, Syrian men experienced that established class structures in Egypt were subject to change: especially bachelors trying to get married in Egypt realized that they were not recognizable as decent, middle-class men anymore and could not rely on what used to define them, as I described in the fourth chapter. Syrian men were unrecognizable because the family of a potential spouse could not access the 'frame of reference' (Rabo 2005) by which a potential groom was socially classified back in Syria; that is, they could not access knowledge about his family's reputation, his place of origin, his upbringing and education. Several young men feared that class differences or the inability to prove one's initial class status would cause rejection. Other bachelors looking for brides, however, realized that Syrians' mutually experienced forced displacement had put them and the bride's family in the same situation and that previous class differences were erased. What is obvious is that traditional class boundaries were differently experienced: some men sensed that they sharpened or kept intact, while others witnessed that they had become blurry and porous. Consequently, I come to the conclusion that traditional barriers and statuses do not remain static, but are subject to change in times of crisis, uncertainty and liminality. Moreover, I observed that the changing values ascribed to class and the unpredictable handlings of and responses to traditional class structures caused confusion, insecurity and uproar. Being recognized as a respectable middle-class man (and groom) was imperative and the experience of having one's previously accumulated resources and masculine identity nullified was extremely painful.

My analysis of Syrian men's longing for being read as middle-class requires an understanding of class as a 'relational and interproductive phenomenon' (Heiman et al. 2012: 13) emerging in relation to other classes. This relational characteristic is obvious when paying attention to Syrian men's implicit creation of 'other' social classes to be able to demarcate and refine their own social position. I suggest that Syrian men created a class structure that functioned as visible markers in relation to which they could define their middle-classness by relating to 'other' men who had chosen less respected life paths or proved to have 'shameful' morals. Syrian men implicitly described themselves as middle class, when they positioned themselves vis-à-vis 'refugees in Europe', who beg and wait for the welfare system to take care of them, or the 'lazy Egyptian worker', who prefers cheating over honest, hard work, presented in the fifth chapter. Consequently, I argue that being middle class should not only be conceptualized as relational and interproductive, but also as both a conscious and an unconscious endeavour (see Rizzo 2015; Bourdieu 1985). Furthermore, it was obvious that class constituted gender and vice versa (Connell 2013; Scott 1999). I observed that Syrian men engaged in actions and efforts to form class and masculinities that were predominantly overlapping. The 'refugee in Europe' is not only an (emasculated) man but an (emasculated) classed man; likewise, the 'lazy Egyptian worker' is not only a man, but a man showing values that do not align with middle-classness. Thus, in the context of forced displacement, in which both masculinities and social class structures are shaken and in need to be actively re-invented, these aspects are not only interrelated and intersecting, but are constituted through each other. Overall, social class proves to be a significant object of analysis in the context of forced displacement, since it sheds light on how men position themselves, try to prove their identity and lay out their life trajectories. The study of aspired social class belonging brings together imaginaries of the future, how men remember and narrate their past, and their struggles and strivings in the present tense. Furthermore, social class should be understood as an instrument of hierarchization and a parameter of judgement of others.

Coping with the nation state

On of the leitmotifs emerging in this work is Syrian men's strong, yet ambivalent and paradoxical relation to the nation state. The significance of the state for Syrian men's lives shows in various forms: firstly, Syrian men were conscious that they had lost a direct, securing connection to the state when they could not do what was defined as one of their duties as citizens, namely, protecting their country. Having lost their trust in the parties and groups involved in the uprising and the civil war, as described in the first chapter, most Syrian men in Egypt felt unable to defend their home country. They did not see a setting for themselves through which they could engage in meaningful protection of their country and consequently had to leave their home country behind. Secondly, Syrian men's understanding of the state is expressed in the image of the abject 'other' embodied by the 'refugee in Europe', which I presented in the second chapter. The discourse around the undignified 'refugee in Europe' proves that, according to Syrian men's understanding, the citizen had the duty to aim for economic self-sufficiency and that depending on the state's welfare was not a dignified option. Furthermore, Syrian men were concerned about the invalidity of their identity papers, such as passports or driving licences, and whether they would be directly accepted by the Egyptian state and its authorities. Syrian men feared loss, expiration or invalidity of documents, which they related to a questioned, unsound personal identity. Closely connected to this theme was Syrian men's awareness of being effectively unprotected by the Syrian and the Egyptian state institutions during their forced displacement. State services, especially from the Syrian embassy, were perceived to be unavailable and the right to be protected from crime and ill will in Egypt seemed out of reach. Turning to alternative service providers, such as UNHCR or other aid organizations, could not restore the stability Syrian men felt to have lost in exile. Missing their secure ground in the form of the citizen-state relationship caused several Syrian men to question themselves as human beings and their consequent right to be in this world, as described in the second chapter. They felt betrayed by a system that used to grant them an identity and rights based on a state-citizen relationship that they could, however, not resort to in Egypt. Their state had provided them with a form of stability and protection that they could not find during forced displacement and thus living in exile translated for most Syrian men to being an apathetic, disrespected, merely tolerated person, a guest, who could not risk behaving as if his citizen-state relationship was still intact. In Chapter 5, I described the nostalgia Syrian men expressed with regard to the UAR and their wish to see Syria turning back into an economically and politically stable state, which holds international relations and is respected in the region and in the world. This discourse symbolizes again men's longing for a state that could function as identity-establishing and as their backbone.

On the one hand, Syrian men expressed in these various ways their difficulties in being without a strong Syrian state that functioned as their mainstay granting them rights, protection, responsibilities, duties and an unquestionable, strong identity. On the other hand, however, men were critical of the nation state's oppressive nature and were haunted by its omnipresent gaze and far-reaching control. They were aware of the state's privileging of certain sects, a theme that emerged in the fifth chapter. Moreover, they struggled to come to terms with the criminality of the Syrian regime: it was known to them that the regime and its authorities engaged in illegal activities, such as accepting bribes, nepotism and corruption, and Syrian men were aware that the state's criminality dragged them into the same illegal structures – the main theme of Chapter 6. They had to comply with a system that was immoral in most men's eyes and they blamed the state for the immorality enforced on them in their interaction with the state and the inability to conform to honourable versions of masculinity. They were aware that the state had major control over their lives, potential, development and aspirations. Furthermore, the state's security apparatus had left a mark on Syrian men, fixing in them a form of suspicion, self-surveillance and anxiety they could not get rid of. Growing up in Syria meant learning to live with an omnipresent and controlling state and this knowledge instilled in Syrian men self-control when it came to the expression of their political opinion, their interests and ideas. Furthermore, the state enforced a militaristic upbringing that men could not circumvent, whether they agreed with this kind of upbringing or were critical of it, as described in the first chapter.

Based on these various forms in which the state appeared in and impacted on Syrian men's lives, I argue that Syrian men had a paradoxical connection to the state that could, on the one hand, reassure them and back them up, but could, on the other hand, severely damage them, plague them, exhaust them and ultimately challenge them in their manhood. The state was a provider of their position as men, but at the same time it robbed them of their manhood. Upon their forced displacement, when their contact to the state had ultimately changed, Syrian men severely critiqued the state but simultaneously bemoaned its loss. Syrian men felt both insecure and fragile in the absence of the state, but at the same time suffocated and tortured in their experiences and encounters with it.

Memories, the present tense and an uncertain future

In an attempt to understand what defines the existential experience of forced displacement, it seems that muddled temporalities and the sinuosity of memories play major roles. The structure of most chapters shows the omnipresence and equal presence of both: aspects pertaining to the here and now in Egypt and to the past in Syria. I found Syrian men's thinking, explanations, actions and practices to be deeply informed by their lives back in Syria as well as their current situation in Egypt. In Syrian men's narratives, there was a 'textual weave, which connects not only past to present but also old country thoughts to new country realities' (Naguib 2018: 290/291). Memories and recollections from the past tainted and coloured the everyday life in Egypt. What came from the past, travelled with Syrian men to Egypt, could sometimes connect to the present in unforeseeable ways. The before and after and the here and there were muddled, sinuous and deeply entangled. In the uncertainty of the first years after the Syrian uprising, Syrian men had not yet managed to put emotions, memories, experiences and atmospheres in order. The condition of enforced change that caused their move to Egypt featured as a prominent rupture in their lives, and the here and there and the before and after were not yet put in their places.

NOTES

Introduction

1   Following Thomassen's (2012: 690) definition of a 'political revolution', what happened in Syria in 2011 and in the years to come cannot be considered a revolution because what is missing is the actual overthrow of the regime. Syrian men and women in Egypt used the terms 'revolution' *(thawra)*, 'events' *(ahdath)* and 'crisis' *(azma)*, when they referred to the situation in Syria in and after 2011. People who called it 'a revolution' were usually considered to be pro-uprising, while people who defined it as 'events' or 'crisis' were assumed to side with the regime.

2   Malkki (1995; 1996) coined the term 'refugeeness' in her research of Hutu refugees from Burundi in Tanzania. She found that the embodiment of refugeeness played out differently in the contexts she analysed. Adopting and embodying refugeeness was also expected on the part of refugee administrators.

3   Kimmel (1994: 128) argues that it is in front of 'other' men that one wants to prove one's manhood and that masculinities achieve meaning 'in opposition to a set of "others" – racial minorities, sexual minorities, and, above all, women' (1994: 120).

4   I watched and translated his speech in September 2015 via the following link: https://m.youtube.com/watch?v=jqfkVupCabs.

5   When I came to Egypt at the beginning of August 2014, it was not my first visit to the Middle East. I had spent a year volunteering in a Coptic orphanage in Cairo directly after I graduated from school in 2007/2008. In the following years, I returned to Egypt for several internships that lasted between two and six months, spent six months in Palestine and visited several other countries in the Middle East. In 2009, I spent six months in Syria studying Arabic at the University of Damascus. This time gave me an idea about the regime, its security apparatus and Syrian society in a nutshell.

6   This could not be taken for granted in Syria. There were several groups in Syria, for instance, approximately 200,000 Syrian Kurds, who were considered 'stateless'.

7   Generally, life for refugees in urban contexts differs notably from the more restrictive experience of encampment. Studies have found that refugees in cities are more often able to generate income, mostly through informal labour. They can more often rely on social capital, that is, local friendships, aid organizations, charity-minded individuals or diasporic communities (Jacobsen 2006: 283). Thus, living in an urban context can translate into social mobility and freedom of movement (Landau and Duponchel 2011: 5). Conversely, however, refugees are struggling under the challenges the receiving cities face, such as over-population, inadequate infrastructure and insufficient public services (Buscher 2013: 17). They may lack support networks, face legal uncertainties due to their status and become victims of xenophobia (see Sommers 2001; Dryden-Peterson 2006; Briant and Kennedy 2004, Sperl 2001; Jacobsen et al. 2012).

8   Luhrmann (1996: vii), among others, used the term '"appointment" anthropology' to describe her fieldwork that was mainly informed by meetings with numerous people individually. I was inspired to apply this term by a lecture entitled '"Ethnography by

Appointment": Studying Muslims in Corporate and Bureaucratic Settings', held by Patricia Sloane-White at the MPI in Halle, Germany in September 2017.

9   Giulio Regeni was a PhD student from Cambridge conducting fieldwork on labour unions in Cairo. He disappeared on the fifth anniversary of the Egyptian revolution and was found dead showing signs of torture in a ditch close to 6th of October City several days later. There is strong evidence suggesting that the Egyptian secret service is responsible for his murder (see Amnesty International 2017; Nassif 2017; Soliman 2017).

10   This concept was introduced by Carrigan et al. (1985). It was then critiqued and partially re-written by Connell and Messerschmidt (2005).

11   Several scholars have expressed their critique of the concept of 'hegemonic masculinity': critiques referring to the nature of men's conformity to hegemonic masculinity (e.g. Wetherell and Edley 1999); the concept's failure to recognize situations in which various hegemonic masculinities coexist (see Cornwall and Lindisfarne 1994: 20); or the constructed dualism of hegemonic and non-hegemonic masculinities (Demitrou 2001).

12   According to Butler (1999: 173), gender is an ongoing bodily performance of imitating what is broadly understood as acceptable acts, behaviours and desires. Nevertheless, performativity is not a choice but a repetitive 'practice of improvisation within a scene of constraint' (2004: 1). Gender norms define how one can appear in public, how the public and the private are distinguished, who becomes subject to stigmatization and who experiences precarity in one's surrounding (2009: iii). Thus, gender performativity is constrained by the boundaries in which a subject becomes eligible for recognition and is perceived and accepted as a living being (2004: 4). I take from Butler's work that being a man is a performance that requires constant work and takes place by positioning oneself within a broader framework of acceptable gender relations and ideals.

13   For a critique of scholarship dealing with masculinities in the Middle East, see Hasso (2018).

14   In the field of (forced) migration studies, there has been a similar turn to researching gender issues and masculinities over the past decades.

15   There has been a long debate among anthropologists researching class whether it is a material phenomenon or an associational category of people striving for similar socio-political goals. A convincing argument is that the very use of the term infers a materialist perspective and invites for an understanding of class as a sociocultural phenomenon and a group experience based on socioeconomic difference (Heiman, Liechty and Freeman 2012: 8/9).

Chapter 1

1   Following Haddad (2012), for rural youth, it was army recruitment that helped them to get access to the heart of Syrian society.

Chapter 2

1   The World Food Program assisted vulnerable Syrian refugees in Egypt since 2013 through food vouchers (https://www.wfp.org/news/wfp-expands-food-assistance-egypt-include-refugees-multiple-countries).

2   The group's action did not mark the first time that the Cairo office of UNHCR was
     severely criticized for major inconsistencies and illegalities leading to an overall sense
     of mistrust among asylum seekers in Egypt (Fiddian 2006: 298/299). In 2005, a major
     protest and sit-in organized by Sudanese refugees in Cairo ended in bloodshed after
     the Egyptian police emptied the protest camp, where people were protesting about
     conditions in Egypt and demanding resettlement in a third country. Anger had
     been rising because of prolonged waiting periods and non-transparent and biased
     procedures (Rowe 2009: 7/8).
3   Ascribing status to a person based on their means of transportation to a new country
     is not unique. In a process of distancing themselves from the newcomers and in order
     to reassert their national belonging, American identity and loyalty, the Arab diaspora
     in Detroit engaged in a process of stigmatization of the newly arrived 'others' by
     calling them 'boaters' (Howell and Shryock 2011: 79/80).

Chapter 3

1   Turner (2019) argues that the perception of Syrian refugees in Jordan's Za'atari camp
     as successful 'refugee entrepreneurs' relates to colonial hierarchies that pervade
     humanitarian work. It confirms a vision of Syrians as 'Levantines' and 'natural
     traders'.
2   The reputation Syrians hold as entrepreneurs varies tremendously in different
     contexts even if these contexts are in close geographic proximity (Turner 2019: 13).
3   According to Ayoub and Khallaf's (2014: 25) study among Syrian refugees, 45.5 per
     cent of their respondents reported work as their only source of income while the rest
     depended on a combination of work, financial aid and/or withdrawing from savings
     to sustain their livelihoods. While a third of the respondents reported to be satisfied
     with their current job, those not satisfied mentioned low wages, difficult work
     conditions, and a mismatch between their jobs and their level of education. Moreover,
     work was perceived as unstable and irregular, and respondents felt they could be
     dismissed at any time (2014: 28).
4   According to Ayoub (2017), irregular income ranging from 300 LE to 1000 LE
     and a rent payment of 250 LE, the condition she found among some of her Syrian
     respondents, are less than the minimum wage for government employees in Egypt
     and slightly above Egypt's domestic poverty line which is equivalent to 326 LE per
     month.
5   Ghannam (2013: 71) elaborates on this aspect. She argues that young men's
     freedom and mobility are perceived as part of their spatial and social knowledge of
     the city.
6   For a similar argument, see Ghannam (2013); Inhorn (2012); Peteet (1994).
7   According to Wentzell (2015: 179), being a man demands different actions depending
     on the specific context. Masculinities are composite collections of action, attitudes
     and performances that are made to hang together to become coherent images. Men
     consciously weave materials available in their current life into a coherent, complete
     selfhood.
8   Changing notions of fatherhood have become a focus of anthropologists in the past
     years. Anthropologists have hinted at the interdependence of cultural and economic

transformations in the ways men engage in parenting and understand their roles as fathers (see, for example, Gutmann (1996)). Like manhood, fatherhood is described as unstable, ever-changing and as being dependent on the various social contexts men encounter in their everyday lives (Inhorn et al. 2015: 7). Fatherhood can have two entirely contradictory repercussions: it can become an arena to prove masculinity or a core challenge to notions of manhood. The specific conditions and challenges that fathers encounter during forced migration have been accounted for: Este and Tachble (2009) find that Sudanese refugee men in Canada suffered from the consequences of underemployment and unemployment on their position as fathers. Fiddian-Qasmiyeh (2010: 307) and Qasmiyeh argue that male asylum seekers and refugees in the UK suffered from the challenge to be a caring, knowledgeable and productive parent. Szczepanikova (2005) suggests that Chechen men in the Czech Republic experience loss of self-esteem because of their difficulties to sustain their families.

9   Muhannad's account echoes Rabo's (2005: 53/90) analysis of the interdependence and needed cooperation of fathers and sons in shops of the *souq* of Aleppo as well as Joseph's (1994: 11/12) classical concept of patriarchal connectivity which describes a person's fluid boundaries and intended involvement with others in a system that is predominantly organized around gendered and aged domination. The relationship of fathers and sons is, according to Joseph (1993), frequently defined by idealization, support and bonding as well as expected compliance by sons.

10   Jaji's (2009: 192) analysis of young refugee men in Kenya comes to mind, in which she argues that the painful situation for men in exile is often triggered by their inability to live up to their pre-flight aspirations and interpretations of the concept of masculinity.

11   Following Ghannam (2013: 105), 'women's support, instructions, and corrections are structured by social norms that define proper men and by a strong desire to see their male relatives become men who are respected and cherished by themselves and others'.

12   The accounts I collected from Syrian men dealing with women's 'natural weakness' resonate with an argument put forward by Barrett (1996: 133), namely, that 'masculinity achieves meaning within patterns of difference'. According to Barrett (1996), 'if success for men is associated with "not quitting" in the face of hardships, femininity becomes associated with quitting, complaining, and weakness'. This follows Kimmel's (1994) argument that notions of masculinity depend on changing definitions of women and gay men who serve as the "others" against which heterosexual men construct and project an identity.'

13   Griffiths (2015: 476/480) found during her research among men who have been refused asylum in the UK that unemployment and poverty were associated with the stigma of idleness and dependency and contributed to a feeling of loss of control. Unemployment was also experienced as a disruption of normality, and the consequent vulnerability was a source of shame. Likewise, Jaji (2009: 182) observed that young refugee men from the Great Lakes Region who settled in Kenya felt marginalized and unable to live up to their own standards of masculinity due to unemployment during their displacement. Unemployed men living with their families sensed that their roles as husband and father were undermined, especially if humanitarian organizations intervened, which caused them to feel inadequate, undignified and insecure (2009: 8/9).

14   Ghannam (2013) highlights the importance of the spousal relationship for men's standing and observes that women would often overemphasize their husband's work

and effort and undermine their own. This behaviour helps support the standing of a man and the woman in this case 'garner[s] for him the kind of public recognition and legitimacy central to a masculine trajectory' (2013: 7).

15 Szczepanikova (2010: 465) argues that male and female refugees from the former Soviet Union in the Czech Republic considered it undignified for a man to ask for help from strangers and acknowledge his helplessness and dependency. This was related to a dominant idea that considers masculinity to be incompatible with asking for help. As a result, men rarely approached the Czech aid organizations but sent their female family members instead.

Chapter 4

1   This does not mean that getting married was an easy endeavour. In fact, age of first marriage for both men and women has risen in many parts of the Middle East and North Africa region. For the context of Egypt, it is the rising cost of marriage, increased poverty, little employment opportunities, among other factors, that delayed marriage (Hasso 2010).

2   The *mahr* is a transaction from the groom and his household to the bride's family. The amount is agreed on before the engagement and is paid before the wedding (Kastrinou 2016: 104). The *mahr* is usually divided into two parts: the first one is the prompt *mahr* (*muqaddam*) to be paid at the time of marriage; the second one is the deferred *mahr* (*mu'ajjal/mu'akhir*) that is paid upon the dissolution of the marriage by death or divorce (Fournier 2013: 141). The amount of the *mahr* is of great significance because it is commonly understood to confirm the 'value' of the bride (see Rabo 2005: 87).

3   Similar wedding customs, habits and negotiations are described for Egypt (see Ghanam 2013; Hoodfar 1997) and other parts of the Middle East (e.g. Adeley 2016; Mundy 1995).

4   In Syria, it is more common to say: 'he was born with a golden spoon in his mouth'.

5   Referring to family engagement as 'the old traditions' versus 'the modern way' of getting to know each other without the family's involvement is a misleading dichotomy. The families' consent is usually of utmost importance, even if couples court without the knowledge or instigation of the families (Adeley 2016). Kreil (2016) argues for the Egyptian context that most marriages are located somewhere along the continuum of a union against the families' will and the families' indifference for the partners' choices.

6   Adeley (2016: 112) sees a similar trend: most of her interviewees believed that a compatible class background and shared cultural norms were the basis for a functioning marriage. Likewise, Kreil (2016) finds that for most Egyptians the spouses' similarities regarding social and family background are highly relevant.

7   Reay et al. (2009) apply the metaphor of the 'fish being out of water' to the context of working-class students in elite universities.

8   Similarly, Johnson et al. (2009: 14/15) describe that commonly experienced economic hardship during the first Intifada made marriage arrangements beyond social classes possible.

9   Before 2011, this was approximately 4,000 US dollars and 6,000 US dollars.

Chapter 5

1   In Syria prior to the war, there were 23 million Syrians of whom around 75 per cent were Sunnis; around 10 per cent Alawis; 10 per cent Christians; and 5 per cent of the populations were Druze, Shia, Ismaili and Yezidis (Bandak 2014; Hokayem 2013; Løland 2019). Regarding its ethnic composition, the majority of Syrians were Arabs and the minorities were Kurds, Armenians and Turcomans (Løland 2019; Van Dam 2017).

2   Zisser (1999: 135) describes the Alawites' trajectory in Syria as a passage 'from ethnic minority to ruling sect'. He defines the central elements in the process of Alawi mastery over Syria as: consolidation of the Alawite community within the army and the Ba'th Party hidden behind the leadership of Hafez al-Asad; the transformation of the community into the main support of the regime; and the establishment of a covenant between the Alawites and other groups.

3   Løland (2019) comes to a similar conclusion with many of her research participants remembering the time before the war as defined by peaceful relations among the different religious groups in society.

4   Faisal al-Qassem is a Syrian Aljazeera host. He is the moderator of the weekly show 'The Opposite Direction', in which two guests discuss key debates of the Arab world (Lynch 2006).

5   This relates to Ismail's (2018: 191) argument that spatial sectarianization had occurred during processes of internal migration and settlement and in patterns of employment and integration into state institutions.

6   According to Kastrinou (2016: 175), *jama'iyyat* are informal groups that are neither registered nor affiliated with the state. These groups, which were pervasive in Syria, comprised networks of friends, families, members of specific occupations, neighbours and sometimes cut across religious and ethnic divides (2016, 2012: 66). Their members meet with the aim of collecting fees from each participant that are paid to a different member of the group each time the group comes together. It is thus best described as a 'rotating credit association' (2012, 2016: 175). Kastrinou (2016: 180) argues that the establishment of *jama'iyyat* supports 'Syrian inventiveness and efficiency in creating spaces that occupy the in-between space of state and household' (2016: 180).

7   Egypt and Syria, under Gamal Abdel Nasser and Sabri al-Asali, proclaimed the Egyptian-Syrian United Arab Republic in February 1958. The unity was declared after Syria stood up and supported Egypt, which was attacked by France, England and Israel in the Suez Crisis. The UAR was perceived as the only option to counter Western hegemony over the Middle East. Podeh (1999: 5–7) describes the widespread appeal of pan-Arabism, the charismatic nature of Gamal Abdel Nasser's leadership and Syria's and Egypt's similar foreign policies as the main factors that encouraged and facilitated the existence of an Egyptian-Syrian union. However, several factors worked against the idea of a union, such as the physical absence of a mutual border, the different composition of the Egyptian and Syrian societies, differences in economies and politics that assured a difficult integration and a perceived superiority to the other existing in both countries (1999: 2–5). Syria held a subordinate role in the Union's government with Gamal Abdel Nasser rejecting a joint leadership with the Syrian Ba'th Party (Meininghaus 2016: 71). Gamal Abdel Nasser also made sure that Syria's political parties were dissolved and that the Syrian army withdrew from political life (Jankowski 2002: 117). Shortly after its formation, the Union faced

internal problems, induced by the introduction of a more centralized governmental structure, tighter controls of foreign trade, reforms of land and labour law. The Union eventually collapsed in September 1961 after a coup staged by Damascene Sunni officers (Joubin 2013: 62).

8   The WFP announced in November 2014 that it was halting its distribution of food vouchers (https://www.theguardian.com/world/2014/dec/01/syrian-refugees-food-crisis-un-world-programme).

9   The community of Arabs in Detroit serves as a telling example of such a process of redefinition of identity followed by a stigmatization of those who do not fit in. Arab Americans had to emphasize their status as 'good', 'loyal' and 'worthy of respect', by distancing themselves from the negative stereotypes ascribed to Muslims in general. They did this by turning away from Arabs in their midst who came closest to these stereotypes (Howell and Shryock 2011: 79).

10   The term 'basha' had an important connotation in the pre-1952 monarchy in Egypt. The Palace bestowed this title on individuals (often large landowners) privileging them and giving them access to positions of power (Eid 2002: 194). It referred to influence, wealth, social status and authority (Eid 2002: 157). Nowadays, if used in an official environment, for example at the workplace or with high officials, it establishes and maintains relations of hierarchy (Shehata 2009: 227).

11   This echoes Kusow's (2004: 179) argument that groups or individuals who experience stigmatization by the society reverse the process and find their own ways to engage in stigmatization of the dominant society. He found that Somali immigrants in Canada ascribed moral and cultural inferiority to Canadian society to draw a symbolic boundary, while they experienced stigmatization on the part of Canadian society because of their skin colour.

12   Shaimaa al-Sabbagh was killed by the Egyptian security forces on 24 January 2015, when she participated in a peaceful protest in Cairo to commemorate the revolution (HRW 2015a).

13   In principle, the narratives echo a study by Marlowe (2012) among Sudanese refugees living in resettlement in Australia, where men expressed that they had to 'walk the line' between connections with the past and what is considered normative within Australian society (2012: 57). This happened sometimes voluntarily and was sometimes enforced on them if they wanted to be successful in Australia (2012: 58). 'Walking the line' meant being able to compromise and to strategize in order to both recognize the present and hold onto the past (2012: 63).

Chapter 6

1   In the 1980s, anti-regime opposition was growing and was led by the Syrian branch of the Muslim Brotherhood. Recurring clashes and violent uprisings took place and the regime was unable to gain the upper hand (Perthes 1995: 137). In 1982, an uprising by the Syrian Muslim Brotherhood in Hama was brutally destroyed by the regime through a siege of the city leaving more than 20,000 people dead (see Lia 2016; Lefèvre 2013). The effects of this period were still visible in Syria up until the uprising in 2011, since thousands of Syrians were still imprisoned, killed or had disappeared (Rabo 2014).

2   This is similar to control and surveillance in other repressive political systems, for example in the German Democratic Republic (see Betts 2010) or in the Soviet Union (see Yurchak 2005).

BIBLIOGRAPHY

3RP Regional Refugee Resilience Plan (2015) *3RP Regional Progress Report June 2015*. Available at: http://www.3rpsyriacrisis.org/wp-content/uploads/2015/06/3RP-Progress-Report.pdf (Accessed 27 January 2016).

Abdelrahman, M. (2015) *Egypt's Long Revolution Protest Movements and Uprisings*. London/New York: Routledge.

Abdulhaq, N. (2016) *Jewish and Greek Communities in Egypt: Entrepreneurship and Business before Nasser*. London/New York: I.B. Tauris.

Adeley, F. (2016) 'A Different Kind of Love: Compatibility (Insijam) and Marriage in Jordan', *Arabic Studies Journal*, 24(2), pp. 102–26.

Aghacy, S. (2009) *Masculine Identity in the Fiction of the Arab East since 1967*. Syracuse: Syracuse University Press.

Ahmed, S. (2004) *The Cultural Politics of Emotion*. Edinburgh: Edinburgh University Press.

Aldoughli, R. (2018) 'Belonging to a Militarized Syria as a Woman', *Syria Untold*. 5 January 2018. Available at: https://syriauntold.com/2018/01/05/belonging-to-a-militarized-syria-as-a-woman/

Ali, A. (2012) 'Egypt's Stake in the Syrian Revolution', *openDemocracy*. Available at: *http://www.opendemocracy.net/arab-awakening/amro-ali/egypt%E2%80%99s-stake-in-syrian-revolution* (Accessed 22 January 2016).

Ali, K. A. (2003) 'Myths, Lies and Impotence: Structural Adjustment and Male Voice in Egypt', *Comparative Studies in South Asia, Africa and the Middle East*, 23(1), pp. 321–34.

Allsopp, J. (2017) 'Agent, Victim, Soldier, Son: Intersecting Masculinities in the European "Refugee Crisis"', in Freedman, J., Kivilcim, Z. and Baklacıoğlu, N. Özgür (eds.) *A Gendered Approach to the Syrian Refugee Crisis*. London/New York: Routledge, pp. 155–74.

AlNahar TV (2015) *Sabāyā al-khayr: Rīhām Saʿīd tuhdy musāʿadāt lillālgʾīn al-sūryīn bil-mukhaymāt*, 3 August. Available at: https://www.youtube.com/watch?v=AFWXpnHM EM4&app=desktop (Accessed 27 January 2016).

Al-Sharmani, M. and Grabska, K. (2009) 'African Refugees and Diasporic Struggles in Cairo', in Singerman, D. (ed.) *Cairo Contested: Governance, Urban Space, and Global Modernity*. Cairo/New York: The American University in Cairo Press, pp. 455–88.

Amnesty International (2017) *Giulio Regeni, Cambridge Student Murdered in Egypt*, 11 February. Available at: https://www.amnesty.org.uk/giulio-regeni-italian-cambridge-student-murdered-egypt (Accessed 1 August 2017).

Anderson, P. (2018) '"Order" and "Civilty": Middle-Class Imaginaries of Citizenship before the Syrian Uprising', *Anthropological Theory*, 18(2–3), pp. 248–70.

Anderson, P. (2013) 'The Politics of Scorn in Syria and the Agency of Narrated Involvement', *Journal of the Royal Anthropological Institute*, 19(3), pp. 463–481.

Appadurai, A. (1998) 'Dead Certainty: Ethnic Violence in the Era of Globalization', *Public Culture*, 10(2), pp. 225–47.

Arendt, H. (1973) [1951] *The Origins of Totalitarianism*. 5th ed. New York: Harcourt Brace Jovanovich.

Assad, R., Binzel, C. and Gadallah, M. (2010) 'Transitions to Employment and Marriage among Young Men in Egypt', *Middle East Development Journal*, 2(1), pp. 39–88.

Ayoub, M. (2017) 'Gender, Social Class and Exile: The Case of Syrian Women in Cairo', in Freedman, J., Kivilcim, Z. and Baklacıoğlu, N. (eds.) *A Gendered Approach to the Syrian Refugee Crisis*. New York: Routledge, pp. 77–104.

Ayoub, M. and Khallaf, S. (2014) *Syrian Refugees in Egypt: Challenges of a Politically Changing Environment*. Paper No 7. Cairo Studies on Migration and Refugees: The American University in Cairo.

Bandak, A. (2014) 'Reckoning with the Inevitable: Death and Dying among Syrian Christians during the Uprising', *Ethnos*, 80(5), pp. 671–91.

Banki, S. (2006) 'Burmese Refugees in Tokyo: Livelihoods in the Urban Environment', *Journal of Refugee Studies*, 19(3), pp. 328–44.

Barbir, K. (1986) 'Review of Thomas Philipp Book's the Syrians in Egypt 1725–1975 [Review of The Syrians in Egypt 1725–1975 by T. Philipp]', *Middle East Journal*, 40(4), pp. 760–61.

Barnes, E. (2002) 'Loving with a Vengeance: Wieland, Familicide and the Crisis of Masculinity in the Early Nation'. Shamir, M. and Travis, J. (eds.) *Boys Don't Cry? Rethinking Narratives of Masculinity and Emotion in the U.S.* New York: Columbia University Press, pp. 44–63.

Barrett, F. J. (1996) 'The Organizational Construction of Hegemonic Masculinity: The Case of the US Navy', *Gender, Work and Organization*, 3(3), pp. 129–42.

Bayat, A. (2010) *Life as Politics: How Ordinary People Change the Middle East*. Stanford/California: Stanford University Press.

Betts, P. (2010) *Within Walls: Private Life in the German Democratic Republic*. Oxford: Oxford University Press.

Birenbaum-Carmeli, D. and Inhorn, M. (2009) 'Masculinity and Marginality: Palestinian Men's Struggles with Infertility in Israel and Lebanon', *Journal of Middle East Women's Studies*, 5, pp. 23–52.

Bonjour, S. and Chauvin, S. (2018) 'Social Class, Migration Policy and Migration Strategies: An Introduction', *International Migration*, 56(4), pp. 5–18.

Booth, M. (2011) 'Constructions of Syrian Identity in the Women's Press in Egypt', in Beshara, A. (ed.) *The Origins of Syrian Nationhood: Histories, Pioneers and Identity*. London/New York: Routledge, pp. 223–5.

Bourdieu, P. (1987) 'What Makes a Social Class? On the Theoretical and Practical Existence of Groups', *Berkeley Journal of Sociology*, 22, pp. 1–17.

Bourdieu, P. (1985) 'The Social Space and the Genesis of Groups', *Theory and Society*, 14(6), pp. 723–44.

Bourdieu, P. (1977) 'The Economics of Linguistic Exchanges', *Social Sciences Information*, 16(6), pp. 645–48.

Bourdieu, P. and Wacquant, L. (1992) *An Invitation to Reflective Sociology*. Chicago: University of Chicago Press.

Briant, N. and Kennedy, A. (2004) 'An Investigation of the Perceived Needs and Priorities Held by African Refugees in an Urban Setting in a First Country of Asylum', *Journal of Refugee Studies*, 17(4), pp. 437–59.

Brun, C. (2000) 'Making Young Displaced Men Visible', *Forced Migration Review*, 9, pp. 10–12.

Buscher, D. (2013) 'New Approaches to Urban Refugee Livelihoods', *Refuge*, 28(2), pp. 17–29.

Butler, J. (2009) 'Performativity, Precarity and Sexual Politics', *AIBR*, 4(3), pp. i–xiii.

Butler, J. (2004) *Undoing Gender*. London: Routledge.

Butler, J. (1999) *Gender Trouble: Feminism and the Subversion of Identity*. New York/London: Routledge.

Cambell, E. (2006) 'Urban Refugees in Nairobi: Problems of Protection, Mechanisms of Survival, and Possibilities for Integration', *Journal of Refugee Studies*, 19(3), pp. 396–413.

Camus, A. (1979) [1955]. *The Myth of Sisyphus. Justin O'Brien (Translator)*. Harmondsworth: Penguin Books.

Carrigan, T., Connell, B. and Lee, J. (1985) 'Towards a New Sociology of Masculinity', *Theory and Society*, 14(5), pp. 551–604.

Charsley, K. and Wray, H. (2015) 'Introduction: The Invisible (Migrant) Man', *Men and Masculinities*, 18(4), pp. 403–23.

Chatty, D. (2018) *Syria: The Making and Unmaking of a Refugee State*. Oxford: Oxford University Press.

Chatty, D. (2010) *Displacement and Dispossession in the Modern Middle East*. Cambridge/New York: Cambridge University Press.

Christensen, A. and Jensen, S. Q. (2014) 'Combining Hegemonic Masculinity and Intersectionality', *NORMA: International Journal for Masculinity Studies*, 9, pp. 60–75.

Cockburn, C. (2009) 'The Continuum of Violence', in Linke, U. and Smith, D. T. (eds.) *Cultures of Fear: A Critical Reader*. London/New York: Pluto Press, pp. 158–73.

Collinson, D. and Hearn, J. (1994) 'Naming Men as Men: Implications for Work, Organization, and Management', in Whitehead, S. M. and Barrett, F. J. (eds.) *The masculinities reader*. Cambridge/Maldon: Polity Press, pp. 144–69.

Connell, R. (2013) 'Embodying Serious Power: Managerial Masculinities in the Security Sector', in Hearn, J., Blagojević, M. and Harrison, K. (eds.) *Rethinking Transnational Men: Beyond, between and within Nations*. New York/London: Routledge, pp. 45–58.

Connell, R. (1998) 'Masculinities and Globalization', *Men and Masculinities*, 1(1), pp. 3–23.

Connell, R. (1995) *Masculinities*. Cambridge: Polity Press.

Connell, R. W. and Messerschmidt, J. (2005) 'Hegemonic Masculinity: Rethinking the Concept', *Gender & Society*, 19(6), pp. 829–59.

Cornwall, A. (2016) 'Introduction: Masculinities under Neoliberalism', in Cornwall, A., Karioris, F. and Lindisfarne, N. (eds.) *Masculinities Under Neoliberalism*. London: Zed Books, pp. 1–28.

Cornwall, A. and Lindisfarne, N. (1994) 'Introduction', in Cornwall, A. and Lindisfarne, N. (eds.) *Dislocating Masculinity: Comparative Ethnographies*. London/New York: Routledge, pp. 1–10.

Crenshaw, K. (1991) 'Mapping the Margins: Intersectionality, Identity Politics, and Violence against Women of Color', *Stanford Law Review*, 43(6), pp. 1241–99.

Dam, N. van (2017) *Destroying a Nation: The Civil War in Syria*. London/New York: I.B. Tauris.

Dam, N. van (2011) [1979] *The Struggle for Power in Syria Politics and Society under Asad and the Bath Party*. London/New York: I.B. Tauris.

Danielson, Nora (2015) 'Demonstabe Needs: Protest, Politics and Refugees in Cairo', in Koizumi, K. and Hoffstaedter, G. (eds) *Urban Refugees: Challenges in Protection, Services and Policy*. London/New York: Routledge, pp. 13–41.

Dardot, P. and Laval, C. (2013) *The New Way of the World: On Neoliberal Society*. London: Verso.

Das, V. (2015) 'Corruption and the Possibility of Life', *Contributions to Indian Sociology*, 49(3), pp. 322–43.

Davis, R. (2016) 'Gendered Vulnerability and Forced Conscription in the War in Syria', *The Long-term Challenges of Forced Migration: Perspectives from Lebanon, Jordan and Iraq. LSE Middle East Centre Collected Papers*, 6, pp. 49–54.

Davis, R., Taylor, A. and Murphy, E. (2014) 'Gender, Conscription and Protection, and the War in Syria', *Forced Migration Review*, 47, pp. 35–8.

Davis, R. Benton, G. Todman, W. and Murphy, E. (2017) 'Hosting Guests, Creating Citizens: Models of Refugee Administration in Jordan and Egypt', *Refugee Survey Quarterly* 36, pp. 1–32.

De Koning, A. (2009) *Global Dreams: Class, Gender, and Public Space in Cosmopolitan Cairo*. Cairo/New York: American University in Cairo Press.

Deardorff Miller, S. (2017) *Political and Humanitarian Responses to Syrian Displacement*. London/New York: Routledge.

Deboulet, A. (2009) 'The Dictatorship of the Straight Line and the Myth of Social Disorder: Revisiting Informality in Cairo', in Singerman, D. (ed.) *Cairo Contested: Governance, Urban Space, and Global Modernity*. Cairo/New York: The American University in Cairo Press, pp. 199–234.

Demitrou, D. (2001) 'Connell's Concept of Hegemonic Masculinity: A Critique', *Theory and Society*, 30, pp. 337–61.

Dolan, C. (2003) 'Collapsing Masculinities and Weak States: A Case Study of Northern Uganda', in Cleaver, F. (ed.) *Masculinity Matters: Men, Masculinities and Gender Relations in Development*. London: Zed Books, pp. 57–84.

Donaldson, M. and Howson, R. (2009) 'Men, Migration and Hegemonic Masculinity', in Donaldson, M., Hibbins, R., Howson, R. and Pease, B. (eds.) *Migrant Men: Critical Studies of Masculinities and the Migration Experience*. New York/London: Routledge, pp. 210–17.

Donner, H. (2015) 'Making Middle-class Families in Calcutta', in Carrier, J. G. and Kalb, D. (eds.) *Anthropologies of Class: Power, Practice and Inequality*. Cambridge: Cambridge University Press, pp. 131–48.

Dream TV Egypt (2017) '"jawla lī-kāmīrā "kalām tānī" mʿa al-sūriyyīn wasaṭ maḥalāthum wa iʿamālhum al-tijāriyya bi-madīna "6 uktūbir"', 5 January. Available at: https://www.youtube.com/watch?v=fIu8dK0LAkc&feature=youtu.be (Accessed 5 June 2017).

Dryden-Peterson, S. (2006) '"I Find Myself as Someone Who Is in the Forest": Urban Refugees as Agents of Social Change in Kampala, Uganda', *Journal of Refugee Studies*, 19(3), pp. 381–95.

Eastmond, M. (2011) 'Egalitarian Ambitions, Constructions of Difference: The Paradoxes of Refugee Integration in Sweden', *Journal of Ethnic and Migration Studies*, 37(2), pp. 277–95.

Eddy, M. and Johannsen, K. (2015) 'Migrants Arriving in Germany Face a Chaotic Reception in Berlin', *The New York Times*, 26 November. Available at: https://www.nytimes.com/2015/11/27/world/europe/germany-berlin-migrants-refugees.html?_r=0 (Accessed 3 April 2017).

Edwards, T. (2006) *Cultures of Masculinity*. London: Routledge.

Eid, M. (2002) *The World of Obituaries Gender across Cultures and Over Time*. Detroit: Wayne State University Press.

El-Gundy, Z. (2013) 'The Shias: Egypt's Forgotten Muslim Minority', *ahram online*, 18 March. Available at: http://english.ahram.org.eg/NewsContent/1/151/67170/Egypt/Features/The-Shias-Egypts-forgotten-Muslim-minority.aspx (Accessed 1 September 2017).

Enloe, C. (2004) *The Curious Feminist: Searching for Women in a New Age of Empire.* Berkeley/Los Angeles/London: University of California Press.

Enloe, C. (1993) *The Morning After: Sexual Politics at the End of the Cold War.* Berkely, California: University of California Press.

Este, D. C. and Tachble, A. (2009) 'Fatherhood in the Canadian Context: Perceptions and Experiences of Sudanese Refugee Men,' Sex Roles, 60, pp. 456–66.

Feldman, A. (2000) 'Violence and Vision: The Prosthetics and Aesthetics of Terror', in Das, V., Kleinman, A., Ramphele, M. and Reynolds, P. (eds.) *Violence and Subjectivity.* Berkeley: University of California Press, pp. 20–46.

Ferguson, F. and Gupta, A. (2002) 'Spatializing States: Toward an Ethnography of Neoliberal Governmentality', *American Ethnologist*, 29(4), pp. 981–1002.

Fiddian, E. (2006) 'RELOCATING: The Asylum Experience in Cairo', *Interventions*, 8(2), pp. 295–318, DOI: 10.1080/13698010600782048.

Fiddian-Qasmiyeh, E. (2010) '"Ideal" Refugee Women and Gender Equality Mainstreaming in the Sahrawi Refugee Camps: "Good Practice" for Whom?', *Refugee Survey Quarterly*, 29(2), pp. 64–8.

Fiddian-Qasmiyeh, E. and Qasmiyeh, Y. M. (2010) 'Muslim Asylum-seekers and Refugees: Negotiating Identity, Politics and Religion in the UK', *Journal of Refugee Studies*, 23(3), pp. 294–314.

Finnan, C. R. (1981) 'Occupational Assimilation of Refugees', *The International Migration Review*, 15(1/2), pp. 292–309.

Fournier, P. (2013) 'Flirting with God in Western Secular Courts: *Mahr* in the West', in Fishbayn Joffe, L. and Neil, S. (eds). *Gender, Religion & Family Law: Theorizing Conflicts between Women's Rights and Cultural Traditions.* Waltham, MA: Brandeis University Press, pp. 140–62.

Freeman, C. (2012) 'Neoliberal Respectability: Entrepreneurial Marriage, Affective Labor, and a New Caribbean Middle Class', in Heiman, R., Freeman, C. and Liechty, M. (eds.) *The Global Middle Classes: Theorizing Through Ethnography.* New Mexico: School for Advanced Research Press, pp. 85–116.

Fritzsche, J. (2013) 'Egypt's Others', *Sada Middle East Analysis*, Carnegie Endowment for International Peace, 5 November. Available at: http://carnegieendowment.org/sada/?fa=53501 (Accessed 8 June 2016).

Gabiam, N. (2015) 'Citizenship and Development: Palestinians in France and the Multiple Meanings of Statelessness', *Studies in Comparative International Development*, 50, pp. 479–99.

Gampel, Y. (2000) 'Reflections on the Prevalence of the Uncanny in Social Violence', in Robben, A. M. and Suárez-Orozco, M. (eds.) *Cultures under Siege: Collective Violence and Trauma.* Cambridge: Cambridge University Press, pp. 48–69.

Gentry, C. (2009) 'Twisted Maternalism', *International Feminist Journal of Politics*, 11(2), pp. 234–52.

Ghannam, F. (2013) *Live and Die Like a Man Gender Dynamics in Urban Egypt.* Stanford/California: Stanford University Press.

Goffman, E. (1961) 'Role Distance', in Goffman, E. (ed.) *Encounters: Two Studies in the Sociology of Interaction.* Indianapolis: Bobbs-Merrill, pp. 84–152.

Grabska, K. (2006) 'Marginalization in Urban Spaces of the Global South: Urban Refugees in Cairo', *Journal of Refugee Studies*, 19(3), pp. 287–307.

Green, L. (1994) 'Fear as a Way of Life', *Cultural Anthropology*, 9(2), pp. 227–56.

Griffiths, M. (2015) '"Here, Man Is Nothing!": Gender and Policy in an Asylum Context', *Men and Masculinities*, 18(4), pp. 468–88.

Gupta, A. (1995) 'Blurred Boundaries: The Discourse of Corruption, the Culture of Politics and the Imagined State', *American Ethnologist*, 22(2), pp. 375–402.

Gupta, A. and Ferguson, J. (1997) 'Culture, Power, Place: Ethnography at the End of an Era', in Gupta, A. and Ferguson, J. (eds.) *Culture, Power, Place: Explorations in Critical Anthropology*. Durham, NC/London: Duke University Press, pp. 1–32.

Gutmann, M. (1996) *The Meanings of Macho: Being a Man in Mexico City*. Berkeley/Los Angeles/London: University of California Press.

Haddad, B. (2012) *Business Networks in Syria: The Political Economy of Authoritain Resilience*. Stanford/California: Stanford University Press.

Hafez, S. (2012) 'No Longer a Bargain: Women, Masculinity and the Egyptian Uprising', *American Ethnologist*, 39(1), pp. 37–42.

Hamzawy, A. (2017) 'Legislating Authoritarianism: Egypt's New Era of Repression', *Carnegie Endowment for International Peace*. 16 March 2017. Available at: http://carnegieendowment.org/2017/03/16/legislating-authoritarianism-egypt-s-new-era-of-repression-pub-68285

Harling, P. and Birke, S. (2013) 'The Syrian Heartbreak. Middle East Research and Information Project', *MERIP*. Available at: *http://www.merip.org/mero/mero041613* (Accessed 22 April 2014).

Hasso, F. (2018) 'Decolonizing Middle East Men and Masculinities Scholarship: An Axiomatic Approach', *Arab Studies Journal* 15/10/2018. Available at: https://www.arabstudiesjournal.org/asj-online/decolonizing-middle-east-men-and-masculinities-scholarship-an-axiomatic-approach (Accessed 10 June 2019).

Hasso, F. (2010) *Consuming Desires: Family Crisis and the State in the Middle East*. Stanford/California: Stanford University Press.

Haugbolle, S. (2012) 'The (Little) Militia Man: Memory and Militarized Masculinity in Lebanon', *Journal of Middle East Women's Studies*, 8(1), pp. 115–39.

Haywood, C. and Mac an Ghaill, M. (2003) *Men and Masculinities: Theory, Research and Social Practice*. Buckingham/Philadelphia: Open University Press.

Hearn, J. & D.L Collinson. (2005) 'Men and Masculinities in Work, Organizations and Management', in Kimmel, M.; Hearn, J. and R.W. Connell (eds.) *Handbook of Studies of Men and Masculinities*, Sage. Thousand Oaks/London/New Delhi: Sage Publications, pp. 289–310.

Heiman, R., Liechty, M. and Freeman, C. (2012) 'Introduction: Charting an Anthropology of the Middle Classes', in Heiman, R., Liechty, M. and Freeman, C. (eds.) *The Global Middle Classes: Theorizing through Ethnography*. Santa Fe: School for Advanced Research Press, pp. 3–33.

Henry, M. (2017) 'Problematizing Military Masculinity, Intersectionality and Male Vulnerability in Feminist Critical Military Studies', *Critical Military Studies*, 3(2), pp. 182–99.

Hinnebusch, R. (2001) *Syria: Revolution from Above*. New York: Routledge.

Hinnebusch, R. and Rifai, O. (2015) 'Syria: Identity, State Formation, and Citizenship', in Meijer, R. and Butenschøn, N. (eds.) *The Crisis of Citizenship in the Arab World*. Leiden/Boston: Brill, pp. 105–28.

Hoffman, S. (2016) *Iraqi Migrants in Syria: The Crisis before the Storm*. Syracuse: Syracuse University Press.

Hokayem, E. (2013) *Syria's Uprising and the Fracturing of the Levant*. Milton Park: Routledge.

Hoodfar, H. (1997) *Between Marriage and the Market: Intimate Politics and Survival in Cairo*. Berkeley: University of California Press.

Hopkins, P. and Noble, G. (2009) 'Editorial: Masculinities in Place, Situated Identities, Relations and Intersectionality', *Social & Cultural Geography*, 10(8), pp. 810–19.

Howell, S. and Shryock, A. (2011) 'Cracking Down on Diaspora: Arab Detroit and America's War on Terror', in Abraham, N., Howell, S. and Shryock, A. (eds.) *Arab Detroit 9/11: Life in the Terror Decade*. Detroit: Wayne State University Press, pp. 67–86.

HRW (2019) *Syria: Events of 2018*. Available at: https://www.hrw.org/world-report/2019/country-chapters/syria.

Human Rights Watch (2017) *World Report 2017*. Available at: https://www.hrw.org/sites/default/files/world_report_download/wr2017-web.pdf (Accessed 5 August 2017).

Human Rights Watch (2015) 'Egypt: Dozens Detained Secretly: National Security Officers Operating Outside the Law', 20 July. Available at: https://www.hrw.org/news/2015/07/20/egypt-dozens-detained-secretly (Accessed 8 August 2017).

Human Rights Watch (2015a) 'Egypt: Protesters Killed Marking Revolution: Prosecutors Should Investigate Excessive Use of Force', 26 January. Available at: https://www.hrw.org/news/2015/01/26/egypt-protesters-killed-marking-revolution (Accessed 10 August 2016).

Human Rights Watch (2013) 'Egypt: Arrests of Syrians Raise Deportation Fears: Asylum Seekers, Legal Residents Taken from Checkpoints', 25 July. Available at: https://www.hrw.org/news/2013/07/25/egypt-arrests-syrians-raise-deportation-fears (Accessed 8 June 2016).

Hull, M. S. (2012) 'Documents and Bureaucracy', *Annual Review of Anthropology*, 41(1), pp. 251–67.

International Labour Organization (2015) *Access to Work for Syrian Refugees in Jordan: A Discussion Paper on Labour and Refugee Laws and Policies*. Available at: http://www.ilo.org/beirut/publications/WCMS_357950/lang--en/index.htm (Accessed 26 February 2016).

Inhorn, M. (2012) *The New Arab Man: Emergent Masculinities, Technologies and Islam in the Middle East*. Princeton/Oxford: Princeton University Press.

Inhorn, M., Chavkin, W. and Navarro, J.-A. (2015) 'Introduction. Globalized Fatherhood: Emergent Forms and Possibilities in the New Millennium', in Inhorn, M., Chavkin, W. and Navarro, J.-A. (eds.) *Globalized Fatherhood*. New York/Oxford: Berghahn Books, pp. 1–30.

Ismail, S. (2018) *The Rule of Violence: Subjectivity, Memory and Government in Syria*. Cambridge: Cambridge University Press.

Ismail, S. (2011) 'The Syrian Uprising: Imagining and Performing the Nation', *Studies in Ethnicity and Nationalism*, 11(3), pp. 538–49.

Ismail, S. (2009) 'Changing Social Structure, Shifting Alliances and Authoritarianism in Syria', in Lawson, F. (ed.) *Demystifying Syria*. London: Saqi Press, pp. 13–28.

Ismail, S. (2006) *Political Life in Cairo's New Quarters: Encountering the Everyday State*. Minneapolis: University of Minnesota Press.

Jackson, M. (2013) *The Wherewithal of Life: Ethics, Migration, and the Question of Well-Being*. Berkeley: University of California Press.

Jackson, M. (2002) *The Politics of Storytelling: Violence, Transgression, and Intersubjectivity*. Copenhagen: Museum Tusculanum Press.

Jacobsen, K. (2006) 'Refugees and Asylum Seekers in Urban Areas: A Livelihoods Perspective', *Journal of Refugee Studies*, 19(3), pp. 273–86.

Jacobsen, K., Ayoub, M. and Johnson, A. (2012) *Remittances to Transit Countries: The Impact on Sudanese Refugee Livelihoods in Cairo*. Cairo: The American University in Cairo.

Jaji, R. (2009) 'Masculinity on Unstable Ground: Young Refugee Men in Nairobi, Kenya', *Journal of Refugee Studies*, 22(2), pp. 177–94.

Jankowski, J. (2002) *Nasser's Egypt, Arab Nationalism, and the United Arab Republic*. Boulder: Lynne Rienner Publisher.

Jansen, S. (2008) 'Misplaced Masculinities: Status Loss and the Location of Gendered Subjectivities amongst 'Non-transnational' Bosnian Refugees', *Anthropological Theory*, 8, pp. 181–200.

Jean-Klein, I. (2000) 'Mothercraft, Statecraft, and Subjectivity in the Palestinian Intifada', *American Ethnologist*, 27(1), pp. 100–27.

Johnson-Hanks, J. (2002) 'On the Limits of Life Stages in Ethnography: Toward a Theory of Vital Conjunctures', *American Anthropologist*, 104(3), pp. 865–80.

Johnson, P., Abu Nahleh, L. and Moors, A. (2009) 'Weddings and War: Marriage Arrangements and Celebrations in Two Palestinian Intifadas', *Journal of Middle East Women's Studies*, 5(3), pp. 11–35.

Jones, A. (2006) *Genocide: A Comprehensive Introduction*. London/New York: Routledge.

Jones, C. (2012) 'Women in the Middle: Femininity, Virtue, and Excess in Indonesian Discourses of Middle Classness', in Heiman, R., Freeman, C. and Liechty, M. (eds.) *The Global Middle Classes: Theorizing through Ethnography*. New Mexico: School for Advanced Research Press, pp. 145–68.

Joseph, S. (1996) 'Gender and Citizenship in Middle Eastern States', *Middle East Report*, 198, pp. 4–10.

Joseph, S. (1994) 'Brother/Sister Relationships: Connectivity, Love, and Power in the Reproduction of Patriarchy in Lebanon', *American Ethnologist*, 21(1), pp. 50–73.

Joseph, S. (1993) 'Connectivity and Patriarchy among Urban Working-class Arab Families in Lebanon', *Ethos*, 21(4), pp. 452–84.

Joseph, S. (1991) 'Elite Strategies for State Building: Women, Family, Religion and the State in Iraq and Lebanon', in Kandiyoti, D. (ed.) *Women, Islam and the State*. Hampshire/London: Macmillan, pp. 145–76.

Joseph, S. (1983) 'Working-Class Women's Networks in a Sectarian State: A Political Paradox', *American Ethnologist*, 10(1), pp. 1–22.

Joubin, R. (2013) *The Politics of Love: Sexuality, Gender, and Marriage in Syrian Television Drama*. Plymouth: Lexington Books.

Kabachnik, P., Grabowska, M., Regulska, J., Mitchnec, B. and Mayorova, O. (2013) 'Traumatic Masculinities: The Gendered Geographies of Georgian IDPs from Abkhazia', *Gender, Place & Culture*, 20(6), pp. 773–93.

Kagan, M. (2011) *Shared Responsibility in a New Egypt: A Strategy for Refugee Protection*. The American University in Cairo: School of Global Affairs and Public Policy.

Kandiyoti, D. (1994) 'The Paradoxes of Masculinity: Some Thoughts on Segregated Societies', in Cornwall, A. and Lindisfarne, N. (eds.) *Dislocating Masculinity: Comparative Ethnographies*. London/New York: Routledge, pp. 196–212.

Kårtveit, B. (2018) 'Being a Coptic Man: Masculinity, Class, and Social Change among Egyptian Copts', *Men and Masculinities*. DOI: 10.1177/1097184X18804000.

Kastrinou, A. M. (2016) *Power, Sect and State in Syria: The Politics of Marriage and Identity amongst the Druze*. London/New York: I.B. Tauris.

Kerr, M. (2015) 'Introduction: For 'God, Syria, Bashar and Nothing Else'?', in Kerr, M. and Larkin, C. (eds.) *The Alawis of Syria: War, Faith and Politics in the Levant*. Oxford/New York: Oxford University Press, pp. 1–26.

Khaddour, K. and Mazur, K. (2013) 'The Struggle for Syria's Regions', *MERIP*. Available at: http://www.merip.org/mer/mer269/struggle-syrias-regions (Accessed 1 August 2017).

Kimmel, M. (1994) 'Masculinity as Homophobia: Fear, Shame, and Silence in the Construction of Gender Identity', in Brod, H. and Kaufman, M. (eds.) *Theorizing Masculinities*. London: Sage, pp. 213–19.

Kingsley, P. (2013) 'Syrian Refugees Serve Up Flavours of Home in Cairo Satellite City', *The Guardian*, 25 July. Available at: http://www.theguardian.com/world/2013/jul/25/syria-refugee-restaurant-food-egypt-city (Accessed 26 February 2016).

Kleinman, A. (2000) 'The Violences of Everyday Life: The Multiple Forms and Dynamics of Social Violence', in Das, V., Kleinman, A., Ramphele, M. and Reynolds, P. (eds.) *Violence and Subjectivity*. Berkeley: University of California Press, pp. 226–41.

Kleist, N. (2010) 'Negotiating Respectable Masculinity: Gender and Recognition in the Somali Diaspora', *African Diaspora*, 3, pp. 185–206.

Knight, M. (2013) '"New markets Must Be Conquered": Race, Gender, and the Embodiment of Entrepreneurship within Texts', *The Canadian Geographer*, 57(3), pp. 345–53.

Kreil, A. (2016) 'The Price of Love: Valentine's Day in Egypt and It's Enemies', *Arab Studies Journal*, 24(2), pp. 128–46.

Kronsell, A. and Svedberg, E. (2012) 'Introduction: Making Gender, Making War', in Kronsell, A. and Svedberg, E. (eds.) *Making Gender, Making War: Violence, Military and Peacekeeping Practices*. London/New York: Routledge, pp. 1–18.

Kusow, A. (2004) 'Contesting Stigma: On Goffman's Assumptions of Normative Order', *Symbolic Interaction*, 27(2), pp. 179–97.

Landau, L. and Duponchel, M. (2011) 'Laws, Policies, or Social Position? Capabilities and the Determinants of Effective Protection in Four African Cities', *Journal of Refugee Studies*, 24(1), pp. 1–22.

Lawson, F. (2016) 'Syria's Civil War and the Reconfiguration of Regional Politics', in Beck, M., Jung, D. and Seeberg, P. (eds.) *The Levant in Turmoil: Syria, Palestine, and the Transformation of Middle Eastern Politics*. Hampshire/New York: Palgrave Macmillan, pp. 13–38.

Lefèvre, R. (2013) *Ashes of Hama: the Muslim Brotherhood in Syria*. Oxford/New York: Oxford University Press.

Lems, A. (2016) 'Placing Displacement: Place-making in a World of Movement', *Ethnos*, 81(2), pp. 315–37.

Levitt, P. and Glick Schiller, N. (2004) 'Conceptualizing Simultaneity: A Transnational Social Field Perspective on Society', *International Migration Review*, 28(3), pp. 1002–39.

Lia, B. (2016) 'The Islamist Uprising in Syria, 1976–82: The History and Legacy of a Failed Revolt', *British Journal of Middle Eastern Studies*, 43(3), pp. 541–59.

Loizos, P. (2007) '"Generations" in Forced Migration: Towards Greater Clarity', *Journal of Refugee Studies* 20(2), pp. 193–209.

Løland, I. (2019) 'Negotiating Paradise Lost: Refugee Narratives of Pre-war Syria – A Discursive Approach to Memory, Metaphors, and Religious Identifications', *European Journal of Cultural Studies*, pp. 1–19.

Lubkemann, S. (2008) *Culture in Chaos. An Anthropology of the Social Condition in War*. Chicago: University of Chicago Press.

Ludwig, B. (2013) '"Wiping the Refugee Dust from My Feet": Advantages and Burdens of Refugee Status and the Refugee Label', *International Migration*, 54(1), pp. 5–18.

Luhrmann, T. (1996) *The Good Parsi: The Fate of a Colonial Elite in a Post-colonial Society*. Cambridge, MA: Harvard University Press.

Lynch, M. (2006) *Voices of the New Arab Public: Iraq, Al-Jazeera, and Middle East Politics Today*. New York: Columbia University Press.

Macklin, A. (2007) 'Who Is the Citizen's Other? Considering the Heft of Citizenship', *Theoretical Inquiries in Law*, 8(2), pp. 333–66.

Macmillan, L. (2011) 'Militarized Children Sovereign Power', in Beier, M. (ed.) *The Militarization of Childhood: Thinking beyond the Global South*. New York: Palgrave Macmillan, pp. 61–76.

Magid, P. (2015) 'TV Presenter under Fire for Disrespecting Syrian Refugees', *Madamasr*, 28 September. Available at: http://www.madamasr.com/sections/politics/tv-presenter-under-fire-disrespecting-syrian-refugees (Accessed 27 January 2016).

Makdisi, U.S. (2000) *The Culture of Sectarianism: Community, History, and Violence in Nineteenth-century Ottoman Lebanon*. Berkeley: University of California Press.

Malkki, L. (1996) 'Speechless Emissaries: Refugees, Humanitarianism, and Dehistoricization', *Cultural Anthropology*, 11(3), pp. 377–404.

Malkki, L. (1995) 'Refugees and Exile: From "Refugee Studies" to the National Order of Things', *Annual Review of Anthropology*, 24, pp. 495–523.

Malkki, L. (1995a) *Purity and Exile: Violence, Memory, and National Cosmology among Hutu Refugees in Tanzania*. Chicago/London: The University Press of Chicago.

Mandour, M. (2015) 'Repression in Egypt from Mubarak to Sisi', *Sada Middle East Analysis*, Carnegie Endowment for International Peace, 11 August. Available at: http://carnegieendowment.org/sada/?fa=60985 (Accessed 27 January 2016).

Maringira, G., Gibson, D. and Richters, A. (2015) '"It's in My Blood": The Military Habitus of Former Zimbabwean Soldiers in Exile in South Africa', *Armed Forces & Society*, 41(1), pp. 23–42.

Marlowe, J. (2012) '"Walking the Line": Southern Sudanese Masculinities and Reconciling One's Past with the Present', *Ethnicities*, 12(1), pp. 50–66.

Mason, V. (2011) 'The Im/mobilities of Iraqi Refugees in Jordan: Pan-Arabism, "Hospitality" and the Figure of the "Refugee"', *Mobilities*, 6(3), 353–73.

McGregor, J. (2008) 'Abject Spaces, Transnational Calculations: Zimbabweans in Britain Navigating Work, Class and the Law', *Transactions of the Institute of British Geographers, New Series*, 33(4), pp. 466–82.

McSpadden, L. A. (1999) 'Negotiating Masculinity in the Reconstruction of Social Place: Eritrean and Ethiopian Refugees in the United States and Sweden', in Indra, D. (ed.) *Engendering Forced Migration: Theory and Practice*. New York/Oxford: Berghahn Books, pp. 242–61.

McSpadden, L. A. and Moussa, H. (1993) 'I Have a Name: The Gender Dynamics in Asylum and Resettlement of Ethiopian and Eritrean Refugees in North America', *Journal of Refugee Studies*, 6(3), pp. 203–25.

Meininghaus, E. (2016) *Creating Consent in Ba'thist Syria: Women and Welfare in a Totalitarian State*. London: I.B. Tauris.

MENA. (2015) 'Sisi Attends Activities of the Youth Week', *State Information Service*, 14 September. Available at: http://www.sis.gov.eg/En/Templates/Articles/tmpArticleNews.aspx?ArtID=96356#. VqikBvmLSUl. (Accessed 27 January 2016).

Mendieta, E. (2009) 'Citizenship and Political Friendship: Two Hearts, One Passport', in Ortega, M. and Alcoff, L. (eds.) *Constructing the Nation: A Race and Nationalism Reader*. New York: Suny Press, pp. 153–78.

Mikdashi, M. (2014) 'Can Palestinian Men Be Victims? Gendering Israel's War on Gaza', *Jadaliyya*, 23 July. Available at: http://www.jadaliyya.com/pages/index/18644/can-palestinian-men-be-victims-gendering-israels-w (Accessed 7 September 2017).

Monterescu, D. (2006) 'Stranger Masculinities: Gender and Politics in a Palestinian-Israel "Third-space"', in Ouzgane, L. (ed.) *Islamic Masculinities*. New York/London: Zed Books, pp. 123–42.

Moors, A. (2003) 'Women's Gold: Shifting Styles in Embodying Family Relations', in Doumani, B. (ed.) *Family History in Middle Eastern Studies: Household Property and Gender*. New York: Suny Press, pp. 101–19.

Morgan, D. H. J. (1992) *Discovering Men*. London: Routledge.

Mundy, M. (1995) *Domestic Government: Kinship, Community and Polity in North Yemen*. London: I.B. Tauris.

Murray, R. (2015) 'Germany: Confronting Challenges at End of the Road', *UNHCR*, 20 October. Available at: http://www.unhcr.org/cgi-bin/texis/vtx/search?page=search& docid=562646636&query=greece (Accessed 3 April 2017).

Myrttinen, H. (2003) 'Disarming Masculinities', *Disarmament Forum: Women, Men, Peace and Security*, 4, pp. 37–46.

Naguib, N. (2018) 'Casualities of Fatherhood: Syrian Refugee Men and Nurturance in the Artic', in Inhorn, M. and Naguib, N. (eds.) *Reconceiving Muslim Men: Love and Marriage, Family and Care in Precarious Times*. New York, Oxford: Berghahn Books, pp. 279–97.

Naguib, N. (2015) *Nurturing Masculinities: Men, Food and Family in Contemporary Egypt*. Austin: University of Texas Press.

Nasser El-Dine, S. (2018) 'Love, Materiality, and Masculinity in Jordan: "Doing" Romance with Limited Resources', *Men and Masculinities*, 21(3), pp. 423–42.

Nassif, H. (2017) 'To Fear and to Defy: Emotions in the Field', *Contemporary Levant*, 2(1), pp. 49–54.

Navaro-Yashin, Y. (2007) 'Make-believe Papers, Legal Forms and the Counterfeit: Affective Interactions between Documents and People in Britain and Cyprus', *Anthropological Theory*, 7(1), pp. 79–98.

Nordstrom, C. (2004) *Shadows of War: Violence, Power and International Profiteering in the Twenty-first Century*. Berkeley/Los Angeles/London: University of California Press.

Norman, K. (2016) 'Host State Responsibility and Capacity in Egypt, Morocco and Turkey', *The Long-term Challenges of Forced Migration: Perspectives from Lebanon, Jordan and Iraq. LSE Middle East Centre Collected Papers*. pp. 31–6.

Norman, K. (2015) 'Co-Ethnicity, Security and Host Government Engagement: Egypt as a Non-traditional Receiver of Migrants and Refugees', *ESPMI Network: Refugee Review: Re-conceptualizing Refugees and Forced Migration in the 21st Century*, 2(1), pp. 77–95.

Ong, A. (2003) *Buddha Is Hiding: Refugees, Citizenship, the New America*. Berkeley: University of California Press.

Parekh, S. (2014) 'Beyond the Ethics of Admission: Stateless People, Refugee Camps and Moral Obligations', *Philosophy and Social Criticism*, 40(7), pp. 645–63.

Pearlman, W. (2016) 'Narratives of Fear in Syria', *Perspectives on Politics*, 14(1), pp. 21–37.

Perthes, V. (2000) '*Si Vis Stabilitatem, Para Bellum*: State Building, National Security, and War Preparation in Syria', in Heydemann, S. (ed.) *War, Institutions and Social Change in the Middle East*. Berkeley/Los Angeles/London: University of California Press, pp. 149–73.

Perthes, V. (1995) *The Political Economy of Syria und Assad*. London: I.B. Tauris.

Peteet, J. (2011) 'Cartographic Violence, Displacement and Refugee Camps: Palestine and Iraq', in Knudsen, A. and Hanafi, S. (eds.) *Palestinian Refugees: Identity, Space and Place in the Levant*. London/New York: Routledge, pp. 13–29.

Peteet, J. (2005) *Landscape of Hope and Despair: Palestinian Refugee Camps*. Philadelphia/Bristol: University of Pennsylvania Press.

Peteet, J. (1994), 'Male Gender and Rituals of Resistance in the Palestinian "Intifada": A Cultural Politics of Violence', *American Ethnologist*, 21(1), pp. 31–49.

Peterson, M. (2011) *Connected in Cairo: Growing Up Cosmopolitan in the Modern Middle East*. Bloomington: Indiana University Press.

Philipp, T. (1985) *The Syrians in Egypt, 1725–1975*. Stuttgart: Franz Steiner.

Phillips, C. (2015) 'Sectarianism and Conflict in Syria', *Third Wold Quarterly*, 36(2), pp. 357–76.

Podeh, E. (1999) *The Decline of Arab Unity: The Rise and Fall of the United Arab Republic*. Brighton: Sussex Academic.

Primo, V. (2015) 'The Syrian Entrepreneurs Starting New Lives in Egypt', *BBC*, 1 October. Available at: http://www.bbc.co.uk/news/business-34380016 (Accessed 26 February 2016).

Proudfoot, P. (2016) *The Living Dead: Revolutionary Subjectivity and Syrian Rebel-Workers in Beirut*. PhD thesis, The London School of Economics and Political Science (LSE).

Pruitt, L., Berents, H. and Munro, G. (2018) 'Gender and Age in the Construction of Male Youth in the European Migration "Crisis"', *Signs: Journal of Women in Culture and Society*, 43(3), pp. 687–709.

Pupavac, V. (2008) 'Refugee Advocacy, Traumatic Representations and Political Disenchantment', *Government and Opposition*, 43(2), pp. 270–92.

Rabo, A. (2014) '"It Has All Been Planned". Talking about Us and Powerful Others in Contemporary Syria', in Butter, M. and Reinkowski, M. (eds.) *Conspiracy Theories in the United States and the Middle East. A Comparative Perspective*. Berlin: Walter de Gruyter, pp. 212–27.

Rabo, A. (2014a) 'Aleppo's Souq: Witness to the Modern Syrian State', *OpenDemocracy*, 30 May. Available at: https://www.opendemocracy.net/author/annika-rabo (Accessed 26 February 2016).

Rabo, A. (2012) '"We Are Christians and We Are Equal Citizens": Perspectives on Particularity and Pluralism in Contemporary Syria', *Islam and Christian-Muslim Relations*, 23(1), pp. 79–93.

Rabo, A. (2005) *A Shop of One's Own: Independence and Reputation among Traders in Aleppo*. London/New York: I.B. Tauris.

Rabo, A. (1996) 'Gender, State and Civil Society in Jordan and Syria', in Hann, C. and Dunn, E. (eds.) *Civil Society. Challenging Western Models*. London/New York: Routledge, pp. 155–77.

Radhakrishnan, S. (2009) 'Professional Women, Good Families: Respectable Femininity and the Cultural Politics of a "New" India', *Qualitative Sociology*, 32, pp. 195–212.

Ramsay, G. (2019) 'Time and the Other in Crisis: How Anthropology Makes Its Displaced Object', *Anthropological Theory*, pp. 1–29, Available at: https://journals.sagepub.com/doi/pdf/10.1177/1463499619840464.

Ratele, K. (2013) 'Masculinities without Tradition', *Politikon: South African Journal of Political Studies*, 40(1), pp. 133–56.

Reay, D. (2004) 'Gendering Bourdieu's Concepts of Capitals? Emotional Capital, Women and Social Class', in Adkins, L. and Skeggs, B. (eds.) *Feminism after Bourdieu*. Oxford/Malden: Blackwell Publishing, pp. 57–96.

Reay, D., Crozier, G. and Clayton, J. (2009) '"Strangers in Paradise"? Working-class Students in Elite Universities', *Sociology*, 43(6), pp. 1103–21.

Rizzo, M. (2015) *Class Acts: Young Men and the Rise of Lifestyle*. Reno/Las Vegas: University of Nevada Press.

Rollins, T. (2015) 'Politicizing Religion: Egypt's Shia', *Madamasr*, 27 October. Available at: http://www.madamasr.com/en/2015/10/27/feature/politics/politicizing-religion-egypts-shia/ (Accessed 6 August 2017).

Rowe, M. T. (2009) *The Experience of Protest: Masculinity and Agency among Sudanese Refugees in Cairo*. Cairo: American University in Cairo Press.

Sa'ar, A. and Yahia-Younis, T. (2008) 'Masculinity in Crisis: The Case of Palestinians in Israel', *British Journal of Middle Eastern Studies*, 35(3), pp. 305–23.

Salamandra, C. (2013) 'Sectarianism in Syria: Anthropological Reflections', *Middle East Critique*, 22(3), pp. 303–6.

Salamandra, C. (2004) *A New Old Damascus: Authenticity and Distinction in Urban Syria*. Bloomington: Indiana University Press.

Salih, R. (2013) 'From Bare Lives to Political Agents: Palestinian Refugees as Avant-Garde', *Refugee Survey Quarterly*, 32(2), pp. 66–91.

Sawah, W. and Kawakibi, S. (2014) 'Activism in Syria: Between Nonviolence and Armed Resistance', in Khatib, L. and Lust, E. (eds.) *Taking to the Streets: The Transformation of Arab Activism*. Baltimore: Johns Hopkins University Press, pp. 136–71.

Schielke, S. (2015) *Egypt in the Future Tense Hope, Frustration, and Ambivalence before and after 2011*. Bloomington/Indianapolis: Indiana University Press.

Schielke, S. (2012) 'Capitalist Ethics and the Spirit of Islamization in Egypt', in Schielke, S. and Debevec, L. (eds.) *Ordinary Lives and Grand Schemes: An Anthropology of Everyday Religion*. New York/Oxford: Berghahn Books, pp. 131–45.

Schneiders, T. G. (2013) 'Der Arabische Frühling in Syrien: Hintergründe, Strukturen, Akteure', in Schneiders, T. G. (ed.) *Der Arabische Frühling: Hintergründe und Analysen*. Wiesbaden: Springer VS, pp. 231–53.

Schrijvers, J. (1999) 'Fighters, Victims and Survivors: Constructions of Ethnicity, Gender and Refugeeness among Tamils in Sri Lanka', *Journal of Refugee Studies*, 12(3), pp. 307–33.

Scott, J. W. (1999) *Gender and the Politics of History*, rev. ed. New York: Columbia University Press.

Segal, L. (2008) 'Gender, War and Militarism: Making and Questioning the Links', *Feminist Review*, 88, pp. 21–35.

Shaaban, B. (1998) 'Persisting Contradictions: Muslim Women in Syria', in Bodman, H. L. and Tohidi, N. (eds.) *Women in Muslim Societies: Diversity within Unity*. Boulder/London: Lynne Rienner Publishers, pp. 101–18.

Shahine, G. (2016) 'Syrians in Egypt: A Heaven despite the Hardships', *Ahramonline* 17 May 2016. Available at: http://english.ahram.org.eg/NewsContent/1/151/217025/Egypt/Features/Syrians-in-Egypt-A-haven-despite-the-hardships.aspx (Accessed 11 May 2017).

Sharma, A. and Gupta, A. (2006) 'Introduction: Rethinking Theories of the State in the Age of Globalization', in Sharma, A. and Gupta, A. (eds.) *The Anthropology of the State*. Oxford: Blackwell, pp. 1–41.

Shehata, S. (2009) *Shop Floor Culture and Politics in Egypt*. Albany: SUNY Press.

Sideris, T. (2004) '"You Have to Change and You Don't Know How!": Contesting What It Means to Be a Man in a Rural Area of South Africa', *African Studies*, 63(1), pp. 29–49.

Singerman, D. (2013) 'Youth, Gender, and Dignity in the Egyptian Uprising', *Journal of Middle East Women's Studies*, 9(3), pp. 1–27.

Singerman, D. (2007) 'The Economic Imperatives of Marriage: Emerging Practices and Identities among Youth in the Middle East', *Middle East Youth Initiative Working Paper*, 6. Available at: http://www.meyi.org/uploads/3/2/0/1/32012989/singerman_-_the_economic_imperatives_of_marriage-_emerging_practices_and_identities_among_youth_in_the_middle_east.pdf (Accessed 10 March 2016).

Skeggs, B. (1997) *Formations of Class & Gender: Becoming Respectable*. London: Sage.

Sluglett, P. (2016) 'Deadly Implications: The Rise of Sectarianism in Syria', in Beck, M., Jung, D. and Seeberg, P. (eds.) *The Levant in Turmoil: Syria, Palestine, and the Transformation of Middle Eastern Politics*. New York: Palgrave Macmillan, pp. 39–56.

Smith, M. D. (2016) 'Rethinking Gender in the International Refugee Regime', *Forced Migration Review*, 53, pp. 65/66.

Soliman, A. (2017) 'Italy Accuses 10 of Killing Regeni, Removes 16 Officials from the List of Suspects', *Madamasr*, 5 April. Available at: https://www.madamasr.com/en/2017/04/05/feature/politics/italy-accuses-10-of-killing-regeni-removes-16-officials-from-list-of-suspects/ (Accessed 1 June 2017).

Sommers, M. (2001) 'Young, Male and Pentecostal: Urban Refugees in Dar es Salam, Tanzania', *Journal of Refugee Studies*, 14(4), pp. 347–70.

Sperl, S. (2001) *Evaluation of UNHCR's Policy on Refugees in Urban Areas: A Case Study Review of Cairo*. Geneva: United Nations High Commissioner for Refugees Evaluation and Policy Unit.

Stacher, J. (2012) *Adaptable Autocrats: Regime Power in Egypt and Syria*. Stanford/California: Stanford University Press.

Stolleis, F. (2004) *Öffentliches Leben in privaten Räumen: muslimische Frauen in Damaskus*. Würzburg: Ergon.

Strathern, M. (1992) *After Nature: English Kinship in the Late Twentieth Century*. Cambridge: Cambridge University Press.

Szczepanikova, A. (2010) 'Performing Refugeeness in the Czech Republic: Gendered Depoliticisation through NGO Assistance', *Gender, Place & Culture: A Journal of Feminist Geography*, 17(4), pp. 461–77.

Szczepanikova, A. (2005) 'Gender Relations in a Refugee Camp: A Case of Chechens Seeking Asylum in the Czech Republic', *Journal of Refugee Studies*, 18(3), pp. 281–98.

Taylor, C. (1994) 'The Politics of Recognition', in Gutmann, A. (ed.) *Multiculturalism*. Princeton: Princeton University Press, pp. 25–74.

Tétreault, M. A. (2000) 'Gender, Citizenship, and State in the Middle East', in Butenschon, N. A., Davis, U. and Hassassian, M. (eds.) *Citizenship and the State in the Middle East: Approaches and Applications*. New York: Syracuse University Press, pp. 70–87.

Thomassen, B. (2012) 'Notes towards an Anthropology of Political Revolutions', *Comparative Studies in Society and History*, 54(3), pp. 679–706.

Thompson, E. (2000) *Colonial Citizens: Republican Rights, Paternal Privilege, and Gender in French Syria and Lebanon*. New York: Columbia University Press.

Toivanen, M. and Baser, B. (2016) 'Gender in the Representations of an Armed Conflict', *Middle East Journal of Culture and Communication*, 9, pp. 294–314.

Treacher, A. (2007) 'Postcolonial Subjectivity: Masculinity, Shame, and Memory', *Ethnic and Racial Studies*, 30(2), pp. 281–99.

Trombetta, L. (2014) 'Beyond the Party: The Shifting Structure of Syria's Power', in Anceschi, L., Gervasio, G. and Teti, A. (eds.) *Informal Power in the Greater Middle East: Hidden Geographies*. London/New York: Routledge, pp. 24–40.

Tucker, J. (2008) *Women, Family, and Gender in Islamic Law*. Cambridge: Cambridge University Press.

Turner, L. (2019) 'Syrian Refugee Men as Objects of Humanitarian Care'. *International Feminist Journal of Politics*, DOI: 10.1080/14616742.2019.1641127.

Turner, L. (2019a) 'The Politics of Labelling Refugee Men as "Vulnerable"', *Social Politics: International Studies in Gender, State and Society*.

Turner, S. (2016) 'What Is a Refugee Camp? Explorations of the Limits and Effects of the Camp', *Journal of Refugee Studies*, 29(2), pp. 139–48.

Turner, S. (2000) 'Vindicating Masculinity: The Fate of Promoting Gender Equality', *Forced Migration Review*, 9, pp. 8–10.

Turner, S. (1999) 'Angry Young Men in Camps: Gender, Age and Class Relations among Burundian Refugees in Tanzania', in *New Issues in Refugee Research*, 9. Geneva: UNHCR.

Turner, V. (1967) *The Forest of Symbols: Aspects of Ndembu Ritual*. Ithaca/London: Cornell U.P.

UNHCR (2011a) *Egypt: Global Appeal 2011 Update*. Available at: http://www.unhcr.org/4cd96bae2c.pdf (Accessed 23 January 2016).

UNHCR (2011b) *Convention and Protocol Relating to the Status of Refugees*. Available at: http://www.unhcr.org/3b66c2aa10 (Accessed 2 November 2016).

Van Eijk, E. (2016) *Family Law in Syria: Patriarchy, Pluralism and Personal Status Laws*. London/New York: I.B. Tauris.

Van Hear, N. (2006) '"I Went as far as My Money Would Take Me": Conflict, Forced Migration and Class', in Crepeau, F., Nakache, D., Collyer, M., Goetz, N., Hansen, A., Modi, R., Nadiq, A., Spoljar-Vrzina, S. and Willigen, M. (eds.) *Forced Migration and Global Processes: A View from Forced Migration Studies*. Oxford: Lexington Books, pp. 125–58.

Vera-Sanso, P. (2016) 'Taking the Long View: Attaining and Sustaining Masculinity across the Life Course in South India', in Cornwall, A., Karioris, F. and Lindisfarne, N. (eds.) *Masculinities under Neoliberalism*. London: Zed Books, pp. 80–98.

Walker, C. and Roberts, S. (2018) 'Masculinity, Labour and Neoliberalism: Reviewing the Field', in Walker, C. and Roberts, S. (eds.) *Masculinity, Labour, and Neoliberalism: Working-Class Men in International Perspective*. Palgrave Macmillan, pp. 1–28.

Watenpaugh, K. (2006) *Being Modern in the Middle East: Revolution, Nationalism. Colonialism, and the Arab Middle Class*. Princeton, NJ: Princeton University Press.

Wedeen, L. (2013) 'Ideology and Humor in Dark Times: Notes from Syria', *Critical Inquiry*, 39, pp. 841–73.

Wedeen, L. (1999) *Ambiguities of Domination: Politics, Rhetoric, and Symbols in Contemporary Syria*. Chicago: University of Chicago Press.

Weiss, M. (2015) 'Community, Sect, Nation: Colonial and Social Scientific Discourses on the Alawis in Syria during the Mandate and Early Independence Period', in Kerr, M. and Larking, C. (eds.) *The Alawis of Syria: War, Faith and Politics in the Levant*. Oxford/New York: Oxford University Press, pp. 63–78.

Wentzell, E. (2015) 'Enhancing Fathering through Medical Research Participation in Mexico', in Inhorn, M., Chavkin, W. and Navarro, J.-A. (eds.) *Globalized Fatherhood*. New York/Oxford: Berghahn Books, pp. 177–96.

Wetherell, M. and Edley, N. (1999) 'Negotiating Hegemonic Masculinity: Imaginary Positions and Psycho-Discursive Practices', *Feminism & Psychology*, 9, pp. 335–56.

Youssef, A. (2015) '500.000 Syrian Refugees Were Received in Egypt: Al-Sisi', *Daily News Egypt*, 13 September. Available at: http://www.dailynewsegypt.com/2015/09/13/500000-syrian-refugees-were-received-in-egypt-al-sisi/ (Accessed 27 January 2016).

Yurchak, A. (2005) *Everything Was Forever, until It Was No More: The Last Soviet Generation*. Princeton University Press.

Yuval-Davis, N. (2006) 'Intersectionality and Feminist Politics', *European Journal of Women's Studies*, 13(3), pp. 193–209.

Yuval-Davis, N. and Anthias, F. (1989) 'Introduction', in Yuval-Davis, N. and Anthias, F. (eds.) *Woman-Nation-State*. New York/Cambridge: Palgrave Macmillan, pp. 1–16.

Yuval-Davis, N. and Stoetzler, M. (2002) 'Imagined Boundaries and Borders: A Gendered Gaze', *European Journal of Women's Studies*, 9(3), pp. 329–44.

Zetter, R. (1991) 'Labelling Refugees: Forming and Transforming a Bureaucratic Identity', *Journal of Refugee Studies*, 4(1), pp. 39–62.

Ziadeh, R. (2013) *Power and Policy in Syria: Intelligence Services, Foreign Relations and Democracy in the Modern Middle East*. London/New York: I.B. Tauris.

Zisser, E. (1999) 'The 'Alawis: Lords of Syria: From Ethnic Minority to Ruling Sect', in Bengio, O. and Ben-Dor, G. (eds.) *Minorities and the State in the Arab World*. Boulder/London: Lynne Rienner Publishers, pp. 129–48.

Ziter, E. (2015) *Political Performance in Syria: From the Six-day War to the Syrian Uprising*. New York: Palgrave Macmillan.

INDEX

Note: Locators with letter 'n' refer to notes.

www.ingramcontent.com/pod-product-compliance
Lightning Source LLC
Chambersburg PA
CBHW071417290326
41932CB00046B/2114